John Locke
and the
Problem of Depravity

John Locke
and the
Problem of Depravity

W. M. SPELLMAN

CLARENDON PRESS · OXFORD
1988

Oxford University Press, Walton Street, Oxford OX2 6DP
Oxford New York Toronto
Delhi Bombay Calcutta Madras Karachi
Petaling Jaya Singapore Hong Kong Tokyo
Nairobi Dar es Salaam Cape Town
Melbourne Auckland
and associated companies in
Beirut Berlin Ibadan Nicosia

Oxford is a trade mark of Oxford University Press

Published in the United States
by Oxford University Press, USA

British Library Cataloguing in Publication Data
Spellman, W. M.
John Locke and the problem of depravity.
1. Locke, John, 1632–1704   2. Sin,
Original—History of doctrines
I. Title
233'.14'0924   BT720
ISBN 0-19-824987-X

Library of Congress Cataloging in Publication Data
Spellman, W. M.
John Locke and the problem of depravity/by W. M. Spellman.
Originally presented as the author's thesis.
Bibliography: p.   Includes index.
1. Locke, John, 1632–1704—Views on original sin. 2. Sin,
Original—History of doctrines—17th century. 3. Ethics,
Modern—17th century. I. Title.
B1298.R4S66 1988   233'.14'0924—dc19   87-28287
ISBN 0-19-824987-X

Typeset by Cotswold Typesetting Ltd.
Printed in Great Britain by
Biddles Ltd., Guildford and King's Lynn

To N. E. Costello

Acknowledgements

JOHN LOCKE's ideas on education were deeply influenced by his broader Protestant vision of the nature of man. While Locke always emphasized the importance of environment and the need for individual guidance in the educational process, he also consistently warned against any over-optimistic estimate of the power of systematic training. Despite the undoubted influence of Lockean ideas in the eighteenth century, and the wide recognition that these ideas have received in books dealing with the history of education, Locke's contribution here was in no fundamental sense unique. There were, it is clear, a number of educational theorists in Locke's day who concerned themselves with conditioning environment as a major factor in shaping Christian character, but most of these individuals remained closely identified with a perspective on human depravity and original sin which made the goal of realizing man's nature as a rational being through education alone virtually impossible. Locke also believed in a doctrine of the Fall, and this belief was the product of personal experiences in early life and especially during the Civil War, friendships made with the Latitudinarian members of the Church of England after 1670, and individual Scriptural exegeses carried out throughout his adult years. Locke's recognition of the limits of enlightened education, and the important influence of his Christian faith on his thought in this area, is a relatively neglected topic which this study seeks to address.

A number of librarians helped facilitate my research over the past two years. In Britain the staff of the Bodleian Library, British Library, University of London Senate House Library, and the Institute of Historical Research made my stay both pleasurable and productive. I would like to thank the Keeper of the Western Manuscripts at the Bodleian for permission to quote from the Locke manuscripts, the editors of the *Journal of Religion* for permission to reprint a version of my article on Locke's *Essay*, and the staff of the Clarendon Press for their patience and helpfulness. My work in Britain would have been impossible without the help of William C. Stinchcombe, Chairman of the History Department at Syracuse University, who generously granted me leave from my duties as a graduate assistant in the Department during the spring of 1984. In Boston the kind professionals at the Boston Athenaeum, the Congregational Library, and the General Theological Library opened their doors and their fine collections to a non-member. Joseph Middleton, reference librarian at the Sawyer Library, Suffolk University, Boston, responded promptly to my many inter-library loan requests. Edward W. Muir of Louisiana State University, John W. Yolton of Rutgers University, and Vernon F. Snow and Ralph L. Ketcham of Syracuse University all read the manuscript at the dissertation stage. I wish to thank Professor Yolton in particular for his criticisms, and for his encouragement of the publication of this study. Special thanks are extended to Joseph M. Levine of Syracuse University for first directing my studies in the history of Stuart England and for serving as my graduate advisor, and to David L. Robbins, Chairman of the Department of History at Suffolk University, who read the entire typescript and saved me from a number of mistakes. Those errors which remain, of course, are entirely my own.

W.M.S.

Contents

Abbreviations

DNB	*Dictionary of National Biography*
Early Draft	*An Early Draft of Locke's Essay, Together with Excerpts from his Journals,* ed. R. Aaron and J. Gibb (Oxford: University Press, 1936).
Essay	*An Essay concerning Human Understanding,* ed. P. H. Nidditch (Oxford: Clarendon Press, 1975).
Essays on LN	*Essays on the Law of Nature,* ed. W. Von Leyden (Oxford: Clarendon Press, 1954).
n.p.	Used in footnotes and bibliography when name of publisher is not provided.
SPCK	Society for Promoting Christian Knowledge.
Thoughts on Ed.	*Some Thoughts concerning Education in The Educational Writings of John Locke,* ed. J. Axtell (Cambridge: University Press, 1968).
Two Tracts	*Two Tracts on Government,* ed. P. Abrams (Cambridge: University Press, 1967).
Two Treatises	*Two Treatises of Government,* ed. P. Laslett (Cambridge: University Press, 1963).
Works	*The Works of John Locke,* 10 vols. (London: Thomas Tegg, 1823).

Introduction

To venture the opinion today that 'all the men we meet with, nine parts of ten, or perhaps ninety nine of one hundred, are what they are, good or evil, useful or not, by their education' is for many observers to call into question a good deal of conventional wisdom about human nature and the origin of evil based upon recent experience; it is to turn one's back upon the more obvious lessons of our own century.[1] But for the men of the seventeenth century, and especially for the men of Restoration England, the opinion struck at the very cornerstone of their intellectual world, a world both deeply Christian in orientation and acutely conscious of the omnipresence of sin. To venture the opinion in the seventeenth century was, in other words, to stand in opposition to the bedrock premiss of organized religion; it was to deny the fundamental import of the Bible story. Few were desirous of expressing, and even fewer were willing to express, such clearly dangerous thoughts, for their expression bespoke a longing to elevate the position of mankind in the larger scheme of things, to remove the notion of rebelliousness from that cluster of words and phrases that first came to mind when one considered the condition of earthly humanity. If education were in fact so central, indeed singular, in shaping moral character,

[1] 'The rationalists', wrote Reinhold Niebuhr after the outbreak of the Second World War, 'always assume that, since men are able to conceive of perfect standards of justice, such standards will be realized as soon as all men become intelligent enough to conceive them. They do not realize that intelligence offers no guarantee of the realization of a standard . . .' (*Beyond Tragedy* (New York: Scribner's Sons, 1941), 13). At the conclusion of that global conflict, Herbert Butterfield, doubtless responding to the whole Enlightenment tradition, gloomily warned: 'It must be emphasized that we create tragedy after tragedy for ourselves by a lazy unexamined doctrine of man which is current amongst us and which the study of history does not support . . . It is essential not to have faith in human nature' (*Christianity and History* (London: Bell, 1949), 46–7). See also Arnold Toynbee's summation of the Western experience since the late seventeenth century in *An Historian's Approach to Religion* (New York: Oxford University Press, 1956), 151–3, and F. Alexander, *Our Age of Unreason: A Study of the Irrational Forces in Social Life* (New York: J. B. Lippincourt, 1942), 19–20. For a criticism of this outlook, and especially of Niebuhr, see M. White, 'Original Sin, Natural Law, and Politics', *Partisan Review*, 2 (1956), 218–36.

then the help of outside intervention—other-worldly assistance, if you will—would plainly become unnecessary. Christ would not matter, vicarious atonement could be ignored.

But who could seriously entertain such ideas in an age when, despite the growing interest in science and empirical philosophy, the majority of men still thought a good deal about religion and the afterlife? The next life was the real business of earthly existence for each and every man—and the business was taken seriously by most. Education was important; no reflective individual in seventeenth-century England would deny that fact. It was important and it was incumbent upon all parents to educate their offspring in the duties associated with their particular station in life—this was the first, the most important parental function.[2] But even the best of efforts in this undertaking were apt to go awry because of the fallen nature of man, because of the ineradicable stain of original sin. The simple fact remained that for most seventeenth-century thinkers education could do precious little to ameliorate the condition of man without the previous infusion of God's saving grace.

So the above words, written by John Locke in the summer of 1684,[3] seem to suggest, at one level anyway, that the philosopher intended to overturn some familiar, firmly held ideas about mankind in hopes of instilling a new sense of confidence in the condition of human nature. At least that is what many of his eighteenth-century readers thought. The French *philosophe* Claude Adrien Helvetius, certainly not one to worry over the many qualifications that Locke made to such statements, expressed the conviction that 'History and experience equally inform us that the understanding is independent of the greater or less acuteness of the senses . . . The principles of Locke, far from contradicting this opinion, confirm it; they prove that education makes us what we are.' And Condillac, always ill at

[2] R. Schlatter, *The Social Ideas of Religious Leaders, 1660–1688* (Oxford: University Press, 1940), 33–4.

[3] Locke to Edward Clarke, 9 July 1684, printed in *The Correspondence of John Locke*, ed. E. S. De Beer, 8 vols. (Oxford: Clarendon Press, 1973–), ii, no. 782. All future references to the correspondence will be from the De Beer edition unless otherwise mentioned and will indicate date, volume, and letter number. Following De Beer, the dates of letters are those of the Old-Style or Julian calendar with one modification: the new year is assumed to begin on 1 January. Locke's claim reappeared in the opening paragraph of his major statement on education (*Thoughts on Ed.* 114).

ease with what he took to be Locke's failure to reduce the origins of all knowledge to a single principle, composed in 1746 a supplement to the famous *Essay concerning Human Understanding* which purported to discover the roots of human knowledge in sensation alone.[4] Now one would doubtless expect the more enthusiastic of the *philosophes* to stretch the truth of the matter a little in support of the good cause, but surprisingly they are not alone in their understanding of Locke. After carefully perusing the philosopher's book on education, Richardson's *Pamela* likened the task of the tutor to a 'skilful gardener, in assisting and encouraging the charming flower, through its several hopeful stages, to perfection', while Chesterfield maintained that 'A drayman is probably born with as good organs as Milton, Locke, or Newton; but by culture, they are much more above him than he is above his horse.' He too had high praise for Locke's book, advising his son that 'People are, in general, what they are made, by education and company, from fifteen to five-and-twenty', and cautioned the young man to 'consider well, therefore, the importance of your next eight or nine years; your whole depends on them'.[5] More recently there has been much scholarly confirmation of the eighteenth-century reading. John Passmore, for example, has argued that Locke deliberately embraced the Pelagian heresy and 'laid the foundations of what was to be one of the most influential forms of eighteenth and nineteenth century perfectibilism, according to which men can be morally improved to an unlimited capacity by education and other forms of social action'.[6] The consensus appears to be that

[4] Helvetius, *A Treatise on Man: His Intellectual Faculties and His Education*, ed. and trans. W. Hooper, 2 vols. (London: Albion Press, 1810), ii. 473; Étienne Bonnot de Condillac, *An Essay on the Origin of Human Knowledge* (1746), trans. T. Nugent (Gainesville: Scholars' Facsimiles, 1971).

[5] Samuel Richardson, *Pamela*, 2 vols. (London: Dent, 1931), ii. 383 (letter no. 90); Philip Dormer Stanhope, *Letters Written by Lord Chesterfield to his Son*, 2 vols. (London: W. Tegg, 1879), i. 192–3, 256. K. MacLean, *John Locke and English Literature of the Eighteenth Century* (New Haven: Yale University Press, 1936), 13, has argued that 'The objective quality of Eighteenth-Century Literature is certainly owing in part to the fact that Locke's demonstration that all ideas originate in sensation induced writers to give almost undue attention to the external world.'

[6] J. Passmore, *The Perfectibility of Man* (London: Duckworth, 1970), 163. See also id., 'The Malleability of Man in Eighteenth Century Thought', in *Aspects of the Eighteenth Century*, ed. E. R. Wasserman (Baltimore, Md.: Johns Hopkins Press, 1965), 23; M. V. C. Jeffreys, *John Locke: Prophet of Common Sense* (London: Methuen, 1967), 75; S. F. Pickering, *John Locke and Children's Books in Eighteenth Century England* (Knoxville, Tenn.:

Locke, whatever his personal misgivings about the applicability
of his more innovative ideas on education, set the philosophical
groundwork for much of what we call the Age of Enlightenment: 'In every branch of intellectual endeavour', says Gerald
Cragg, 'his influence was supreme'.[7] Locke's interpretation of
the human mind and his subsequent pedagogical injunctions,
we are told, constituted the ideological backdrop to the myriad
schemes for reform in the years immediately after his death.
Without Locke the supremacy of reason and the malleability of
the human mind, so much a part of enlightened thought during
the eighteenth century, would have been practically inconceivable.

Now there is a good deal to be said in support of this
argument, and one should exercise caution in any attempt to
alter the general picture. Still, it might be of some use to return
to Locke himself, especially on this very basic question of the
nature of man, in order to identify whether or not the
philosopher deliberately broke with the historic Christian view
of man as is so readily assumed. Given the significance of Locke's
Essay concerning Human Understanding, his *Thoughts concerning
Education,* and his *Reasonableness of Christianity* for the men of the
eighteenth century, the question is of considerable import for the
historian. For if in fact the philosopher was less than sanguine
about the implications of his radical empiricism for the future of
educational endeavour, if he remained within an older, more
traditional frame of reference when considering the nature of
man—if he remained an orthodox Protestant—then our

University of Tennessee Press, 1981), 7–8; W. S. and M. L. Sahakian, *John Locke*
(Boston: Twayne Publishers, 1975), 49–50, 53; M. J. M. Ezell, 'Locke's Images of
Childhood', *Eighteenth Century Studies,* 17 (1983–4), 149; N. Wood, *The Politics of Locke's
Philosophy* (Berkeley, Calif.: University of California Press, 1983), 129–35; *The
Educational Writings of John Locke,* ed. W. Adamson (Cambridge: University Press, 1922),
Introduction; R. R. Rusk, *Doctrines of the Great Educators* (New York: St Martin's Press,
1967), 127–49; P. Gay, *The Enlightenment: An Interpretation* (New York: Norton, 1969), ii.
511; G. R. Cragg, *Reason and Authority in the Eighteenth Century* (Cambridge: University
Press, 1964), 1–27; A. Cobban, *In Search of Humanity: The Role of the Enlightenment in
Modern History* (New York: George Braziller, 1960), 72–4; P. Hazard, *The European Mind*
(New York: Meridian, 1960), 239–51; R. Quintana, *Two Augustans: John Locke and
Jonathan Swift* (Madison, Wis.: University Press, 1978), 24–5, 28; J. T. Moore, 'Locke's
Concept of Faith', University of Kansas (Ph. D. thesis, 1970), 170–1.

[7] Cragg, *Reason and Authority,* 6.

perspective on Locke both as a thinker and as an educator is bound to change.

What follows, then, is an analysis of one relatively brief episode in the history of the theory of human nature, or, as Arthur Lovejoy once succinctly described the field, 'of men's ideas about men'.[8] We will attempt to gauge the impact of the Christian view of human nature, and in particular the special view of the Reformed Churches, on the mind of one who is often considered to have been amongst that select few of intrepid Englishmen who threw off what were perceived to be the stultifying encumbrances of a dying age. At the centre of the Christian view was the idea of Adam's fall from grace in Paradise, of original sin. Here was the starting-point for any Christian estimation of the human situation and the human prospect. The Christian, if he wished to be recognized as such, had to concede that despite whatever advances man might make over the world of nature, whatever victories over both the contrived and the fortuitous evils of this world, in the end substantive improvement in the quality of this life, and salvation in the next, were impossible without God's help. John Locke, of course, was born in an age grown infamous for its religious quarrels. That he rejected much of what he thought had contributed to those quarrels is obvious; that he retained an unshakeable faith in the larger Christian view of man is less so. And while his understanding of the meaning of the Christian story came in for a good deal of criticism by those who suspected the worst of a man who in so many spheres questioned established authority, still his essential premiss was very much congruent with theirs. His critics, locked in the heat of battle, denied it, his successors ignored it, and, until recently, his biographers did not over-much care. But the fact remains.

Throughout the corpus of his published and manuscript writings there exists a definite strain of pessimism about human nature in general and about his immediate contemporaries in particular. As John Dunn has recently observed, Locke was more than anything else a 'tragic thinker, who understood in advance some of the deep contradictions in the modern conception of human reason, and so saw rather clearly some of

[8] A. D. Lovejoy, *Reflections on Human Nature* (Baltimore, Md.: Johns Hopkins Press, 1961), 13.

the tragedy of our own lives which we still see very dimly indeed'.[9] His own upbringing, experience as an educator, physician, and political adviser, not to mention his considerable efforts in the search for a more plausible theory of knowledge—one in better harmony with the discoveries of seventeenth-century science—provided him with the empirical evidence necessary to conclude that the Christian view of man was, after all, an accurate one. And although he worked tirelessly to encourage men along the road to spiritual and temporal advancement, he remained nevertheless acutely aware of the failure of most to help themselves. He ended his days penning commentaries on the Epistles of St Paul, surely nothing out of the ordinary for a devout Christian, but instructive in that it was Paul, as we shall soon discover, who first brought the Christian concept of Adam's sin and its consequences to centre-stage, who made it a living principle for all subsequent generations. Locke was never one to waste his time on unimportant subjects.

While his continuing importance for most of us rests chiefly on his spirited defence of contractual and constitutional government, his assertions on behalf of majority rule, and, more controversially, his alleged justification of the unlimited acquisition of private property,[10] the merits of his ideas on liberal democracy and the assumptions about human rationality which that political theory purportedly embodies should not preclude our studying what the philosopher actually did think and say during his lifetime about human reason and its opposite. Perhaps in this way Locke's vision of the liberal State and the assumptions behind it, issues that remain of some concern in our own day, might be brought into sharper focus, might serve to further illuminate the context in which those issues were originally raised. That Locke should emerge something other than the precursor and prophet of the European Enlightenment, as is so often argued, does not of itself lessen the

---

[9] J. Dunn, *John Locke* (Oxford: University Press, 1984), p. vii.

[10] C. B. Macpherson, *The Political Theory of Possessive Individualism* (Oxford: University Press, 1979), 221, writes that Locke's theory of property 'is a justification of the natural right not only to unequal property but to unlimited individual appropriation'. J. Tully, *A Discourse on Property: John Locke and his Adversaries* (Cambridge: University Press, 1980), challenges Macpherson's interpretation and places Locke's understanding of property rights within a natural-law framework where (p. 124) 'Property is conditional upon its use to perform our positive duties to God.'

significance of his place in that wider movement of ideas. It is only to suggest that Locke would have been somewhat surprised at various of the claims made on his behalf by many who followed him in the eighteenth century, and by some who wrote about him in the twentieth.

1

Original Sin before Locke

FOR most Christians living in late-Stuart England, the centuries-old doctrine of original sin was no amusingly quaint or incidental concept, no ancillary notion to be treated with perfunctory contempt or, what is worse, silent indifference. Rather the doctrine which found its basis in the story of Adam's fall from grace occupied a pivotal and living position within the spiritual life of the Church and within the intellectual community as a whole, despite the very real inroads that had been made by Deism and scepticism towards the end of the era. The real meaning of what had transpired in the third chapter of Genesis had been authoritatively defined in 1563, after both the frenzied years of Protestant reform under Edward VI and the sanguinary reaction carried out by Mary in the 1550s. In that year Elizabeth's newly appointed bishops declared in Convocation that 'Original Sin standeth not in the following of Adam . . . but is the fault and corruption of every man, that naturally is ingendred of the offspring of Adam.' This sin was so heinous an offence that every man, woman, and child, living and dead, 'deserveth God's wrath and damnation'. And the essence of the Fall was such that no one could any longer, out of his own volition and natural strength, so much as even turn towards his Maker in repentance and prepare himself for salvation. 'We are accounted righteous before God', said the bishops, 'only for the merits of our Lord and Saviour Jesus Christ by faith, and not for our own works and deservings.' Indeed, man's voluntary works of repentance, as they precede Christ's meritorious sacrifice, 'have the nature of sin'. The Elizabethan religious establishment, long considered by many scholars to have been the progeny of politic compromise and studied ambiguity in both organization and doctrine, was at least clear on this one important issue, the central issue in the drama of the Christian faith since its inception.[1]

[1] *The Thirty-Nine Articles and the Constitutions and Canons, of the Church of England* (London: John Baskett, 1724), Articles 9, 11, and 13; H. Davies, *Worship and Theology in*

With the adoption of these and other like-minded resolutions as the basis of the Church of England's theology, the Elizabethan bishops were making even more stark the opposition between what had always been Christianity's two disconsonant views of human nature. On the one hand, man was considered to be God's special handiwork, occupying a unique and enviable place in the great cosmic chain of being, the master and guardian of earthly creation, and designed for even greater things once this brief passage was at an end. Contrariwise, man was viewed as the great apostate, the thankless offspring who, knowing full well the consequences of his disobedience, deliberately crossed God's single injunction in Paradise and thereby condemned himself and all of his posterity to eternal damnation.[2] The paradox, though seemingly insoluble, engaged the serious attention of all thoughtful individuals in Tudor and Stuart England perhaps more than any other single issue. To live with the paradox meant the sacrifice not only of logical consistency, but also of any conviction in the substantive improvement of mankind through the application of one's natural faculties. It meant, in other words, that the idea of

England: From Cranmer to Hooker (Princeton, NJ: University Press, 1970), 17–25; C. S. Meyer, *Elizabeth I and the Religious Settlement of 1559* (St Louis, Mo.: Concordia Press, 1960), 158–61; W. H. Frere, *A History of the English Church in the Reigns of Elizabeth and James I, 1558–1625* (London: Macmillan, 1904), 96–7. Joel Hurstfield, 'Church and State, 1558–1612: the Task of the Cecils', in *Freedom, Corruption and Government in Elizabethan England* (Cambridge, Mass.: Harvard University Press, 1973), 81, says that the Anglican Church was both Calvinist in theology and Catholic in much of its ceremony and all of its organization. Although Puritans in the Parliaments of 1566 and 1571 challenged certain aspects of the Thirty-Nine Articles, on doctrinal matters 'There was no quarrel between Anglican and Puritan' (J. E. Neale, *Elizabeth I and her Parliaments*, 2 vols. (London: Cape, 1953), i. 205). This conclusion is seconded by W. MacCaffrey, *The Shaping of the Elizabethan Regime* (Princeton, NJ: University Press, 1968), 61; S. R. Gardiner, *History of England*, 10 vols. (London: Longman, 1883), i. 17–18, and by E. J. Bicknell, *A Theological Introduction to the Thirty-Nine Articles* (London: Longman, 1919), 20–21.

[2] 'We should never let ourselves forget that the orthodox scheme of salvation was pervasive in the Elizabethan Age' (E. M. W. Tillyard, *The Elizabethan World Picture* (London: Chatto and Windus, 1943), 16, 19, 60–73); T. Spenser, *Shakespeare and the Nature of Man* (New York: Macmillan, 1942), 1–45; E. A. Burtt, *The Metaphysical Foundations of Modern Physical Science* (Garden City, NJ: Doubleday, 1960), 17–18; A. Koyre, *From the Closed World to the Infinite Universe* (Baltimore, Md.: Johns Hopkins Press, 1957), 43; A. O. Lovejoy, *The Great Chain of Being* (Cambridge, Mass.: Harvard University Press, 1936), 102; id., 'Pride in Eighteenth Century Thought', in *Essays in the History of Ideas* (Baltimore, Md.: Johns Hopkins Press, 1948), 63.

changing the world and the men in it for the better, the idea of perfection on earth, could not be honestly entertained.[3]

But what of the historical roots of these grim articles now to be accepted as dogma by all Englishmen? Certainly, the emergence and codification of these ideas concerning man's nature and present status must be approached within the context of Reformation Europe, but their real roots extend beyond that crucial episode in the life of the Church, back to the very foundations of the faith itself. Only within this larger setting can the seventeenth century's understanding of the issues be fully appreciated.

Like their Catholic opponents at the Council of Trent, the sixteenth-century Protestant reformers had quite naturally turned to St Paul and St Augustine for Biblical support in interpreting the story of man's expulsion from the Garden and its consequences. After all, there was precious little evidence to be found in the Old Testament to buttress their views. For in that ancient book the inherent sinfulness of man is not specifically or consistently identified as the result of Adam's transgression. More importantly, there is nothing in the Genesis narrative to suggest that the first sin automatically infected all of Adam's posterity with an internal natural corruption capable of being transmitted by physiological heredity. The narrative recounts Adam and Eve's expulsion from Paradise, the denial of access to the tree of life or immortality, and man's exposure to the physical ills of this life, but not a word is to be found about inborn sinfulness or moral infirmity inherited from our first parents.[4] This is not to deny, however, that the Old Testament

---

[3] The belief in man's irreversible depravity was given additional 'empirical' confirmation by overseas explorers from the sixteenth century, all of whom brought back to Europe stories of variant religious practices which were taken as evidence of mankind's loss of virtue and degradation. See E. A. Burtt, *Man Seeks the Divine: A Study of the History and Comparison of Religions* (New York: Harper and Brothers, 1957), 74–5.

[4] Robin Scroggs, *The Last Adam: A Study in Pauline Anthropology* (Philadelphia, Pa.: Fortress Press, 1966), 10, 15; R. Bultmann, *The Old and the New Man* trans. K. R. Crim (Richmond, Va.: John Knox Press, 1967), 61; S. Cave, *The Christian Estimate of Man* (London: Duckworth, 1946), 15; H. W. Robinson, *The Christian Doctrine of Man* (Edinburgh: T. and T. Clark, 1947), 55–60; F. R. Tennant, *The Sources of the Doctrines of the Fall and Original Sin* (Cambridge: University Press, 1903), 90–1, 104–5; id., 'Original Sin', in *Encyclopedia of Religion and Ethics* (1917). The paucity of supportive evidence did not prevent some clergymen from citing Old Testament passages in support of original sin, especially Ps. 51: 7. See, for example, Jonathan Edwards, *The Doctrine of Original Sin* (Oxford: Henry Clements, 1711), 12.

from first to last assumes the universality of sin, but this assumption was largely the result of conscious experience, particularly the post-exilic experience and the moral struggle consequent to that great disaster. The words of Hosea: 'O Israel, return unto the Lord thy God; for thou hast fallen by thine iniquity', sum up this sentiment precisely.[5]

When we come to Christ himself, the same difficulties arise, and the men of the seventeenth century knew it. He too accepted the universality of sin without troubling to explain its ultimate origins. His words in Matthew: 'Repent ye, for the kingdom of God is at hand', succinctly demonstrate his recognition of the former fact. Still it was of no real importance to his immediate public ministry to concern himself with the roots of man's hardness of heart. Jesus was not, as Kenneth Latourette has indicated, 'a philosopher dealing in abstract terms and concepts. He never talked about the problem of evil'. The practical nature of his work and the shortness of his public life prevented him from dwelling upon the question. It was evidently enough for him to recognize the overarching power of sin in the world and to counter its pernicious influence. His sole recorded reference to the first man, in fact, occurs in the context of a discussion of divorce.[6]

The Adamic theory of the Fall as the root cause of original sin was first given definitive exposition by St Paul in his Epistles. Like his Old Testament forebears, Paul's sense of the omnipresence of sin dominated his consciousness; finding himself unable to fulfil the rigid obligations of the Mosaic law, Paul abandoned the futile attempt to merit salvation and committed himself to absolute faith in the saving grace of God in Christ. For Paul salvation was no longer to be earned, since this had proved impossible—only faith in the crucified Christ could release one

---

[5] N. P. Williams, *The Ideas of the Fall and Original Sin* (London: Longman, 1929), 85; Hos. 14:1.

[6] Matt. 3: 2, 17; 19: 4; K. S. Latourette, *A History of Christianity*, 2 vols. (New York: Harper and Row, 1975), i. 43; Robinson, op. cit. 92–5; Williams, op. cit. 98–112; Cave, op. cit. 16–24; D. R. Scott, *Christ, Sin and Redemption* (London: James Clarke and Co., 1927), 13–23. Williams (pp. 87–8) says that there were three theories of the origin of sin current at the beginning of the Christian era. The first identified the ground of moral evil in a hereditary taint introduced into the world by unnatural angel marriages, the second claimed that the basis of sin consists in an 'evil impulse' which is not hereditary but implanted by the Creator in each individual at birth, and the third was related to the Genesis Fall story.

from the oppression of the law. Man as sinner was an irremediable fact of life; the origins of this situation were first alluded to by the apostle in 1 Cor. 15: 21–2, where he declared that as physical death came to all by the actions of one man (Adam), so by another (Christ) the faithful shall be brought to life after death. But it is in his well-known Epistle to the Romans that the historic proof-text for the later dogmatic theory can be identified. Here we find Paul, in language so ambiguous that this passage has defied exegetical consensus to this day, declaring that 'as through one man sin entered into the world, and death through sin; and so death passed unto all men, for that all have sinned'.[7] This crucial and controversial passage will demand a good deal of our attention in this study, precisely because agreement on Paul's meaning here was so difficult to obtain. Was he premissing some hereditary infection or moral debility consequent upon Adam's primal transgression, or was the apostle simply confirming the obvious fact of man's mortality and liability to the ills of this world which was first promulgated in the third chapter of Genesis? The way one answered this difficult question had more than a little significance for the larger problem of man's essential nature and the thorny issue of the role played by human merit in the quest for eternal salvation.

Finding the origin of sin in Adam's fall from grace, Paul seemed to identify the seat of sin in each individual with the body or flesh. His confession of this apparent dualism is best summed up in Romans: 'For I delight in the Law of God, after the inward man. But I see another Law in my members, warring against the Law of my Mind, and bringing me into captivity to the Law of sin, which is in my members. O wretched man that I am: who shall deliver me from the body of this death?'[8] In this passage Paul seems close to what might be called, for convenience's sake, the classical view of human nature, that amalgam of Platonic, Aristotelian, and Stoic elements which

---

[7] Rom. 5: 12; R. N. Flew, *The Idea of Perfection in Christian Theology* (Oxford: University Press, 1934), 45. On the varied interpretations of Rom. 5: 12, see C. E. B. Cranfield, *Romans: A Shorter Commentary* (Grand Rapids, Mich.: Eerdmans Publishing Co., 1985), 112–15. On Corinthians see C. K. Barrett, *A Commentary on the First Epistle to the Corinthians* (New York: Harper and Row, 1968), 352.

[8] Rom. 7: 22–4.

identifies reason or spirit with what is unique and essential to man's real nature, while the body is associated with imperfection, mutability, and decay. The truly divine in man, reason or spirit, must constantly struggle to free itself from the dross of the sensible and the material. And this is best accomplished through the exercise of reason, by divorcing oneself from the transient and contingent and focusing on the life of the mind. The uniqueness of this classical outlook lay in the fact that it found no essential defect at the centre of man's personality. His real nature, according to Plato, 'most clearly resembles the divine and immortal', and his perfection is to be achieved, and can be achieved, through individual self-discipline and the knowledge of the good. The fully rational man, it was believed, could only act in a virtuous manner. For all intents and purposes, reason and virtue were synonymous. In the end man's dependence was rejected, his autonomy restored, and his perfection declared a real possibility.[9]

Not so for Paul, however. The argument that the apostle found the flesh to be inherently evil is a fallacious one; he made no Hellenistic distinction between a sinful body and a perfect soul. His doctrine of man was the product of ancient Hebrew thought patterns, patterns that had originally known no severance between mind and body, but instead viewed man as a corporate whole where physical attributes took on a psychical quality. For the early Hebrews the idea of a pre-existent soul or spirit which inhabited a material body previously prepared for it was completely alien. Their accepted idea of personality was that of an animated body, one where the various bodily parts performed designated mental duties. Paul's refusal to consider the flesh as evil by nature is seen in his description of the body as 'a temple of the Holy Ghost' and later when he enjoins men to 'cleanse our selves from all filthiness of the flesh and spirit, perfecting holiness in the fear of God'. Instead of identifying the

---

[9] R. Niebuhr, *The Nature and Destiny of Man*, 2 vols. (London: Nisbet and Co., 1945), i. 4–12; Passmore, *Perfectibility of Man*, 28–67; H. Baker, *The Dignity of Man: Studies in the Persistence of an Idea* (Cambridge, Mass.: Harvard University Press, 1947), 100–5, 173; Plato, *Phaedo*, quoted in Passmore, p. 40; J. Hick, *Evil and the Love of God* (New York: Harper and Row, 1966), 31–3. Because 'both Plato and the orthodox Christian believed that man could rise above his imperfections and reach towards heavenly perfection, it was easy to identify the Platonic and Hebrew doctrines' (Tillyard, *Elizabethan World Picture*, 19).

flesh as sinful in and of itself, Paul was of the belief that the weak flesh becomes subject to sin, invaded as it were, by the little-understood forces of sin. This onslaught from without found its most convenient and pliable base of operations in the flesh. But more importantly, Paul saw the origin of sin as a conscious individual rebellion against God and an accompanying exal-tation of the self. Sin had taken root with man's full co-operation; it was at bottom the natural result of his efforts to return to the lost state of immortality unaided. Here lay the central meaning of the Genesis story for the apostle—voluntary transgression, 'one man's offence', a premeditated act of rational will—in short, an act of inexcusable disobedience. Paul's estimate of man, and the Christian estimate ever since, places evil at the very centre of man's personality, in his refusal to accept his creatureliness and in his arrogant demand to know good and evil. 'Because that, when they knew God,' he argued, 'they glorified him not as God, neither were thankful, but became vain in their imaginations, and their foolish heart was darkened. Professing themselves to be wise, they became fools.' The Hellenistic view of man reaching for perfection through natural means was truly impossible for Paul to countenance; it was of the nature of the first sin itself.[10]

In light of his later influence on Christian thought, it is interesting to note that Paul's unique analysis of original sin failed to immediately engage subsequent Church thinkers. It was not until late in the second century, when the Gnostic controversy forced the Church to clarify its position on the issue, that we witness a re-emergence of the Adam story. The whole controversy itself might be viewed as one result of the expansion of the Church after the apostolic age. As an increasing

---

[10] 1 Cor. 6: 19; 2 Cor. 7: 1; Rom. 1: 21–2; 5: 17; W. Barclay, *The Mind of St Paul* (New York: Harper and Row, 1975), 200–5; C. K. Barrett, *A Commentary on the Epistle to the Romans* (London: A. and C. Black, 1957), 112; id., *From First Adam to Last: A Study in Pauline Anthropology* (New York: Scribner's Sons, 1962), 15–17; R. Bultmann, *Primitive Christianity in its Contemporary Setting*, trans. R. H. Fuller (New York: Meridian Books, 1956), 46–7; K. E. Kirk, *The Vision of God: The Religious Doctrine of the Summum Bonum* (London: Longman, 1931), 88–92; E. Gilson, *The Spirit of Medieval Philosophy*, trans. A. H. C. Downes (London: Sheed and Ward, 1936), 171; Robinson, *Christian Doctrine of Man*, 11–26, 153; Niebuhr, *Nature and Destiny of Man*, i. 11–18; Cave, *Christian Estimate of Man*, 32–46; Williams, *Ideas of the Fall*, 113–48. Werner Jaeger traces early Christian borrowings from Greek culture in *Early Christianity and Greek Paideia* (Cambridge, Mass.: Belknap Press, 1961).

percentage of the new converts came from pagan ranks, some Christians adopted Gnosticism as a means of attracting the educated amongst their godless neighbours by making the new faith more intellectually appealing. The Gnostics considered the Adamic version of the origin of sin as altogether too puerile; instead they associated sin with the spirit's captivity within matter, the product, ultimately, of man's materiality. Christ's mission had been to save this spirit from the world of material darkness. Thus even to conceive of the saviour of man suffering the indignity of bodily crucifixion was inconsistent with the spiritual nature of his deity. Striking back at this denial of the Incarnation as antithetical to the Christian belief, Iranaeus and Tertullian returned to the Genesis story and reaffirmed the mysterious hereditary taint involved in Adam's sinfulness. Yet while challenging the Gnostic vision of the origin of sin, neither of these early Church Fathers insisted upon the absolute depravity of men; that charge would have to wait until the beginning of the fifth century, when a new set of dangerous circumstances, a new threat to the Pauline doctrine of salvation by faith alone, emerged in the person of an obscure British monk lately arrived in the capital of Western Christendom.[11]

The story of Pelagius' arrival in Rome and his shock at what he perceived to be the moral laxity in evidence there, and of his eventual clash with the great Bishop of Hippo, Augustine, is fairly well known. It should be recalled at the outset, however, that Augustine, despite what many today see as his exaggerated position on the question of man's essential nature, stands second only to Scripture as an authority in the Western Christian Churches, Catholic and Protestant alike. To a certain extent his mature views were the product of his own personal experience as a youthful sinner of no mean proportion. His early life before his conversion to Christianity was filled with moral transgressions which were not so much the product of a weak flesh as, so he tells us, a deliberate preference for evil. A youthful prank involving

---

[11] H. Chadwick, *The Early Church* (Reading: Penguin, 1984), 35–8, 80; J. Tulloch, *The Christian Doctrine of Man* (New York: Scribner, Armstrong, and Co., 1875), 55–6; Latourette, *History of Christianity*, i. 123–5; Williams, op. cit. 179, 246–8, 313; Passmore, *Perfectibility of Man*, 86–7. Irenaeus claimed that Adam and Eve in the Garden were as children, without perfect understanding, thus the cause of their disobedience: see Cave, op. cit. 52, 64–73.

the theft of some pears from a neighbour's garden was 'compelled neither by hunger, nor poverty, but through a distaste for well-doing, and a lustiness of iniquity'. Likewise his mother's warnings against fornication 'appeared to me but womanish counsels, which I should blush to obey'. This wilful preference for that which he acknowledged was evil caused Augustine a good deal of anguish, especially since most philosophers at that time were in basic agreement with the Platonic notion that men will naturally seek the good and that evil is only perpetuated out of ignorance. How to explain this deliberate perversity of will was perhaps Augustine's highest priority. A solution had to be found because his own actions were no aberration; the phenomenon was universal. No one was free from this sort of sinful behaviour, not even the new-born infant. The tell-tale signs of human corruption appeared at birth and continued throughout the course of everyone's life.[12]

For Augustine the only plausible explanation for this state of affairs seemed to rest in the Pauline interpretation of the Fall pushed to its furthest limits. This meant an acceptance of the idea that all men existed potentially in Adam and thus participated in his disobedience—his defiance of God and claim to independence—and his consequent guilt.[13] Augustine drew from this the severest conclusion: human nature had been so corrupted by the Fall that man could not even will the good. There was absolutely no quarter given to human merit in this system, no opportunity for the sinner to work his way towards salvation with the help of God's grace. All grace was prevenient, salvation was the free gift of God who arbitrarily chose some of the guilty to participate in the glories of eternal life. Again the Bishop of Hippo's personal experience played a crucial role in his interpretation of Paul. His own wilfully sinful youth convinced him that he had been saved in spite of himself, by an infusion of grace working inexorably to redeem him from sin.

---

[12] H. Pope, *Saint Augustine of Hippo* (New York: Image Books, 1961), 82–94; W. C. Placher, *A History of Christian Theology* (Philadelphia, Pa.: Westminster Press, 1983), 108; Baker, *Dignity of Man*, 165–76; Hick, *Evil and the Love of God*, 43; Augustine, *The Basic Writings of Saint Augustine*, 2 vols., ed. W. J. Oates, i. (New York: Random House, 1949), *Confessions*, bk. 1, chs. 4, 7; bk. 2, chs. 3, 4.

[13] Augustine agreed with Paul that sin preceded and caused the corruption of the flesh: 'The corruptible flesh made not the soul to sin, but the sinning soul made the flesh corruptible' (*City of God* ed. John Healey, 2 vols. (London: Dent, 1945) ii. 29.)

'Can they do anything by the free determination of their own will?' he asked of men in the *Enchiridion*. 'Again I say, God forbid. For it was by the evil use of his free will that man destroyed both it and himself'. Spurious claims made on behalf of man's free will and work towards perfection, he felt, served only to undermine the majesty and omnipotence of God. They constituted an affront to the divine essence, another example of the irrepressible pride of Adam at work in all men.[14]

Augustine was the first churchman to detail how Adam's sin was transmitted from one generation to the next. This fearful taint was imparted, he argued, through the act of sexual intercourse—not because the act was evil in itself, but because the sexual organs were not under the control of the will guided by reason. As Adam had rebelled against God, so man's body rebelled against the dictates of the will. Augustine demonstrated a basic hostility towards the desires of the flesh which seemed to reflect his study of classical literature, especially Plato, and this ascetic temperament would become one of the more important hallmarks of medieval Christianity. In so far as sin was derived from this source, it reinforced his basic conviction that only through the special intervention of the Creator could men be saved from the eternal damnation which they all so justly deserved.[15]

Pelagius, on the other hand, found the Augustinian principles of predestination and inherited corruption both morally enervating and pernicious. He thought that much of the moral laxity which he had discovered in Rome could be traced directly to Augustine's doctrine. For Pelagius, the whole notion of mankind's frailty and corruption seemed an all too convenient excuse for those nominal Christians who had no real intention of checking their sinful inclinations and acknowledging their responsibilities to God. Pelagius disputed the Augustinian view of man and sought to place the onus of responsibility with regard

---

[14] Augustine, *The Enchiridion*, in *Basic Writings*, i. 673, 675; E. Gilson, *The Christian Philosophy of St Augustine* (New York: Random House, 1960), 151–2; id., *A History of Christian Philosophy in the Middle Ages* (New York: Random House, 1955), 78–9.

[15] Augustine, *City of God*, ii. 53–5; H. Chadwick, *Augustine* (Oxford: University Press, 1986), 112–14; Tennant, 'Original Sin'. Also *Encyclopedia of Religion*, 1945 edn., article on 'Original Sin'. Baker, *Dignity of Man*, 166–7, correctly points out that while the Greeks 'shared a general distrust of matter', Augustine's severe asceticism owes much to its rigour to Paul.

to salvation squarely on the shoulders of the individual by restoring free will and the possibility of perfection through a sinless life. 'Everything good, and everything evil,' he declared, 'on account of which we are either laudable or blameworthy, is not born with us but done by us: for we are not born fully developed, but with a capacity for either conduct; and we are procreated as without virtue, so also without vice; and previous to the action of our own proper will, that alone is in man which God has formed.' The Pelagian God was a just God, one who would not impose upon men obligations and duties which they could never possibly fulfil. Where there was no freedom of will, where sin was unavoidable, there it was no sin. Obligation would never be greater than ability; this was the bedrock position of Pelagius. Deny free will and the rational nature of man, he insisted, and one might as well give licence to all those who, like the youthful Augustine, would just as soon wait to be saved from above while enjoying the debaucheries of this world as demonstrate any seriousness of purpose about salvation by living correctly. Why, he asked, avoid the sins of this world if in the final analysis behaviour does not really matter?[16]

The moral rigour behind Pelagianism is often overlooked. Pelagius did not eliminate the idea of hereditary sinfulness merely to create a cheerier view of human nature, nor simply to reintroduce the Hellenistic idea of unaided perfection; rather he sought to shift responsibility for all sins, large and small, back to men possessed of free will and reason so that in the end there would be no excuse for even the most venial of moral transgressions.[17] Sin became a conscious, avoidable defiance of God's will, a voluntary repudiation of his sovereignty and wisdom. Now even the smallest infraction, because it could be avoided, carried with it the possibility of eternal punishment.

---

[16] B. B. Warfield, 'Augustine and the Pelagian Controversy', in *Two Studies in the History of Doctrine* (New York: Christian Literature Co., 1897), 3–12; P. Tillich, *A History of Christian Thought* (New York: Harper and Row, 1968), 124–5; *Encyclopedia of Religion and Ethics*, 1917 edn., article on 'Pelagianism and Semi-Pelagianism'. Quote from Pelagius contained in Augustine's *On Original Sin* in *Basic Writings*, i. 628. Chadwick, *Early Church*, 228, writes that while Pelagius was accused of denying man's need for grace, he 'was much misrepresented in the course of the controversy. In fact he affirmed that in the forgiveness of sins there is an unmerited gift of grace.' The best biography is J. Ferguson, *Pelagius* (Cambridge: Heffer, 1956).

[17] This fact should be kept in mind when we come to discuss the seventeenth-century Latitudinarians.

Augustine believed to the last that Pelagianism made the saving work of Christ unnecessary, that it undermined the central drama of the New Testament. Pelagius had made men independent of God in the sense that their salvation was entirely in their own hands.[18] The issue which engaged these two religious giants, then, was one that remained central to the life of the Church down to the seventeenth century and beyond. Was the salvation which all men hoped for the free gift of God, was it the product of man's independent efforts, or was it some combination, some ill-defined amalgam of the two?

Pelagius seems to have been the loser in the immediate aftermath of his clash with the Bishop of Hippo. Although Pope Zosimus had initially come out in defence of his orthodoxy, the hostile decisions taken against Pelagius' ally Caelestius at the Council of Carthage in 418, coupled with the edict of the Emperor Honorius condemning Pelagian opinions, convinced the Pontiff that his preliminary finding had been incorrect.[19] Still, Augustine's extreme views concerning predestination and the irresistible power of God's prevenient grace were not immediately endorsed by the Church. Even at the same Council of Carthage where Pelagius was censured, and where the Bishop's influence must have been great, the final canons made no mention of these concepts. The legitimate fear that Augustine's tenets might be used to condone moral laxity led some contemporaries who had no sympathy for Pelagianism as a whole to insist none the less that the first movement of faith originates with man and that God's assisting grace is subsequent to this human initiative. Finding themselves torn between the merits of a system which glorified God at the possible expense of moral nihilism and one where man seemed arrogantly equipped to begin the process of salvation on his own, the bishops of the sixth-century Church determined that the latter formulation constituted the greater danger to Christianity. Thus the so-called doctrine of Semi-Pelagianism was declared anathema at

---

[18] T. A. Burkill, *The Evolution of Christian Thought* (Ithaca, NY: Cornell University Press, 1978), 126–7; Chadwick, *Augustine*, 110; Passmore, *Perfectibility of Man*, 94–5; Placher, *History of Christian Theology*, 115–16; Cave, *Christian Estimate of Man*, 16; Williams, *Ideas of the Fall*, 333–4, 355–7.

[19] C. J. Hefele, *A History of the Councils of the Church, from the Original Documents*, 5 vols. (Edinburgh: T. and T. Clark, 1876), iii. 458–69.

the Council of Orange in 529 when the delegates announced that 'without grace, and merely from natural powers, we can do nothing which belongs to eternal salvation'. The Augustinian understanding of the Genesis story seemed a necessary corollary to this harsh pronouncement, so the implications of Adam's sin were detailed yet once again. Man was helplessly mired in corruption, left in a condition of sinning necessarily, and subject to the death of both body and soul. Here the matter stood, with the canons of the Council of Orange receiving the approval of the Papacy and thus becoming orthodox teaching until the High Middle Ages.[20]

The Council of Orange had spoken plainly on the issue of prevenient grace, but Augustinian predestination remained an anomalous and an ambiguous point within the Church for centuries to come.[21] In fact the whole problem of man's nature began to recede from prominence as the Church was forced to direct its greatest energies towards the assimilation and conversion of the pagan invaders who had overspread Western Europe in the years after the fall of Roman power. The forced return to rural life and subsistence agriculture, together with the high illiteracy rate amongst the new peoples, compelled the Church to shift its focus away from the intellectualized brand of Christianity previously used to attract educated pagans and in the direction of a clearer, simpler gospel message. Under these difficult circumstances, where thousands were in need of conversion and immediate instruction, predestinarian theology seemed largely impractical, indeed counterproductive. Through the introduction of auricular confession and penance, the cult of the saints and the efficacy of the other sacraments, the early medieval Church hoped to encourage men and women in the practice of moral reform in hopes of receiving the saving grace of God. All told, this vast and constantly expanding panoply of Church dogma and ritual made the pronouncements

---

[20] Ibid. iv. 155–7; Latourette, *History of Christianity*, i. 182; *Encyclopedia of Religion and Ethics*, 1917 edn., article on 'Pelagianism and Semi-Pelagianism'.

[21] J. Pelikan, *The Growth of Medieval Theology, 600–1300* (Chicago: University of Chicago Press, 1978), 81. According to John H. Leith (ed., *Creeds of the Churches* (Atlanta, Ga.: John Knox Press, 1977), 37) 'Orange represents the victory of a moderate Augustinianism.' The Council condemned the belief that some are predestined to evil: Latourette, op. cit. i. 182.

at Orange seem strangely inadequate to the task at hand.[22]

This movement in the direction of meritorious acts was not to dismiss Augustine, however. He remained a revered figure and authoritative Church Father, but certain elements of his teaching were necessarily discounted while others received new emphasis. The medieval monastic movement, and the early Benedictine rule in particular, best exemplified the situation. Monasticism, after all, was firmly committed to the idea of moral struggle and working one's way towards salvation, but at the same time it deprecated the flesh (especially carnal pleasures) as a central prerequisite for achieving that goal. The roots of this attitude were many; there had always been an ascetic strain in early Christian practice, and recurring fears of the imminent end of the world were likely to strengthen this tendency. Moreover, the writings of Sts Paul and Augustine were easily interpreted in a dualistic sense, and the continuing influence of Neoplatonism and Gnosticism provided additional justification for the self-abnegating ideal that was maintained by these special Christian communities.[23] By the thirteenth century, when the mendicant orders of Dominicans and Franciscans were founded, the monastic life-style had achieved firm intellectual credibility within the Catholic Church despite its implicit criticism of the worldliness and pomp of the higher clergy and of the papacy itself. The propriety of man's seeking salvation through works of self-denial and charity undercut the whole predestinarian platform while maintaining an implicit distrust of the world and its practical allurements.

St Thomas crystallized medieval Catholic thinking on the issue of man's nature in a vast synthesis of knowledge and belief completed in the late thirteenth century. His *Summa Theologica* adhered closely to Augustine's analysis of the transmission of sin through Adam. 'According to Catholic Faith,' he said, 'we are bound to hold that the first sin of the first man is transmitted to his descendants, by way of origin.' He also remained in

---

[22] Placher, op. cit. 122, 126. The ninth-century monk Gottschalk fell foul of the Church for rediscovering Augustinian predestination. His views represented a threat to the efficacy of the sacraments; he was eventually condemned and imprisoned (A. Harnack, *History of Dogma*, 7 vols. (New York: Dover, 1961), v. 292–9).
[23] Burkill, *Evolution of Christian Thought*, 136–45, 159–62. On Augustine's influence between the sixth and twelfth centuries, see Baker, *Dignity of Man*, 176–9.

concordance with Pauline teaching by identifying the formal cause of original sin with Adam's wilful turning against God. Once this happened, Adam and his posterity forfeited control over the various powers of the soul. Man's subsequent preoccupation with impermanent sensual gratification or concupiscence in the larger sense constituted the material cause of sin in all. But Thomas could not ignore the experience of the medieval Church with its ongoing commitment to conversion and education. He could not believe that man's nature was as hopelessly corrupt as Augustine had suggested. Sin diminishes man's 'natural inclination to virtue' which all possess by reason of their God-given rational nature, but since sin 'cannot entirely take away from man the fact that he is a rational being', his basic good nature cannot be fully extinguished. The state of original sin, he suggested, was one in which a special divine gift had been withdrawn from man, a gift which in Paradise had enabled him to subdue 'the lower parts of the soul, while reason itself was perfected by God in being subject to him'. This gift could be restored by supernatural grace alone, for man's efforts to merit salvation would always fall short of that which was required. That this infusion of special grace could never be expected outside the institutional Church with its sacramental system Aquinas took for granted, knowing full well that to doubt the Church's intermediary function would be to call into question the whole spirit of medieval theology.[24]

At length the Church was forced to codify its position on the question of man's essential nature in order to check the inroads being made by the sixteenth-century Protestant reformers. At the Council of Trent the Catholic bishops found themselves in the unenviable situation of having to deal with both the Protestant menace and a serious theological split within their own ranks. During the sessions the Augustinian-leaning Dominicans clashed with the combined forces of the Franciscans and the newly formed Society of Jesus over the alleged Semi-Pelagianism of the latter orders. After considerable wrangling

---

[24] St Thomas Aquinas, *The Basic Writings of St Thomas Aquinas*, ed. A. C. Pegis, 2 vols. ii. (New York: Random House, 1945), *Summa Theologica*, qu. 81, art. 1; qu. 85, art. 2; qu. 85, art. 3. See also F. C. Copleston, *Aquinas* (Harmondsworth: Penguin Books, 1982), 156–98; Gilson, *Christian Philosophy in the Middle Ages*, 375–81; G. P. Fisher, *A History of Christian Doctrine* (New York: Scribner's Sons, 1901), 240–1.

the Council followed the Augustinian view of the taint inherited through the Fall, declaring that Adam and his posterity had been 'changed for the worse in body and soul', but then went on to reject the equally Augustinian idea that concupiscence was 'truly and properly sin in the regenerate'. Rather, so the bishops reasoned, concupiscence carried guilt only for those who freely consented to its impulses. On the issue of justification the Council seemed to reaffirm the Thomist definition, but their final position on what constituted the formal cause of justification, or what it was that truly justified men before God, served to exacerbate the growing friction between loyal Catholics and those who were beginning to question the whole temper of Roman theology. It was concluded that man's free will, although doubtless impaired by the Fall, had not been completely extinguished. And while Christ's prevenient saving grace was needed to move men in the performance of good works, once that grace had been bestowed through baptism and the sacraments each person could either accept or reject its helping power. It was the infusion of inherent righteousness through the grace of Christ which justified, not, as the reformers would claim, the imputation of Christ's righteousness to the ever-sinful offspring of Adam. Christ remained the 'first mover' in this Catholic process of justification, then; but men had to choose to love God, hate sin, and live the life of the spirit or righteousness. Predestination received scant attention at this Counter-Reformation gathering. Its declining stock within the Catholic Church could only be expected after Trent had dedicated so much effort to clarifying the sacramental system. The growing influence of the Jesuit Order and the forced suppression of Jansenism in the late seventeenth century only further signalled the eclipse of rigid Augustinianism within the Church militant.[25]

So the Catholic lines in the struggle against Protestantism were firmly drawn by 1563. Because of Adam's fall no one could save themselves or even begin to merit salvation without the

---

[25] On the canons and decrees issued at Trent, see Leith, ed., *Creeds of the Churches*, 400–46; Cave, *Christian Estimate of Man*, 118–25; Fisher, op. cit. 326–30; Latourette, op. cit. ii. 868–9; J. H. Froude, *Lectures on the Council of Trent* (London: Longman, 1896), 194–235. The quarrel between Catholic and Protestant on the important issue of formal cause in justification is discussed by C. F. Allison, *The Rise of Moralism: The Proclamation of the Gospel from Hooker to Baxter* (New York: Seabury Press, 1966), 1–30.

infusion of Christ's saving grace, first bestowed in the sacrament of baptism and subsequently renewed during the course of one's life through the other sacraments. With this grace, however, men were enabled to engage in works of righteousness, to co-operate, as it were, with prevenient grace. The whole process of salvation was in this manner given a strong ethical component while still salvaging much, or so Catholics thought, of the Augustinian heritage.[26]

The traces of Pelagianism inherent in this position might have gone unchallenged were it not for the general decline in the spirit and practice of the late medieval Church—those myriad abuses which exposed the official Catholic world to the blows of Wycliffe's heresy, the ridicule of Erasmus's pen and, ultimately, to the sting of Luther's revolt. What Luther did, of course, was to undercut the entire rationale of institutional Christianity and the whole fabric of the hierarchical Church by returning to the Pauline conception of salvation by faith alone, faith that was the unmerited gift of God to certain select individuals.[27] The Pelagian tendencies within sixteenth-century Catholicism were for Luther brought home with particular force by the aggressive salesman-like antics of John Tetzel in 1517. The marketing of indulgences, Luther believed, had taken the always suspect notion of human merit to its furthest mercenary limits. In reaction both to this and to his failure to find inner peace with the formulae provided by his own religious order, Luther threw himself entirely upon the grace of God; and because he defined this grace as simple forgiveness for the transgressions that he could never hope to overcome, he thereby rejected the Catholic belief that grace somehow transformed men in this life so that they could act righteously in the future. Luther's idea of freedom lay in the recognition that the saved man was no longer beholden to the law, no longer in constant fear of God's wrath by

---

[26] The Catholic position after Trent, writes H. Outram Evennett, 'may be rated humanistic in that it proceeded on the belief that each man's destiny for all eternity was partly in his own power to make or mar' (*The Spirit of the Counter-Reformation* (Notre Dame, Ind.: University Press, 1970), 41). See also M. R. O'Connell, *The Counter-Reformation* (New York: Harper and Row, 1974), 103.

[27] G. R. Elton, *Reformation Europe, 1517–1559* (New York: Harper and Row, 1963), 17. The creedal formulation of this position is contained in the Augsburg Confession, drawn up by Philip Melanchthon and presented at the 1530 Diet of Augsburg. The Confession's articles of faith and doctrine are printed in Leith, op. cit. 67–79.

virtue of the fact of every man's sinfulness. Works of merit, under whatever guise, had no efficacy in the drama of salvation. They were performed by Christians not out of hopes of reward but as natural concomitants to Christian temperament, the fruits of true faith.[28] The Reformed Churches joined Luther in his attack upon the sacramental and hierarchical system and pushed Augustinian predestination as an essential plank in their programme to restore the uninhibited majesty of God. It was Calvin who best defined what Protestants took to be the essential error in Catholic doctrine when he suggested that the principle of co-operation with God's grace in effect declared that the whole man had not fallen with Adam. Churchmen had followed pagan exhaltations of reason too far, he thought, pretending that even in fallen man 'Reason ... like a lamp illuminates with its counsels, and like a queen governs the will; for that it is so irradiated with Divine light as to be able to give the best counsels, and endued with such vigour as to be qualified to govern in the most excellent manner'. In opposition to this, Calvin argued that the whole man was infected by the Fall, mind and body together. The divine image in man 'was obliterated, he was punished with the loss of wisdom, strength, sanctity, truth, and righteousness'; and to suggest that we could in any sense co-operate with the workings of grace was tantamount to repudiating the Fall in its entirety: 'For man has not only been ensnared by the inferior appetites, but abominable impiety has seized the very citadel of his mind and pride has penetrated into the inmost recesses of his heart.' In his present condition, so devoid of even the least intrinsic power to obey God's law, 'oil might be extracted from a stone sooner than we could perform a good work'.[29]

---

[28] Latourette, op. cit. ii. 705–8. Ernst Troeltsch (*The Social Teachings of the Christian Churches*, trans. O. Wyon, 2 vols. (London: Allen and Unwin, 1931), ii. 465–84) offers a useful discussion of some of the implications of Luther's thought.

[29] A. C. McGiffert, *Protestant Thought Before Kant* (London: Duckworth, 1911), 20–46; John Calvin, *Institutes of the Christian Religion*, trans. H. Beveridge, 3 vols. (Edinburgh: Calvin Translation Society, 1845), i. 2. 1. 9, 2. 2. 9; ii. 3. 14. 15. In his commentary on Rom. 5:12 Calvin observed: 'For as Adam, by his first creation, as well received for himself as for his posterity the gifts of God's grace; so he, falling from the Lord, corrupted, vitiated, defiled, and destroyed our nature in himself' (*Commentary upon the Epistle of Saint Paul to the Romans*, ed. H. Beveridge, trans. C. Rosdell (Edinburgh: Calvin Translation Society, 1844), i. 135).

The impact of Calvin's thought upon Reformation figures in England should not be underestimated. The returning Marian exiles, girded by the powerful cross-currents of continental thought during their years of exile, were not the only ones influenced by the logic of the *Institutes*.[30] Both the incipient Puritan party and their Anglican opponents shared common ground on a broad range of fundamental issues.[31] Differences there were, and they should by no means be ignored. But these had more to do with the institutional and ceremonial side of religion than with such core problems as the nature of man, predestination, the conversion experience, and the role of Providence. The old picture of the Puritan movement as a sort of militant phalanx, initially checked by the wily Elizabeth, then re-emerging in pulpit and press under the indolent Stuarts, and slowly but surely snowballing its way towards spiritual and political hegemony by the 1640s, has of late been corrected.[32] That the Puritans throughout the period 1558–1640 did revile their Anglican counterparts with accusations of Arminianism and Roman Catholicism while Anglicans retorted with charges of Antinomianism might at one level suggest irreconcilable differences between the two camps. Yet another, perhaps more fruitful, way of viewing the whole quarrel might be to place it within the wider context of the central role played by religion in the everyday lives of sixteenth- and seventeenth-century

---

[30] H. Baker, *The Wars of Truth* (Cambridge, Mass.: Harvard University Press, 1964), 25, 37; C. and K. George, *The Protestant Mind of the English Reformation, 1570–1640* (Princeton, NJ: University Press, 1961), 35; Dewey D. Wallace, Jr. ('The Doctrine of Predestination in the Early English Reformation', *Church History*, 43 (1974), 201–15) argues that Calvinist teaching had been adopted in England prior to the return of the Marian exiles.

[31] The term 'Anglican' is anachronistic, being a 19th cent. invention. I retain it here for convenience's sake. 'Puritan' was more often than not a general term of derision in the late 16th and 17th cents. See C. Hill, *Society and Puritanism in Pre-Revolutionary England* (London: Panther Books, 1969), 15–30; C. Russell, *Parliaments and English Politics* (Oxford: Clarendon Press, 1979), 27. It seems to have first been used during the Elizabethan Vestiarian Controversy: see M. M. Knappen, *Tudor Puritanism: A Chapter in the History of Idealism* (Chicago: University Press, 1939), 488.

[32] W. Haller, *The Rise of Puritanism* (New York: Columbia University Press, 1938) is the classic statement of Puritan determinism. For background on the Marian exiles and the Elizabethan experience as a whole, Knappen's *Tudor Puritanism* is still valuable. N. Tyack, 'Puritanism, Arminianism and Counter-Revolution', in C. Russell, ed., *The Origins of the English Civil War* (New York: Barnes and Noble, 1973), and C. Russell, *The Crisis of Parliaments* (New York: Oxford University Press, 1971), 210–17 challenge Haller's thesis.

Englishmen. The dispute then becomes part and parcel of the honest and heartfelt desire on both sides to establish the basis of a true religious reformation in England after centuries of what everyone agreed had been the debilitating effects associated with the quasi-magical hocus-pocus of medieval Catholicism.[33]

In a highly stratified, overwhelmingly rural and ignorant society where almost half the population was regularly under-employed and earning less than they consumed, where the average life-expectancy of even the well-to-do was not much more than twenty-nine years, where in the capital city at least half the inhabitants perished before their sixteenth summer, where chronic epidemics, uncontrollable fires, and the accepted humoural medical practice all took their deadly annual tolls; in other words, where sickness, death, and disaster were the granite-like constants of everyday life, the interpretive and consultatory role played by official religion was immense. And where natural science and medicine as yet offered no real solution to man's daily sufferings, the recognized queen of the sciences, theology, provided men with a fully developed and highly credible interpretation of the whole of life's experiences. The theological interpretation of suffering held by all Protestants centred on man's personal relationship with God and on the overarching power of God's providence.[34] From world-shaking events like the defeat of the Spanish Armada to the more pedestrian (and all too frequent) death of an unnamed infant, the providence of God was at work within the world. In the final analysis this interpretation viewed suffering as the direct result of man's sinfulness, as a punishment from God for calculated lapses perpetrated out of pride and conceit. The most influential member of the spiritual brotherhood, William Perkins, whose

---

[33] For the Anglican view of the Reformation, see H. R. McAdoo, *The Structure of Caroline Moral Theology* (London: Longman, 1949), 5 and id., *The Spirit of Anglicanism* (New York: Scribner's Sons, 1965). Dewey D. Wallace (*Puritans and Predestination: Grace in English Protestant Theology* (Chapel Hill, NC: University of North Carolina Press, 1982), 100) argues that for English followers of Calvin, the idea of merit 'made Arminianism in their view no different from the religion of Rome'.

[34] K. Thomas, *Religion and the Decline of Magic* (Harmondsworth: Penguin Books, 1984), 3–20; C. Hill, *The World Turned Upside Down: Radical Ideas During the English Revolution* (New York: Viking, 1972), 121–2; C. Bridenbaugh, *Vexed and Troubled Englishmen, 1590–1642* (New York: Oxford University Press, 1968), 25–8; J. Viner, *The Role of Providence in the Social Order* (Philadelphia, Pa.: American Philosophical Society, 1970), 6–9.

books on practical divinity instructed generations of seventeenth-century Puritan divines, put the matter succinctly. God's reproof took many forms: 'In the bodie diseases, aches, paines: in the soule blindnesse, hardness of heart, horror of conscience: in goods, hindrances and losses: in name, ignominie and reproach: lastly, in the whole man, bondage under Sathan the prince of darknesse.'[35] For the helpless individual subject to the cruel vicissitudes of life and toil, secure knowledge of God's immediate disposition towards him, of the condition of his immortal soul, and of the possible means whereby he might reform and be accorded saving grace—all these things were of utmost importance. Religion mattered, was the most serious of businesses, because its definitions, its perceived ability to unscramble the real meaning of this troublesome, painful passage, its authoritative resolution of man's relationship with his Maker, furnished its adherents with both a comprehensible world-view and with a buffer against the hammer-blows of sudden calamity.

It is within the context of this larger setting that the theological testiness of both Anglican and Puritan must be viewed. Questions concerning the place and form of worship, church order, the authority of the hierarchy, and a host of other practices were every one of them thrown into the cauldron of dispute because a satisfactory resolution of them seemed imperative if the English Church were to stand united against the ever-constant menace of Counter-Reformation tyranny and obscurantism. Fortunately for both sides, however, there did exist a broad common ground that could serve as a touchstone when the above matters were under discussion.[36] From Calvin

---

[35] William Perkins, *The Foundation of Christian Religion, Gathered into Six Principles*, in *Works*, 3 vols. (Cambridge: John Legate, 1608), i. 4. Perkins's great influence is discussed in an otherwise controversial essay by Christopher Hill ('William Perkins and the Poor', in *Puritanism and Revolution* (New York: Schocken Books, 1970), 215–18), and by H. C. Porter (*Reformation and Reaction in Tudor Cambridge* (Cambridge: University Press, 1958), 288–313). Providence touched every aspect of life in the 16th and 17th cents.: see J. S. McGee, *The Godly Man in Stuart England* (New Haven, Conn.: Yale University Press, 1976), 34; Baker, *Wars of Truth*, 12–25.

[36] Patrick Collinson (*The Elizabethan Puritan Movement* (London: Cape, 1967), 26) says that the real differences between Anglican and Puritan were ones of emphasis rather than ones of kind. Conrad Russell writes that 'The Thirty-Nine Articles were too carefully drafted to commit the Church of England to a Calvinist theology, but they were readily compatible with it, and a high proportion of the Jacobean bench of bishops

(and ultimately from Sts Paul and Augustine) all English Protestants had inherited a firm conviction in the depravity of men and in the doctrine of justification by faith alone, faith which was the unmerited gift of God. That a Puritan like Perkins could argue in the strongest terms that 'Every man is by nature dead in sinne as a loathsome carrion' really surprises no one, so inured are most of us to dark descriptions of the Puritans inculcated when we were schoolchildren; but that a supposedly moderate Anglican such as Bishop James Ussher could use precisely the same forbidding language is more of a surprise.[37] The first great Anglican pulpit figure, Lancelot Andrewes, claimed without hesitancy that 'the darkness we are subject to is manifold: there is a darkness inward, not only in the understanding . . . but in the heart'. And in a similar spirit John Owen, Dean of Christ Church, Oxford, in the 1650s (when John Locke was a youthful undergraduate there and doubtless in attendance at many of the Dean's sermons) stated that 'The mind of man by nature is wholly vain, under the power of vanity, and is an endless, fruitful womb of all malicious births.' Agreement on this most fundamental of matters was dictated by the long-standing need to refute the Catholic gradual and sacramental approach to salvation. All would have agreed with Perkins's strictures against the efficacy of Catholic ritual. The Papists wrongfully believed 'that Original sinne is so farre forth taken away after baptisme, that it ceaseth to be a sinne properly'. Every Protestant could easily espy the damnable motives behind the delusory opinion that the divinely infused righteousness of a regenerate person was sufficient to merit

shared with the Puritans the theology which was derived from Calvin and Perkins' (*Crisis of Parliaments*, 211). And John F. H. New (*Anglican and Puritan: The Basis of their Opposition* (Stanford, Calif.: University Press, 1964), 6) argues that both sides 'accepted the doctrine of total depravity, the fall from Grace, and its attendant consequences, the doctrine of justification by faith alone'. See also M. Powicke, *The Reformation in England* (Oxford: University Press, 1961), 125–6; McGee, op. cit. 24, 44, 57; Wallace, *Puritans and Predestination*, 36–7; and footnote 1 above.

[37] Perkins, *Foundations of Christian Religion* (above, n. 35), 3. James Ussher, *Body of Divinity* (1645) quoted in C. and K. George's *Protestant Mind*, 143. For a discussion of the continuing influence of Augustinian ideas in Church of England theology during Locke's lifetime and beyond, see D. Greene, 'Augustinianism and Empiricism: A Note on Eighteenth Century English Intellectual History', *Eighteenth Century Studies*, 1 (1967), 43–51.

salvation; Catholics sought only to 'uphold some grosse opinions of theirs, namely, that a man in this life may fulfill the law of God: and doe good works void of sinne; that he might stand righteous at the barre of God's judgment by them'.[38]

For the English Protestant, salvation was to be achieved only through divine regeneration, whereby a man is enabled to respond to God's call through faith. The process begins and ends with God, however. Those who are justified or acquitted from the penalties of the law by the imputation of Christ's sacrifice on the Cross are then sanctified, or given the strength to pursue the good in their own lives. And though the saved man will continue to sin in this life, his faith will guarantee the final victory. 'The faith therefore of the true believers,' said the celebrated defender of the Elizabethan Church, Richard Hooker, 'though it may have many and grievous downfalls, yet doth it still continue invincible; it conquereth and recovereth itself in the end.'[39] Still, it is God alone who, out of his infinite mercy to fallen man, calls some to a new life and empowers them to respond to this wholly gratuitous election. Thomas Hooker, the Puritan founder of the Connecticut colony in New England, epitomized the entire process from Fall to regeneration before leaving for the New World where he hoped to work out his vision of a pure Church without hindrance:

They [Adam's Posterity] departed from the God of all holiness, glory and consolation, unto all baseness, desolation and misery, which cannot be conceived. They being thus departed from the Lord, recovered again they cannot be into the state of spiritual life and goodness unless they be brought again to him who is the fountain of life and good to all that shall have it, namely, to the living God. And brought they will never be but by faith; for man being bound to live the spiritual life of grace, and to please God, he must either live by

---

[38] Lancelot Andrewes, *A Preparation to Prayer*, Sermon 2 in *Works*, 11 vols. (Oxford: Henry Parks, 1854), v. 318; John Owen, *A Discourse Concerning the Holy Spirit*, in *Works*, 6 vols. (Philadelphia, Pa.: Protestant Episcopal Book Society, 1860), iii. 254; M. Cranston, *John Locke: A Biography* (London: Longman, 1957), 41; Perkins, *The Reformed Catholic*, in *Works*, i. 554. Both Ussher and Andrewes had been deeply influenced by Puritanism in their youth: M. M. Knappen, 'The Early Puritanism of Lancelot Andrewes', *Church History*, 2 (1933), 95.

[39] Richard Hooker, *A Learned and Comfortable Sermon of the Certainty and Perpetuity of Faith in the Elect*, in *The Works of Mr Richard Hooker*, 2 vols. (Oxford: Clarendon Press, 1865), ii. 593.

himself or by another. By himself he cannot, being dead in sins and trespasses; therefore he must live by another.[40]

Lancelot Andrewes was even more blunt about the whole matter when he wrote that 'we ought not to boast of our ability, because we have none', but his meaning was doubtless the same. Man's utter helplessness in the face of sin was even acknowledged by that obdurate nemesis of the Puritans, William Laud. The allegedly Catholicizing Archbishop was doing no more than expressing a universally shared Protestant assumption when he declared in the midst of a quarrel with the Jesuit John Fisher that 'Man lost by sin the integrity of his nature, and can not have light enough to see the way to heaven but by grace.'[41] Anglicans, it is true, placed more emphasis upon the importance of doing good works in this world—and were duly excoriated by Puritans for doing so—but they categorically denied that these works were of any real moment in facilitating the process of spiritual regeneration without the support of divine grace.[42]

In fact, the emphasis which is often placed upon Puritan bibliolatry, on their supposed utter distrust of human reason unaided by grace, tends to distort the extent to which they clashed with the Anglicans at this juncture. The misunderstanding owes a good deal to early Protestant notions concerning the nature of the conversion process itself. Calvin had of course included man's reason in his analysis of the Fall, and consequently sixteenth-century English Protestants were drawn towards an understanding of conversion which excluded all

---

[40] Thomas Hooker, 'Epistle to the Reader of John Roger's *The Doctrine of Faith*' (1627), in *Thomas Hooker: Writings in England and Holland*, ed. G. H. Williams *et al.* (Cambridge, Mass.: Harvard University Press, 1975), 143. For a discussion of the conversion process see P. Miller, *The New England Mind: The Seventeenth Century* (Boston: Beacon Press, 1964), 21–7, and E. Morgan, *Visible Saints: The History of a Puritan Idea* (New York: New York University Press, 1963), 67–71.

[41] William Laud, *A Relation of a Conference between William Laud and Mr Fisher the Jesuit*, in *Works,* 7 vols. (Oxford: J. H. Parker, 1847), ii. 280; E. C. E. Bourne (*The Anglicanism of William Laud* (London: SPCK, 1947), 50–74) discusses the Puritan–Anglican split. J. P. Kenyon concludes that while Laud's theological views are obscure, 'it was possible to combine strictly orthodox Calvinism with a belief in episcopacy by divine right' (*The Stuart Constitution* (Cambridge: University Press, 1966), 147); Andrewes, *Preparation to Prayer*, sermon 1 (*Works*, v. 302). The above statements were consonant with Articles 9, 10, 11, and 12 of the Church of England.

[42] We shall presently discover that John Locke was in entire agreement with this viewpoint.

human involvement. The story of Paul's sudden seizure on the road to Damascus, described in Acts 22: 6–11, was the ideal model taken for the norm. All ideas of preparation for grace were rejected out of hand; God would call the sinner for reasons of his own and the question of whether or not those who were so chosen had conformed to the moral standards of their own puny intellects was of no consequence. Man's reason counted for nothing in the process, its dilapidated and depraved nature having disqualified it from service.

But by the last quarter of the sixteenth century, English Puritans, sensitive to the requirements of their role as proselytizing Christians, began, however haltingly, to exhort men towards a preparation for the moment when God might call them as one of his Elect.[43] By preparation the Puritan normally meant intensive self-analysis and introspection, but it would often also mean a renewed concentration on behaviour. During the seventeenth century this shift in emphasis was given new urgency by the Antinomian controversy, where certain aberrant souls became convinced that the Elect of God, once chosen, were thereby released from the sanctions of the law. The most famous chapter in this schism within the ranks was played out in the recently settled Zion of Massachusetts Bay, where Mistress Anne Hutchinson was brusquely expelled from the colony for her dangerous opinions. Surely the most efficacious means of checking this ruinous strain of thought, it was agreed, was to concentrate on the necessity of godly living, tempered by reason, in hopes of salvation.[44]

And reason, oddly enough, was the key here. The Puritan had never fully abandoned it during the opening stages of the Reformation struggle, and by the seventeenth century it had

---

[43] N. Pettit, *The Heart Prepared: Grace and the Conversion Process in Puritan Spiritual Life* (New Haven, Conn.: Yale University Press, 1966), 7–20.

[44] W. K. B. Stoever, *A Faire and Easie Way to Heaven: Covenant Theology and Antinomianism in Early Massachusetts* (Middletown, Conn.: Wesleyan University Press, 1978), 10–11, 23–33; E. Morgan, *The Puritan Dilemma* (New Haven, Conn.: Yale University Press, 1958), 134–54. The English Antinomians of the Civil War period constitute the single, though important, exception to an otherwise commonly shared Protestant vision of human depravity. Gertrude Huehns (*Antinomianism in English History* (London: Cresset Press, 1951), 15, 92) writes that 'it was impossible for them to recognize the existence of evil in themselves as in God'. The Antinomian 'accepted the idea of original sin in order to contrast it with his own unconditional redemption'. See also Hill, *World Turned Upside Down*, 147–54; Wallace, *Puritans and Predestination*, 113–20.

come to play a crucial role in readying the unregenerate for God's call. There was no guarantee that the call would come, of course—all Protestants understood that—and if it did not come despite the most arduous of preparations, one received no more and no less than what one truly deserved. 'The Lord will not stand bent to thy bow and give thee grace when thou wilt', cautioned Thomas Hooker; but it was nevertheless incumbent upon every man to play his assigned part, to live uprightly and 'wait upon God in the use of the means'. God alone must save us; that fact was beyond question, 'yet he will not do it without us, because we are *reasonable* [emphasis mine] men and women, and God affords us the means; and therefore we are to wait upon the Lord in the use of the means, and let the Lord do what he will, and let us do what we should'.[45] And what were the specific means available to frail humanity? Most Puritans would place hearing the Word at the top of the list (much to the consternation of the Laudians), then prayer, the administration of the sacraments, and a godly deportment and life-style.[46] Although the best works that we can do are 'more the matter of damnation than of salvation', though the blemish of original sin can only be purged 'by the merits and power of Christ's death', though God has from the beginning of time 'proposed in himselfe to shewe mercie on some men, and to passe by others, shewing his justice on them for the manifestation of the glory of his own name', still it was imperative that moral standards be defined and upheld to the best of one's impaired ability.[47] At the end of the century, when the godly experiment in Massachusetts had seemingly gone awry in the face of increasing prosperity and a new charter which stripped the Elect of their monopoly over political power, one could still hear the indefatigable Increase Mather admonishing his by now weary audience to action: 'Sinners can do more towards their own Conversion than they do or will do. They should give diligence to make sure of their being effectively called. They should strive to enter in at the

---

[45] Thomas Hooker, *The Poor Doubting Christian Drawn Unto Christ*, in *Writings in England and Holland*, 158, 176.

[46] The popular Perkins briefly outlined the steps for his readers in *The Foundations of Christian Religion* (*Works*, i. 1–4).

[47] Perkins, op. cit. 6, and *An Exposition of the Symbole or Creed of the Apostles* (*Works*, i. 284).

strait gate.' William Laud's Arminian devotees could not have agreed more.[48]

The Puritans' respect for learning, both religious and classical, is well documented and further attests to their acknowledgement of man's diminished yet still respectable powers of reason. Their every reference to classical models, their grudging admiration for notable heathen moralists, and their utter disdain for unlettered enthusiasm in religion, reveals that the Puritans' fallen man, as Perry Miller remarked, 'was not quite a contemptible worm'. While they always placed more emphasis upon Biblical literalism when discoursing on Church government, worship, and ethics than did most Anglicans, the Puritans continued to call upon men to exercise rational control over the unruly passions and affections, and it is unlikely that their bibliolatry would have been of much practical use had they denied a place to natural reason in their mandate for reform.[49]

The practical danger inherent in this joint Puritan-Anglican call for moral reform and preparation for salvation was, obviously, the unpalatable yet surely possible danger of slipping over into the Catholic position regarding the role of merit or works of righteousness. In fact most Puritans felt quite sincerely that Charles I's Church of England had done just that in the 1620s. Ominous signs were all around: there was the upgrading of ceremony and the Laudian preoccupation with what the Archbishop euphemistically called 'things indifferent'; there was the dismissal of Puritan preachers, the suspect Court headed by a Catholic queen, the pro-Spanish foreign policy of the first Stuart king, the callous abandonment of continental Protestants fighting for their lives and their faith, and a whole host of other

---

[48] Increase Mather, *Awakening Truths Tending to Conversion*, in *The Puritans*, ed. P. Miller and T. Johnson, (Boston: American Book Co., 1938), 337. R. H. Tawney pointed out the more deleterious consequences of covenant theology for the social order in *Religion and the Rise of Capitalism* (Gloucester, Mass.: Peter Smith, 1962), 253–73.

[49] Miller and Johnson, eds., *The Puritans*, 23; J. S. Coolidge, *The Pauline Renaissance in England: Puritanism and the Bible* (Oxford: Clarendon Press, 1970), 3; R. D. Linder, 'Calvinism and Humanism: The First Generation', *Church History*, 44. 2 (1975), 167–81; Baker, *Wars of Truth*, 102. 'To charge the intellect with perpetual blindness,' wrote Calvin, 'so as to leave it no intelligence of any description whatsoever, is repugnant not only to the Word of God, but to common experience' (*Institutes*, 2. 2. 12). On the importance of education for the Puritans, see R. Greaves, *The Puritan Revolution and Educational Thought* (New Brunswick, NJ: Rutgers University Press, 1969).

equally repugnant developments, all of which would not be countenanced for long by a just God intent upon punishing those who dared cross him.[50] But in truth there did exist a particularly fine line that both sides were attempting to walk between the need for preparation and the arbitrariness and sufficiency of God's election. Lancelot Andrewes had early on worked to clear up the ambiguity by insisting that even our first movement in preparation, since it clearly had to be viewed as a good action on our part, was in effect inaugurated by God. But even this analysis could be easily misunderstood. For on the one hand 'The means to obtain this grace at the hands of God is by prayer', and if 'in humility we seek for grace from God, knowing that we have it not of ourselves, we shall receive it from God'; one senses in this statement that Andrewes was discussing the efficacy of merit, in that men could petition for grace and receive it after fulfilling specific conditions (that is, by prayer and humility). But in the next breath the Bishop said that even our seeking was in vain without prior grace, 'Seeing that there is in us no ability, no not so much as to think any thing'.[51] All ability comes from God, he maintained; men turn towards their Maker only when he enables them to do so.

It is clear from statements such as these that the differences between Anglican and Puritan on matters theological were primarily ones of emphasis. Yet the subject was always an extremely volatile one—a question of eternal life and death, one might say. That misunderstanding and mutual recrimination was often the result does not of itself invalidate the shared premises, even in light of the fact that the less substantive differences played their part in the final resort to arms during the 1640s.

Perhaps the worldly-wise Clarendon, a moderate Anglican who early in his career had come under the influence of the Latitudinarian members of the Great Tew Circle just outside Oxford, can be taken as the best example of someone who balked at the political excesses of the Puritan party while sharing most of their basic assumptions about the nature of man, the significance of Christ's sacrifice, and the role of reason and

---

[50] For details see P. Zagorin, *The Court and the Country: The Beginning of the English Revolution* (New York: Atheneum, 1971), 40–73.

[51] L. Andrewes, *Preparation to Prayer* (*Works*, v. 310).

merit in the search for salvation.[52] For here was a man acutely sensitive to the danger lurking behind Protestantism's debasement of human nature. In his concern he echoed the perennial warnings of the monk Pelagius, predicting that most of his contemporaries would happily accept the Augustinian estimation of man's capacity in order to excuse themselves from all their wilful transgressions. His own solution to the dilemma was to maintain, again like Pelagius, that men took 'Great Pains' to assist in the corruption of nature; that the unthinking masses, in refusing to cultivate and give good direction to their minds, to curb their passions, and to reform their ill affections, consciously contributed to their own degradation. This self-destructive tendency, he thought, must be overturned lest all moral effort be banished from the world. 'Neither Virtue or Piety', he said, 'come by Nature or Chance, but are learned and taught and studied.'[53] A more Pelagian statement would be difficult to find in the seventeenth century. We will discover later that John Locke would employ similar language while wrestling with essentially the same problem. But for now it is important to notice that Clarendon adamantly refused to abandon Protestant orthodoxy in spite of this statement. The Pauline-Augustinian-Calvinist frame of reference, an authoritative perspective on human nature seemingly borne out by the bloody events of Clarendon's own lifetime, prescribed and delimited his religious outlook.

Clarendon believed no sin to be more inconsistent with true Christianity than the sin of presumption, the arrogant conviction that whatever shred of integrity and innocence one possessed was the sole product of one's own 'Wit, Reason, and Observation'. Man merits absolutely nothing from even the most exhaustive obedience to duty that he is capable of working on his own. And while no one should perplex themselves 'with hard Words of Justification and Merit, which signify no more, or less, than they who use them intend they should', still everyone

---

[52] On Clarendon and the Tew Circle, see B. H. G. Wormald, *Clarendon* (Cambridge: University Press, 1951), 243–56; Barbara Shapiro, *Probability and Certainty in Seventeenth Century England* (Princeton, NJ: University Press, 1983), 80–2.

[53] Edward Hyde, *Of Human Nature*, in *A Collection of Tracts of the Right Honourable Edward, Earl of Clarendon* (London: T. Woodward, 1727), 89; *On An Active and On a Contemplative Life* (ibid. 168).

should be fully conscious of the fact that 'We can neither refrain from doing ill, nor persevere in well-doing, without the immediate Support and Influence of his good Spirit.'[54] Not a moment of our lives, thought Clarendon, should pass in which we neglect to contemplate God's mercy or implore his assistance. That assistance, for Anglican and for Puritan, for Laud and for Perkins, for Cranmer and for Cromwell, was mankind's only hope of overcoming the otherwise ineradicable stain of Adam's sin, a sin that Catholics had assayed to remove with the false solvent of priestly and sacramental mystery-mongering, but which most seventeenth-century Englishmen recognized was only giving the lie to a very hard fact of life.

In agreeing that the Bible was authoritative in points of doctrine, then, Anglicans and Puritans were demonstrating their close adherence to the bedrock principles of Reformed Christianity. The Puritans, we know, would go on to claim for the Bible equal authority in questions concerning every aspect of life—modes of conduct, the order of worship, the form of Church government, and, ultimately, the form of temporal government—while Anglicans, led by Richard Hooker, insisted that such an extreme position would only abrogate the limited and legitimate role of God-given reason and natural law in settling matters of lesser import.[55] To agree with Hooker, however, was not to reject the Pauline understanding of man's nature. That would remain an almost instinctive assumption upon which everyone could agree. Predestined to salvation or damnation, the Protestant was left in a state of constant doubt as to the condition of his soul. Expected to live as though he were in fact one of the Elect, the backsliders and the indolent alike jeopardized their already slim prospects. 'The husbandman may not therefore burn his plow,' wrote Richard Hooker, 'nor the mechanic foresake his trade, because God hath promised "I

---

[54] Edward Hyde, *Contemplations and Reflections on the Psalms of David* (ibid. 390, 414, 458). Clarendon's sentiments were echoed by the Puritan John Preston: 'A Natural Man may pay a certain debt of dutie and obedience to God, but he pays it in a counterfeit coin that hath the stamp, and colour, and similitude of true coin, yet it consists of base mettal' (*Sermons* (1630), quoted in C. and K. George, *Protestant Mind*, 43).

[55] Davies, *Worship and Theology*, 53; J. S. Marshall, *Hooker and the Anglican Tradition: An Historical and Theological Study of Hooker's Ecclesiastical Polity* (London: A. and C. Black, 1963), 117–18. F. J. Shirley (*Richard Hooker and Contemporary Political Ideas* (London: SPCK, 1949), 35–6) discusses his influence.

will not foresake thee".[56] Together lay the call to action and the burdensome knowledge of its hollow character. By the end of the Stuart century, important steps had been taken to mitigate the severity of the latter Christian dictum, and the philosopher John Locke would play a not insignificant role in the developments. But he too, as we shall see, refused to dispense with a view of man then close on eighteen hundred years old and still being given fresh credibility by the cruel empirical evidence that was mid-seventeenth-century England.

[56] Richard Hooker, *Works*, ii. 598.

2

From Pensford to Oxford

JOHN LOCKE was born at Wrington, Somerset, on 29 August
1632 and spent his childhood years in the village of Pensford,
some six miles outside Bristol. Details concerning the philosopher's early life are scanty; thus, suggestions regarding his
'Puritan' upbringing and its impact upon his later life and
thought must remain no more than that.[1] His father, a
small-time lawyer in and around the city of Bristol and a minor
clerk to the Justices of the Peace in Somerset, sided with the
Parliamentary forces in the struggle against Charles I after 1640
and became captain of a troop of horse under his friend and
patron Colonel Alexander Popham. When the Royalists took
control of Bristol and the surrounding countryside in 1643, John
Locke senior returned to the obscurity whence he had so
recently emerged, this time as clerk to the commissioner of
sewers for the county of Somerset. His connection with Popham
eventually paid off, however, when as MP for Bath after 1647
the colonel was able to secure a place for Locke's eldest son in the
prestigious Westminster School.[2] The Master of the institution
was the indomitable Richard Busby, a dedicated Royalist whose
ability to maintain his place after a Parliamentary committee
had taken charge of the school in 1645 is a testimony both to his

---

[1] Dunn, *John Locke*, 9; P. Abrams, ed., *Two Tracts on Government* (Cambridge:
University Press, 1969), 50; J. L. Mabbott, *John Locke* (Oxford: University Press, 1970),
106; Cranston, *John Locke*, 1–3; R. I. Aaron, *John Locke* (Oxford: University Press,
1955), 2; G. Parry, *John Locke* (London: Allen and Unwin, 1978), 27; M. Johnson, *Locke
on Freedom* (Austin, Te.: Best Printing Co., 1977), 6; all assume that Locke's early
environment was deeply Puritan. Damaris Masham wrote after Locke's death that the
philosopher 'was born and studied at a time when Calvinism was the fashion in England'
and that the ideas of men like her father Ralph Cudworth were 'new to him' (letter to
Philip Limborch, 19 September 1705, printed in John Locke, *Epistola de Tolerantia*, ed.
R. Klibansky and J. W. Gough (Oxford: Clarendon Press, 1968), pp. xv–xvi).
[2] Cranston, op. cit. 17. Thomas G. Barnes (*Somerset, 1625–1640* (Cambridge, Mass.:
Harvard University Press, 1961), 15) says that Somerset 'proved to be predominantly
Puritan in religious sympathy' during the Civil War: see pp. 147–9 for a description of
the duties assigned commissioners of sewers. On Popham see *DNB* xvi. 143.

abilities as a teacher of considerable repute and to his skill as a political survivor.

During Busby's tenure of some fifty-seven years (1638–95) a number of important seventeenth-century figures attended Westminster—Christopher Wren, Robert South, John Dryden, George Hooper—and all of them, including John Locke, spent the bulk of their days drilling in Latin and Greek grammar (Busby wrote his own grammars in both languages for use in the school), translating from these ancient languages into English and back again, engaging in declamations on classical topics, and competing with each other for the honour of being elected, at the end of their long ordeal, to a Studentship at either Christ Church, Oxford, or Trinity College, Cambridge. The basic grammar-school fare at this time, as one scholar has written, 'was in the main pagan, and the English schoolboy was brought up on the same classics as his counterpart in ancient Rome'.[3] Locke would later protest against the seemingly endless routine of grammar lessons in Latin and Greek and the overall impracticality of the grammar-school curriculum for a gentleman's son,[4] but we should remember that classicism in the seventeenth-century grammar school was not pursued as an end in itself, but rather served as a handmaiden to sound religious instruction, and, perhaps just as importantly, as a prerequisite to enlightened public service and statecraft. Busby was seeking a greater good than scholarship at his school; the real end of learning was religion and civility, whereby the student would be brought to the practice of piety and probity through a solid knowledge of the 'holy languages', those undisputed keys to the study of the Bible and its unalterable rule of life. Classical knowledge was useful knowledge in the seventeenth century, useful in the pursuit of Christian duty and godly living. And useful also in the sense that the humanists in England since the

---

[3] M. L. Clarke, *Classical Education in Britain, 1500–1900* (Cambridge: University Press, 1959), 7. On the curriculum at Westminster see J. Sargeaunt, *Annals of Westminster School* (London: Methuen, 1898), 113–34; R. Airy, *Westminster* (London: Bell, 1902), 21–36; Clarke, op. cit. 36–7; and H. L. Fox Bourne, *The Life of John Locke*, 2 vols. (London: Henry King, 1876), i. 20–1.

[4] 'A great part of the Learning now in fashion in the schools of Europe, and that goes ordinarily into the round of Education, a Gentleman may in good measure be unfurnished with, without any great Disparagement to himself, or Prejudice to his Affairs' (*Thoughts on Ed.*, 196).

time of Colet, More and Erasmus had rediscovered in the classics the vision of the orator as the exemplary statesman, where individuals skilled in the art of public speaking, whose judgement, experience, and practical knowledge had been carefully cultivated through the study of classical prose and poetry, would be best fitted to take up positions of leadership in a society growing daily more complex. Expanding government, unprecedented economic growth and the social dislocations that accompanied it, religious disquiet and an emerging animus towards the perceived intellectual aridity of medieval scholastic method—these developments challenged sensitive Tudor and Stuart educators to formulate, articulate, and implement a new educational programme, one capable of coming to terms with the changing needs of men living in the early modern nation-state and geared to the propertied classes who were fast replacing clergymen in key political positions.[5] This being the case, there was really little need for those subjects which made up the medieval quadrivium: arithmetic, geometry, astronomy, and music. Nor were such modern innovations as vernacular languages and natural science apt to contribute to achieving one's goal in life.[6] The Master of Westminster felt confident that his rigorous standards were in the best interests of his scholars

[5] R. M. Ogilvie, *Latin and Greek: A History of the Influence of the Classics on English Life from 1600 to 1900* (London: Routledge and Kegan Paul, 1964), 5–8; R. S. Crane, 'The Idea of the Humanities', in *The Idea of the Humanities and Other Essays*, 2 vols. (Chicago: University Press, 1967), i. 5–28. 'Like their Italian forerunners,' writes Joan Simon (*Education and Society in Tudor England* (Cambridge: University Press, 1979), 103), 'the northern humanists consistently emphasized that close and detailed study of classical tongues and authors, both as regards form and content, was the best and most useful preparation for life, whether active or scholarly.' See also A. B. Ferguson, *The Articulate Citizen and the English Renaissance* (Durham, NC: Duke University Press, 1965), 405; F. Caspari, *Humanism and the Social Order in Tudor England* (Chicago: University Press, 1954), 17; L. Stone, *The Crisis of the Aristocracy* (Oxford: Clarendon Press, 1965), 672–83. In the 1690s the first two combatants in the quarrel between the ancients and moderns, William Temple and William Wotton, were of one mind concerning the superiority of the ancients in eloquence and poetry, and in the advantages of classical imitation for the educated man of their day: J. M. Levine, 'Ancients, Moderns and History: The Continuity of English Historical Writing in the Later Eighteenth Century', in *Studies in Change and Revolution: Aspects of English Intellectual History, 1640–1800*, ed. Paul Korshin (Menston: Scolar Press, 1972), 45–7.

[6] F. Watson, *The English Grammar Schools to 1660* (New York: Frank Cass and Co., 1908), 60, 63, 118, 536; id., *The Beginnings of the Teaching of Modern Subjects in England* (London: Pitman, 1909), introd.; W. A. L. Vincent, *The State and School Education in England and Wales, 1640–1660* (London: n.p., 1958), 16; W. Notestein, *The English People on the Eve of Colonization* (New York: Harper Torchbooks, 1962), 116–29.

and would fully prepare them for success in a world full of bad habits and vile temptation.

Wood described Busby as 'a person eminent and exemplary for piety and justice, an encourager of virtuous and forward youth, of great learning and hospitality, and the chief person that educated more youths that were afterwards eminent in the Church and the State than any master of his time', but Thomas Pierce was perhaps more to the point about Busby's real strength as a teacher and role-model when he observed that besides the man's obvious depth of knowledge and wisdom, 'that which gained him my reverence was the greater sanctity of his life . . . for his mastery over his Passions and his diffusiveness of his substance as well as of himself (to all at least who are deserving as well as needy), I have heard few persons commended more'.[7] Busby exerted his greatest energies in the religious education of his charges. Not willing to see their preparation abandoned upon graduation, he offered to estab-lish two catechistical lectures, one at each university, with endowments of £100 per annum, for instructing all undergra-duates in the Christian faith, but the authorities balked when the benefactor made his offer contingent upon the lectures being made compulsory for all students and required that everyone be successfully examined by the catechist as a condition of their graduation.[8] Despite this set-back, Busby did his utmost to prepare his best students who stood for the annual election to the universities. Locke was to repeat Busby's own educational path—first at Westminster, then on to Christ Church, and finally as a college tutor—and notwithstanding Busby's repu-tation for severity, Locke thought a great deal of his Royalist teacher. Writing to his father in Pensford concerning the coming election for the school year 1656, the younger Locke said that 'your letter to Mr Busby I have delivered and he hath promised me to doe what he can which I can not doubt of haveing soe many assureances of his love he hath made choice of my oration

[7] Anthony Wood, *Athenae Oxonienses*, ed. P. Bliss, 4 vols. (London: n.p., 1820), iv. 418. Pierce is quoted in G. F. R. Barker, *Memoir of Richard Busby, D.D.: With Some Account of Westminster School in the Seventeenth Century* (London: Lawrence and Buller, 1895), 29. Locke later commented upon the harsh discipline at Westminster in a letter to Edward Clarke (26 Feb. 1692: iv, no. 1471).

[8] Barker, op. cit. 29–30; A. Kippis, *Biographia Britannica*, 7 vols. (London: n.p., 1747), iii. 52–6; *DNB* iii. 481–3.

before any of the rest to be perhaps spoken at the Election'.[9] He would leave Westminster a twenty-year-old scholar whose interests in life were rapidly drawing him away from the mundane concerns of provincial Pensford, but whose sense of studied commitment to Protestant religious values and assumptions about the nature of man were being forged within the context of civil war and the excesses of enthusiasm and bloodshed which it fostered.

'I no sooner perceived myself in the world but I found myself in a storm, which has lasted almost hitherto', admitted Locke at the start of the Stuart Restoration.[10] While at Westminster School he had been in close proximity to the spot where a king by divine right had been executed in January 1649, but Master Busby kept his school in session and his scholars in prayer for the soul of their martyred monarch. Upon his arrival at Oxford in 1652, Locke found himself entering a Puritan stronghold recently reformed after the decline of learning and the debauchery of life-style which had marked the tenure of the Stuart court in that city during the years 1642–6. Cromwell was now Chancellor and his personal chaplain John Owen was both Dean of Christ Church and Vice-Chancellor of the University.[11] Locke would later be as critical of the university curriculum as he was of the grammar-school fare, but these sentiments and his own leaning towards natural science outside the official university community should not be interpreted as a disparagement of the quality of the traditional learning that went on under the rule of the Puritans.[12] Their commitment to

[9] Locke to his father (4 May 1652: i, no. 3). On 11 May 1652 (i, no. 4) he wrote to his father that Busby had spoken to the electors on his behalf.

[10] *Two Tracts*, 119.

[11] H. L. Thompson, *Christ Church* (London: F. E. Robinson and Co., 1900), 65–78; C. Mallet, *A History of the University of Oxford*, 3 vols. (New York: Longman, 1924), ii. 370–96; C. V. Wedgwood, *The King's War, 1641–1647* (London: Collins, 1958), 156–7; Anthony Wood, *Life and Times*, ed. Andrew Clark, 5 vols. (Oxford: Clarendon Press for Oxford Historical Society, 1891–1900), i. 60, 71–4, 83–4.

[12] Locke's friend Lady Masham wrote to Jean Le Clerc on 12 Jan. 1705 that Locke 'never loved the trade of disputing in publick in the schools, but was always wont to declaim against them as being rather invented for wrangling or ostentation than to discover truth' (excerpt from a letter printed in Cranston, *John Locke*, 38). Jean Le Clerc ('The Life and Character of Mr Locke' (1706), trans. T. F. P., printed in Locke's *An Essay concerning Human Understanding*, ed. M. W. Calkins (Chicago: Open Court, 1917), pp. x–xii), details Locke's dissatisfaction with the 'peripatetick' philosophy then known at Oxford. The undergraduate course of study during this period is discussed by M.

educational rigour was unassailable, despite the acrid criticism of sectaries eager to disassociate piety from erudition. Even Clarendon, certainly no admirer of things Puritan, took exception to those who questioned the Cromwellian dedication to a learned ministry and intelligent laity. In point of fact the Lord Chancellor believed that the Puritan rule at Oxford had brought forth 'a harvest of extraordinary good and sound knowledge in all parts of learning and the practice of virtue: so that when it pleased God to bring King Charles the Second back to his throne, he found that University abounding in excellent learning, devoted to duty and obedience, and little inferior to what it had been before its desolation'.[13]

Owen was an important figure in this revival of learning at Oxford, preaching regularly at Christ Church and, after June 1651, ordering scholars to report to their tutors on the contents of the Sunday sermon. But to discuss the extent of his immediate influence on Locke is, as in the case of Busby, problematical.[14] Moving from Presbyterianism to Independency in 1646, Owen despite his own strongly Calvinist convictions, had become a firm believer in the principle of religious toleration for all Protestants provided that civil peace was maintained. Locke,

Curtis, *Oxford and Cambridge in Transition, 1558–1642* (Oxford: Clarendon Press, 1959), 83–90; W. N. Hargreaves-Mawdsley, *Oxford in the Age of Locke* (Norman, OK: University of Oklahoma Press, 1973), 96–101; W. Costello, *The Scholastic Curriculum at Early Seventeenth Century Cambridge* (Cambridge, Mass.: Harvard University Press, 1958), 14–35; R. L. Greaves, *Puritan Revolution*, 9–15; J. B. Conant, 'The Advancement of Learning During the Puritan Commonwealth', *Proceedings of the Massachusetts Historical Society* 65 (1942), 3–31; Thompson, op. cit. 73–8.

[13] Edward Hyde, *A History of the Rebellion and Civil Wars in England*, ed. W. D. Macray, 6 vols. (Oxford: Clarendon Press, 1888), iv. 283. See also C. Hill, *God's Englishman: Oliver Cromwell and the English Revolution* (New York: Harper Torchbooks, 1970), 197, and Wood, *Life and Times*, i. 300–1, where he grudgingly acknowledges Puritan learning and discipline at Oxford.

[14] P. Toon, *God's Statesman: The Life and Work of John Owen* (Grand Rapids, Mich.: Zondervan Publishing, 1973), 55, 57; W. Von Leyden, in his edition of Locke's *Essays on the Law of Nature* (Oxford: Clarendon Press, 1954), 17, suggests that Owen's influence on Locke was significant, but he gives no reference. Fox Bourne believed that Owen shaped Locke's ideas on religious toleration, but Abrams's recently published *Two Tracts* disproves that theory. A letter from Samuel Tilly to Locke (11 Sept. 1655: i, no. 23) seems to indicate Locke's respect for Owen. The Dean's intervention on behalf of the man whom Locke respected most at Oxford, the staunch Royalist and oriental scholar Edward Pococke, to prevent his being deprived of his living in 1655, probably increased Locke's estimation of Owen (see Thompson, op. cit. 70). Pococke was for Locke an 'extraordinary' example of learning and virtue 'in so degenerate an age' (*Works*, x. 300).

however, had great difficulty in accepting this permissive viewpoint during his years at Oxford.[15] Religious enthusiasm in general, and the actions of the Quakers in particular, disturbed him greatly during these years. Witnessing the appearance of some Quakers who had been called before a parliamentary commission in 1656, Locke indicated to his father his belief in the 'dangerous' nature of these 'mad folks'. His deep disdain was again revealed in his contemptuous description of James Nayler, alleged to have been one of the leading Quakers, who had been brought before a committee of the Commons for claiming to be the Messiah and re-enacting Christ's entry into Jerusalem in the city of Bristol earlier that year. 'I am tired of the Quakers', he told Locke senior, and this wariness of religious excess would carry over to the Restoration and beyond, conditioning his reaction to that great event and the type of society which he envisioned it would be in the best interests of all Englishmen to create.[16]

Christ Church became Locke's principal residence for the next fourteen years (1652–66). After graduating BA in 1656, he continued for the MA (1658) and was subsequently appointed Reader in Greek (1660), Rhetoric (1662), and Censor in Moral Philosophy (1664).[17] The Studentship to which he had been elected was for life, on condition that he remain single and enter into Holy Orders when appointed to one of four senior Studentships. As this latter position, with its potentially awkward requirement, was awarded strictly on the basis of seniority, Locke had little immediate worry in the 1650s. At Oxford he was relatively insulated from the whirl and tumble of

---

[15] S. R. Gardiner, *History of the Commonwealth and Protectorate*, 3 vols. (London: Longman, 1897), ii. 26; Kippis, *Biographica Britannica*, v. 3291–4; *DNB* xiv. 1318–22; Cranston, *Locke*, 41; Thompson, op. cit. 69–71; Mallet, *History of Oxford Univ.* ii. 390, 393–6. W. K. Jordon thinks Owen's advocacy of toleration was minimal before the Restoration, extending little beyond the confines of the Calvinistic Churches (*The Development of Religious Toleration in England*, 4 vols. (London: Allen and Unwin, 1938), iii. 425–6). Wallace (*Puritans and Predestination*, 150) places Owen's theology in the 'high Calvinist' camp, particularly on the matter of justification by faith alone.

[16] Locke to his father (25 Oct. 1656: i, no. 29; 15 Nov. 1656: i, no. 30). Locke's distrust of the Quakers continued until at least 1675: see MS Locke, c. 27, fol. 30. On Nayler see E. Fogelklou, *James Naylor: The Rebel Saint*, trans. L. K. Yapp (London: Benn, 1931), 191–204; G. F. Nuttall, 'James Naylor: A Fresh Approach', *Journal of the Friends Historical Society*, Supplement 26 (1954); C. Hill, *The Experience of Defeat: Milton and Some Contemporaries* (New York: Viking, 1984), 138–42.

[17] Cranston, op. cit. 37, 38, 69, 71, 73, 78; Fox Bourne, *Life of Locke*, i. 86–7.

Interregnum politics, and while living the life of a dedicated student, his interests expanded beyond the normal academic subjects to encompass chemistry, botany, and medicine, all in the company of men of similar leisure and intelligence.[18] These new intellectual interests made visits to Pensford more than a little trying at times. He would normally return home during holidays, but the ever-widening gulf between life at Oxford and in rural Somerset became increasingly pronounced as the years progressed. Reporting on local conditions for an inquisitive Locke ensconced in his Christ Church chambers in 1658, an envious John Maggs ruefully observed 'att Penceford we nothinge but Toyle and labour and sweet [*sic*], like Asses groaneing under our burthens . . . but Christs Church is a safe shelter from outward discontentments'. That never-ending toil was apparently too much for Locke to bear when he finally visited Pensford the next year. Spending the summer months with his father, he lamented his unhappy circumstances in a letter to an Oxford acquaintance. It seems that at Pensford he was forced to converse with 'animals' who had nothing to say of import to a man of liberal training: 'I am in the midst of a company of mortall [*sic*] that know noething but the price of corne and sheepe that can entertaine discourse of noething [but] fatting of beast and dungging of ground and never thanke god for any thing but a fruitfull yeare and fat bacon.' This, coupled with the presence of the insufferable Quakers 'with light in their brest and smoake in their mouth', made the experience altogether unpalatable. Were it not for the expectation of his father's recovery from ill health, he declared, he would be on his way back to the seat of 'learning' and 'civility' amongst his many friends and colleagues. Contact with the common folk in and about Pensford would leave Locke with a lifelong distrust of and disdain for their limited capacities and selfish proclivities. The backwardness and mental torpor which characterized rural life would constitute for Locke a major stumbling block to any plans

---

[18] Kenneth Dewhurst (*John Locke, Physician and Philosopher: A Medical Biography* (London: Wellcome Historical Medical Library, 1963), 1–32) gives the best coverage of Locke's interest in natural science while at Oxford. See also P. Romanell, *John Locke and Medicine: A New Key to Locke* (Buffalo, NY: Prometheus Books, 1984), 36–8. Members of this 'Invisible College' included John Wilkins, Robert Hooke, Thomas Willis, Locke's friend Richard Lower, and, after 1660, Robert Boyle: Dewhurst, op. cit. 4–7.

for the improvement of society through the medium of education and the exercise of reason.[19]

Still, no matter how idyllic the life of study at Oxford was for Locke, no one could for long remain unaffected by the wider political developments taking place after the death of the Lord Protector in September 1658. Earlier Locke had contributed to a volume of congratulatory poems, organized and published by Dean Owen, that honoured Cromwell after the defeat of the Dutch in 1653.[20] In that juvenile exercise Locke had stressed the advantages of peace to the nation, a theme which would re-emerge in a Restoration poem of 1660.[21] With Cromwell's untimely death and the collapse of his son Richard's short protectorate in May 1659, the future of the nation was again thrown into confusion. The resuscitated Long Parliament immediately clashed with the army leadership, and a show-down was precipitated when the legislators attempted to remove Fleetwood and Lambert in the autumn. The response of the army to this action was immediate: the parliament was dismissed by the threat of force and the soldiers resorted once again to rule by committee.[22] For his part Locke could only lament these foreboding developments and attempt to take refuge in the fatalistic hope that God's providence would in the end resolve all for the best. At any rate, he thought, there was at least a modicum of security in the knowledge that what becomes of this world was of no great consequence; 'this tumbling world' was but an evanescent thing and one's preparation for and faith

[19] John Maggs to Locke (*c.* 1 Apr. 1658: i, no. 42); Locke to Isaiah Ward (Aug. 1659: i, no. 68). E. J. Hundert ('The Making of *Homo Faber*: John Locke between Ideology and History', *Journal of the History of Ideas*, 33 (1972), 6) writes that 'Locke considered the majority of workers an inferior order of men, while he viewed the working class as a whole from the standpoint of a defective rationality.' This view is echoed by C. B. Macpherson, *Political Theory of Possessive Individualism*, 222–3. Locke's father was not an unreflective man, as excerpts from a memorandum book indicate that he had given some thought to problems in ethics. Excerpts printed in Fox Bourne, op. cit. i. 70–1. Impatience with life at Pensford seems to have begun while Locke was still an undergraduate: see Locke to Samuel Tilly (Sept. 1655: i, no. 22).

[20] Fox Bourne, op. cit. i. 51–2.

[21] This latter piece is printed in *Two Tracts*, 51–2.

[22] D. Ogg, *England in the Reign of Charles II* (Oxford: University Press, 1972), 3–5. G. Davies, *The Restoration of Charles II* (San Marino, Calif.: Huntington Library, 1955) treats these events in greater detail. The most recent survey is R. Hutton, *The Restoration: A Political and Religious History of England and Wales, 1658–1667* (Oxford: Clarendon Press, 1985), 42–67.

in the next life served as an effective bulwark against despair. Yet he still could not refrain from expressing his deep disappointment in mankind as a whole and in his country, where the promises of the Puritan Revolution had so clearly been betrayed, in particular. Locke's pessimism at this point in his life was indeed pronounced. Order and security, he thought, could only be restored in an atmosphere of trust and rational deliberation, and it was these very attributes which were in such short supply throughout the land. The week following Lambert's expulsion of the Long Parliament, Locke demanded of his friend Thomas Westrowe what had become of reason in a world crazed with passion. The truth of the matter, he could only conclude, was that what often passed for reason in the minds of men was in fact the uncontrolled operation of distorted fancy. ''Tis our passions that bruiteish part that dispose of our thoughts and actions', he observed in language easily recognizable by any Protestant; 'When did ever any truth settle it self in any ones minde by the strength and authority of its owne evidence? Truths gaine admittance to our thoughts . . . by their handsome dresse and pleaseing aspect . . . and are entertaind as they suite with our affections, and as they demeane themselves towards our imperious passions.'[23] Nor did he regard himself as immune from this pernicious disease, this fixed attribute of human nature. 'I am one of the mad men too in this great Bedlam England,' he wrote in the following weeks, 'and shall thinke myself happy enough if I can but order my fits and frenzys any way to the advantage of my friends.' He counselled an ascetic rejection of the world to the extent that that was possible, insisting that once ensnared in the 'frippery' of practical affairs a man would never be satisfied in this life.[24]

Locke's lowly estimation of the powers of reason and his realistic appraisal of the inexorable influence of selfish interest and fickle passion, prepared him to welcome the restoration of Charles II in a society adrift and searching for foundation. 'O for a Pilot that would steare the tossed ship of this state to the haven of happinesse!', he told Westrowe in the late autumn of

---

[23] Locke to his father (22 June 1659: i, no. 59); Locke to Thomas Westrowe (20 Oct. 1659: i, no. 81). Similar sentiments would appear again in the *Essay*, 1. 3. 26; 1. 4. 22; 2. 2. 37; 2. 21. 67.

[24] Locke to Westrowe (8 Nov. 1659: i, no. 82).

1659. To his father he intimated an intention to take up arms himself; the only thing that prevented him from doing so, he wrote with bitter sarcasm, was his inability to decide on which side to fight, afraid that whatever his efforts might be, the advantage would only accrue to ambitious men bent upon pursuing their own interests at the expense of the nation. What Locke wanted more than anything else in 1660 was security, political stability, law and order: ''tis the great misery of this shattered and giddy nation that warrs have produced noething but warrs and the sword cut out worke for the sword'.[25] It was well-nigh time for a respite. If the price of that most precious of commodities required the sacrifice of certain liberties, well, that was a small penalty indeed. When Charles returned in May there was at last an opportunity to quiet the passions that had all but engulfed the British Isles since 1640. That Locke would emerge a steadfast conservative in these circumstances is really no surprise. Puritans like Milton might lament the passing of the godly Commonwealth; Locke lamented even more the instability which that experiment had visited upon the body politic. Busby's tutorials, Owen's Christ Church sermons, and universal Protestant assumptions about the nature of man had readied Locke for the return of the monarchy and all that it promised—a well-regulated polity designed to stem the influence of human sinfulness whenever and wherever it reared its ugly head. 'I have long since learnd not to rely on men', he said as early as 1659. For Locke in 1660 the monarchy could still stand for something above the vertiginous and fatal enthusiasms of individual political actors. At least, he thought, the Restoration presaged better things than the just-concluded episode in English history: authoritarianism seemed necessary.[26]

With the Restoration an accomplished fact by the summer of 1660, Locke turned his attention to the question of religious toleration and its implications for civil society in the context of the previous twenty years, when political unrest had been the natural concomitant of religious dispute. In September of that year his fellow-Student at Christ Church, Edward Bagshaw,

---

[25] Locke to Westrowe (8 Nov. 1659: i, no. 82); Locke to his father (9 Jan. 1660; i. no. 91); J. Dunn, *The Political Thought of John Locke* (Cambridge: University Press, 1969), 18.
[26] Locke to his father (22 June 1659: i, no. 59).

published a tract entitled *The Great Question Concerning Things Indifferent in Religious Worship* in which he argued for complete freedom of conscience in the area of religious ceremony. Bagshaw had been a favourite of Owen before the latter's removal as Dean of Christ Church in 1659. He had also quarrelled with Richard Busby during a brief tenure as Assistant Master at Westminster (1657–9), their disagreement over teaching assignments partially obscuring a deeper rift over matters of religious practice.[27] In his tract Bagshaw argued that since responsible Christians seemed to agree that religious ceremonies were indifferent things left unspecified by God's law, the magistrate should have no coercive authority in this area; that variety was of no harm to the practice of true religion. At one level Locke professed agreement with this position. In a response to Bagshaw that remained unpublished until the present century, Locke observed that 'if men will only suffer one another to go to heaven every one his own way, and not out of a fond conceit of themselves pretend to greater knowledge and care of another's soul and eternal contentment than he himself', then yes, toleration would be to the advantage of society and Locke would be the first to endorse its adoption.[28] Unfortunately, he pointed out, the realities of the human situation made this otherwise laudable doctrine unworkable. For Locke, one of the obvious conclusions to be drawn from the experience of the recent past was that the uninhibited quest for religious perfection had led to nothing but violence and destruction, to fratricidal civil war, and to the repudiation of reason. Disputes over matters indifferent to the core of religion, such circumstantial considerations as posture during services, appearance in church, time and place of worship, had all stirred up the worst elements within the human breast. 'Grant the people once free and unlimited in the exercise of their religion,' he inquired, 'and

[27] *Calamy Revised*, ed. A. G. Matthews (Oxford: Clarendon Press, 1934), 21–2; *DNB* i. 874–5; Wood, *Athenae*, iii. 944–5. In addition to telling Busby that his teaching of Arabic was a waste of time and that Busby's Greek grammar could stand improvement, Bagshaw refused to remove his hat when inside the Abbey: Sargeaunt, *Annals*, 86; Airy, *Westminster*, 25.

[28] *Two Tracts*, 161. According to John Colman (*John Locke's Moral Philosophy* (Edinburgh: University Press, 1983), 17) Locke's opposition to Bagshaw 'is not dictated by a regard for uniformity, but by a fear of those who see themselves conscientiously bound to impose their beliefs on others': cf. *Two Tracts*, 10. The larger topic of religious freedom during the Interregnum is treated by Jordon in vol. 3 of his *Development of Religious Toleration*.

where will they stop, where will they themselves bound it, and will it not be religion to destroy all that are not of their profession? And will they not think that they do God good service to take vengeance on those that they have voted his enemies?'[29] This pessimism born of experience carried Locke well beyond a simple interdiction against freedom in matters relating to religious ceremony, for he also took occasion in his rebuttal of Bagshaw to challenge the author's underlying assumptions concerning man's essential nature. In his tract Bagshaw seemed to be offering a picture of social relations where individuals demonstrated a live-and-let-live attitude in religious matters, implying a degree of intelligence, sanity, and good will that Locke found irresponsibly naïve. Without strong government and the power of coercion to enforce order, said Locke, there would be 'no peace, no security, no enjoyments, enmity with all men and safe possession of nothing, and those stinging swarms of misery that attend anarchy and rebellion'.[30] Surely Thomas Hobbes could not have expressed it in language more poignant. In fact, Professors Gough and Cranston argue for a Hobbesian influence here. It is possible that Locke may have been echoing the philosopher of Malmesbury in this passage; his Somerset neighbour and Oxford friend Henry Stubbe knew Hobbes quite well.[31] But it is not necessary to make this rather tenuous connection in order to discover the roots of Locke's outpouring. His feelings were, after all, very much of a piece with contemporary Protestant attitudes on the same topic; they were, in other words, prosaic utterances, platitudes even.[32] The

---

[29] *Two Tracts*, 159.

[30] Ibid. 156. A similar argument would reappear in the *Two Treatises* (1689), 2. 3. 21. According to John Dunn's analysis of the *Two Tracts*, Locke felt that 'Men because of their historical lapse are notoriously sinful.' In addition, 'The cognitive insouciance and the insubordinate disposition of fallen men necessitate an elaborate structure of human authorities to bring this law [God's law] to bear upon their diverse situations' (op. cit. 15). Colman (op. cit. 12) argues that 'a deeply pessimistic view of mankind pervades the Two Tracts'.

[31] Cranston, *Locke*, 62; J. Gough, *John Locke's Political Philosophy* (Oxford: Clarendon Press, 1950), 180. On Stubbe, see J. R. Jacob, *Henry Stubbe: Radical Protestantism and the Early Enlightenment* (Cambridge: University Press, 1983); Wood, *Athenae*, iii. 1067–83; and Locke to Stubbe (Sept. 1659: i, no. 75) in which Locke takes exception to Stubbe's plea for toleration in his *Essay in Defence of the Good Old Cause*. Stubbe befriended Hobbes in 1656 and with his approval began translating *Leviathan* into Latin: Jacob, op. cit. 10.

[32] 'English and Scottish Presbyterians anticipated Hobbes in teaching that it was the function of civil government to restrain the depravity natural to all men . . . nobody denied the wickedness of the multitude until the multitude began to speak for itself' (Hill, *World Turned Upside Down*, 125, 126).

orthodox view of human nature, what Locke in his unpublished *Tracts* called man's state of 'improved corruption', constituted the basis of his picture of the human personality: 'Ever since man first threw him self into the pollution of sin, he sullies whatever he takes into his hand, and he that at first could make the best and perfectest nature degenerate cannot fail now to make other things so too.' Locke did not believe that man's proclivity for evil in this disordered state could be overcome by individual merit alone; his 'slavery to sin' was in effect irreversible without the redeeming work of Christ.[33] In this state of affairs, one so obvious to most of Locke's contemporaries that it rarely needed conscious articulation, Bagshaw's claim for toleration was plainly unacceptable. It was precisely because God had left some things indifferent that the magistrate, the origins of whose authority Locke declined to examine here, must step in and impose some good order. Grant toleration for all in matters not specifically commanded by God and the result would be a plethora of fanatics similar to James Nayler and his sorry band of benighted peasants stirring up trouble throughout the countryside, feeding the suspicious passions of the multitude, that majority of Englishmen 'always craving, never satisfied', forever 'reaching at and endeavouring to pull down'.[34] This situation had to be prevented at all costs.

Since his less than sanguine view of man had been vindicated by the Civil Wars, military rule, and the selfishness of Interregnum political manoeuvring after Cromwell's death, Locke turned with enthusiasm towards the Stuart monarchy and the Anglican faith in hopes that the peace and quiet which he so cherished might be re-established under royal auspices.[35] It was the duty of the Christian monarch, he thought, to enforce the order and ceremony of the established faith as the best means of fulfilling the higher injunction of God that men maintain decency and tranquillity in their daily lives. And the perversity of men being what it was (and always would be), the magistrate

---

[33] *Two Tracts*, 142, 155.

[34] Ibid. 158–9.

[35] Locke's interest in the Anglican establishment is indicated in a letter from Gabriel Towerson offering to forward the recently published defence of the 'doctrine, discipline, and ceremonies of the Church of England' by Dr John Pearson: Towerson to Locke (23 Oct. 1660: i, no. 104). On Pearson see *DNB* xv. 613–18.

must be the absolute arbiter of things indifferent if society itself was to survive.[36] In 1660 Locke assumed that the restored monarch would exercise wisdom in ensuring that his decisions were in harmony with the ends of God's higher injunctions; and in making this assumption he betrayed the extent of his longing for peace and stability, as well as the lengths to which he was willing to go to realize them. For his assumption entailed the notion that somehow the magistrate's understanding was by its very nature complete and impartial. A dangerous conjecture was being made by Locke in 1660, one he would later come to reject once he had devoted more time to the problem of natural law and man's knowledge of its contents. Over the course of the next decade he would begin to realize that Charles II had no better understanding of God's law than the bulk of his subjects, that in fact specific knowledge of the contents of divine law was exceedingly difficult for even the most erudite and best-intentioned of men to acquire. But in 1660 this thoroughly academic man of twenty-eight—weary of the insecurity born of revolution and religious fanaticism in the name of liberty, and carrying the weighty intellectual baggage of Calvinist anthropology—turned for succour to monarchical authority. 'All the remedy that can be found', he asserted, 'is when the prince makes the good of the people the measure of his injunctions and the people without examining the reasons, pay a ready and entire obedience.'[37] It was an act of faith, this trust in the Stuart solution, and like most faiths it was adopted as much out of fear as out of any sense of genuine conviction. Yet in 1660 the fear was a real one and Locke was not alone in admitting as much. The 'overheated zeal' of those calling for toleration had to be controlled before the 'authority of conscience', the refuge of the designing and the disaffected, 'kindles a blaze among the populace capable of consuming everything'.[38] Puritan sagacity on the matter of human nature had unhappily never been equalled in the realm of political power. In 1660 the Puritan political experiment, the godly Commonwealth, was brought to an inglorious conclusion, but the political failure had ironically

---

[36] *Two Tracts*, 20–4, 232; R. Kraynak, 'John Locke: From Absolutism to Toleration', *American Political Science Review*, 74 (1980), 55–60.
[37] *Two Tracts*, 119.
[38] Ibid. 211.

added new credibility to what had always been the central dogma of that exceptional movement: the irreversible corruption and inherent sinfulness of all men. The lesson was never to be lost on Locke.

In the quarrel with Bagshaw both men were obliged to assume that if there existed areas where God's commands did not reach, then men must perforce possess more than a general knowledge of those things which were covered by the divine law. For Puritans and Nonconformists like Bagshaw, the specific contents of the divine law were to be found exclusively in Scripture. All things left indeterminate by Holy Writ were for him matters of Christian liberty, to be decided according to conscience. Locke, on the other hand, surveying the scale of disagreement over the meaning of Scripture demonstrated throughout the Interregnum, began to examine the possibility of better determining the precise content of God's commands through the study of natural law. He began this undertaking sometime in the late 1650s in discussions with his friend and Fellow of All Souls, Gabriel Towerson, and furthered his study during the early 1660s, eventually utilizing the manuscript notes which he had compiled as his principal source for a series of lectures delivered in 1664 while he was Censor of Moral Philosophy at Christ Church.[39] The idea of natural law being somehow synonymous with the essential law contained in Scripture goes back to the medieval schoolmen and remained in Locke's day an important axiom of Christian humanism. Aquinas had stressed that mankind had in its power dual access to the Word of God, the way of faith and the way of reason; and Richard Hooker, whose first book on the *Laws of Ecclesiastical Polity* Locke had read before setting to work on his own *Essays on the Law of Nature*, echoed Aquinas in his equating 'the Laws of well-doing' with 'the dictates of right reason'.[40] Probably the

[39] Colman, op. cit. 24; W. Von Leyden, ed., *Essays on LN*, introd. 10–11. Locke never published these essays during his lifetime. Gabriel Towerson to Locke (23 Oct. 1660: i, no. 104).

[40] R. Hoopes, *Right Reason in the English Renaissance* (Cambridge, Mass.: Harvard University Press, 1962), 76; Gough, *Locke's Political Philosophy*, 1–3; Richard Hooker, *Laws of Ecclesiastical Polity*, in *Works*, i. 168. Hobbes, of course, had shocked his contemporaries by denying the existence of a universal law of nature binding upon all men, and Locke's unpublished *Essays on LN* can be viewed in the context of that debate.

central assumption of natural-law theory was the identification of God's eternal will with the order of reason. Divine reason, it was thought, might be above the comprehension of man, but the difference was one of degree only. God voluntarily obliged man by enjoining only those things capable of being grasped by human reason. Puritan fideism, on the other hand, took the position that the inscrutable will of the Creator was not to be fathomed, but only obeyed. The futile attempt to anticipate God's reason represented the height of folly and arrogance for the Puritan. Thus Locke's investigation at this juncture of his career can be seen as a rejection of one important component of his Puritan heritage.

But the search for the content of God's decrees in natural law did not result in Locke's abandonment of ethical voluntarism, something easily accomplished by exponents of natural-law theory. The Puritans were firm believers in voluntarism and Locke found it impossible to jettison this doctrine even though he recognized its pitfalls. According to this theory, moral principles are obligatory solely because they are every one of them the product of God's omnipotent will, his personal fiat. The major danger here involved the consequences that this theory had for another, equally important Christian belief: the unquestioned wisdom and omniscience of God. For if the Deity possesses these latter characteristics of goodness and knowledge, it follows that there are some things that he would never will because of their unchanging evil nature and, conversely, others that he must will on account of their essential goodness. But once this is accepted, a possible next step is to claim that man, blessed with God-given reason and for ever enjoined to exercise that faculty, can begin to uncover on his own the distinction between moral good and evil. The Cambridge Platonist Ralph Cudworth was only one of many who took this bold step in the second half of the seventeenth century, arguing that moral standards exist independent of the will of God in the realm of eternal reason itself, in the immutable nature of things. According to Cudworth, 'the bare Will of God himself could not beget an Obligation upon any to Do what he Willed and Commanded, because the Nature of things do not depend upon Will' but rather upon 'Natural Justice' and the 'Necessity of their own Nature'.[41] Plainly one faulty step here and God would become peripheral to the ethical rationalists, the Creator's now subjective wisdom of no concern to man unless it reflected the dictates of eternal, independent right reason.

The Puritans escaped from this logical dilemma by insisting that man's feeble mind was ill-fitted to determine the rectitude of God's doings, to set the absolute standards to which God must adhere. Injunctions that may seem unjust, said the Puritan, were in point of fact in harmony with a greater, suprarational moral rule of right and wrong. As Calvin pointed out in the *Institutes*, 'Every event which happens in the world is governed by the incomprehensible counsel of God' and the proper function of fallen humanity was simply to obey in the knowledge that whatever God wills is undoubtedly designed for the best.[42]

As mentioned before, Locke was unwilling to follow the voluntarist argument to these lengths. He consistently refused to believe that God would impose upon his greatest creation obligations that flew in the face of human reason. In the *Essays* he attempted to steer a middle course between what he saw as the deficiencies of both the rationalist (or intellectualist) and voluntarist schools. On the one hand Locke rejected the non-theistic implications of the rationalists. Moral right and wrong would be unintelligible for him without the existence of God, the command of a superior will being an absolute necessity before the moral 'ought' could be considered truly obligatory. The 'right which the Creator has over His creation' and the 'liability to punishment' which awaits those who disobey suggest that Locke's view of human nature was such that rationalist ethics, laudable though they might be in theory, could never sufficiently motivate men in the performance of their Christian duties.[43] On the other hand, to concur with the Puritans that

---

[41] Ralph Cudworth, *A Treatise Concerning Eternal and Immutable Morality* (London: James and John Knapton, 1731), 16, 20, 23; J. Passmore, *Ralph Cudworth: An Interpretation* (Cambridge: University Press, 1950), 40–50; F. J. Powicke, *The Cambridge Platonists* (London: Dent, 1926), 137–9. See also Samuel Clarke's Boyle Lectures for 1704–5 printed as *A Demonstration of the Being and Attributes of God, the Obligation of Natural Religion, and the Truth and Certainty of the Christian Revelation* (London: W. Botham, 1728), 121–5, 174–224.

[42] Calvin, *Institutes*, i. 1. 17. 2.

[43] *Essays on LN*, 183. According to John Yolton (*John Locke: An Introduction* (Oxford: Blackwell, 1985), 23), 'It is clear that he [Locke] considered knowledge of good, of what one ought to do, as an insufficient motive for one to act, unless one has been systematically guided and trained for many years.' Cf. Colman, op. cit. 48.

God's reason was unknowable struck at the very roots of man's claim to superiority over the mere sentient beasts. Following Aristotle's argument in the *Nicomachean Ethics*, Locke concluded that man's special gift and unique function in life was the exercise of his rational faculties. In consideration of this, the Creator had voluntarily fashioned all moral duties in such a way that human reason could comprehend them fully. Thus, for Locke God's majestic will stood as the formal cause of obligation while the facts of human nature, man's rational powers, determined the specific content of that obligation. In this way he hoped to preserve the absolute sovereignty of God while enabling man to discover the content of the moral law outside the much-disputed ambit of Scripture.[44] The sovereign will of God remained an indispensable part of his moral theory and no matter how much he elevated the innate, God-given faculty of reason as the instrument by which the moral law was best discovered, reason's apprehension of that law carried with it, alone, no obligation whatsoever. Cudworth believed that the intrinsic moral worth of certain actions perceived by reason would be sufficient to obligate men; Locke would have none of this. That man was created a rational being, he would not deny: that most men would exercise reason and remain faithful to its dictates, he emphatically rejected.

With the discovery of reason as the one characteristic whereby men were to be distinguished within God's larger creation, Locke, like Aristotle centuries before him, concluded that no gift, especially one so dignified as reason, could be considered superfluous. The world of the *Essays* was a teleological one and the man who did not fully exercise the discursive faculty of reason was to all intents and purposes rejecting his true nature—and, what was worse, defying the will of his Maker.[45] The fact that the majority of men refused to live in accord with

---

[44] Aristotle, *Nicomachean Ethics*, trans. D. P. Chase (London: Dent, 1920), 1. 7. Locke's position reappears in the *Essay* (2. 21. 49), where he says: 'And if it were fit for such poor finite Creatures as we are, to pronounce what infinite Wisdom and Goodness could do, I think, we might say, That God himself cannot choose what is not good; the Freedom of the Almighty hinders not his being determined by what is best.' In the *Two Treatises* (1. 6. 58) Locke insisted that reason places man 'almost equal to Angels'.

[45] Tully, *Discourse on Property*, 41–5. John Yolton ('Locke on the Law of Nature', *Philosophical Review*, 67 (1958), 434–5) writes that for Locke 'to violate these laws [the Law of Nature] is tantamount to renouncing one's humanity'. Cf. *Two Treatises*, 2. 2. 63.

what reason indicated was not in itself sufficient proof that the obligation was invalid. This sorry situation had already been considered by Hooker in the *Laws*. There he had observed that any government hoping to perfect itself must take into consideration the widespread antipathy towards reason, must presume 'the will of man to be inwardly obstinate, rebellious, and averse from all obedience unto the sacred law of his nature'.[46] In the *Essays* Locke took a similar measure of man's penchants, but the language was less explicit. A full understanding of natural law, he explained, required considerable diligence, reflection, and attention to detail on the part of every individual. Its discovery was made contingent upon the natural ability of men to reason systematically from things known to things unknown, beginning with the evidence provided by sense experience and progressing to abstract truths and moral relations whose validity could be proved by demonstration. Innate ideas of right and wrong were ruled out entirely, the strongest evidence against them being the very fact that so many ignored the mandate of reason in their daily lives. 'Admittedly this is an easy and very convenient way of knowing,' he said of inborn ideas, 'and the human race would be very well off if men were so fully informed and so endowed by nature that from birth they were in no doubt as to what is fitting and what is less so.'[47] Unfortunately the facts of experience belied innateness.

The Lockean method of acquiring rational knowledge of one's moral duties was an exacting one: indeed, as fraught with danger for the majority of men as the equally formidable search through Scripture. The requirements, at any rate, appeared too stringent to be practicable for most. Some men, he believed, reared in vice and ill habits, followed their evil ways without giving much thought to possible alternatives, while others, incapacitated by natural defect, could not be expected to exercise reason in their lives. But the most disappointing fact was that so many actually 'prefer darkness' to voluntary self-improvement, and for these persons Locke thought that there was little hope for reform. Indeed 'not even the sun shows a man the way to go, unless he opens his eyes and is well prepared for

---

[46] Hooker, *Works*, i. 185; Marshall, *Hooker and Anglican Tradition*, 104.
[47] *Essays on LN*, 127.

the journey.' Most persons, he admitted, happily discover their rules of conduct in faulty custom and tradition, finding this an easier avenue to acceptable behaviour than intensive self-enquiry.[48]

It is an unflattering assessment of man's condition made by Locke in these early *Essays*, but one which should be of little surprise given his previous statements in the *Two Tracts* and in his early letters. He concluded with a melancholy observation to the effect that any lives lived in opposition to the law of nature (meaning the lives of most of his contemporaries) were really lives 'lived badly and without reason'. The optimistic implications of Locke's natural-law theory, the challenge which it represented in terms of man's innate ability to master the process of discursive reasoning and thereby to discover a non-Scriptural rule of life, was thus overshadowed by his gloomy estimation of human commitment to the way of reason in all walks of life. As Geraint Parry has written, Locke was very much 'a Christian writer who has in mind man as portrayed in Christian theology, capable of reason but sinful, swayed by passions. Only a few may seriously infringe the law of nature, but this is a propensity in all men. Infringements of the law are therefore all too likely.'[49] While people seemed strangely eager to engage their opponents in hard-fought battles over the meaning of each and every passage in the Bible, to marshal overwhelming (and to us quite monotonous) evidence in defence of their personal exegeses, they all the while remained smugly indifferent towards the requirements of the alternative, and surely less bloody, avenue to truth and felicity.

Gabriel Towerson, whom Locke first engaged in what seems to have been prolonged discussion concerning the law of nature, eventually published his own account of God's natural promulgation of the eternal law.[50] On the problem of man's disobedience of the law of his own being, Towerson concurred with

---

[48] Ibid. 115.

[49] Ibid. 143. Parry, *Locke*, 58. Later Locke indicated that men who 'follow the herd' in morality are no better than 'brute beasts, since they do not allow themselves the use of their reason, but give way to appetite' (*Essays on LN*, 203).

[50] Gabriel Towerson, *An Explication of the Decalogue or Ten Commandments, with Reference to the Catechism of the Church of England* (London: J. Macock, 1676), ch. 1; MS Locke e. 7, fol. 35: draft of a letter to Towerson where Locke says: 'I should never have gone out of my way had you not engagd me in the Journey.'

Locke, saying that deductions from first principles, necessary for a proper understanding of natural law, required exceptional efforts of the sort that few men were willing to engage in on a consistent basis. Addressing the issue directly, he blamed this reluctance on the 'depravedness' of man's will and affections, a depravedness which resulted in the single-minded pursuit of any and every present pleasure or advantage. Locke too had a good deal to say about the short-sightedness of men in his manuscript, but he stopped at the point of discussing their inherited depravity. In his one reference to the fall of Adam, introduced while treating the issue of innate ideas, he said by way of excuse for the omission that the question of the Fall 'does not particularly concern philosophers'. But in commenting upon how many men 'follow the herd in the manner of brute beasts, since they do not allow themselves the use of their reason, but give way to appetite', Locke, I believe, was really talking about the voluntary repudiation of human nature, the conscious, deliberate refusal to measure up to the standard set for them by a loving God.[51] And in that sense at least, he was alluding to more than simple human error, more than forgetfulness or inadvertency.

Another early Oxford friend, James Tyrrell, probably discussed the contents of the *Essays* with Locke in the 1660s; and after Locke had published the *Essay concerning Human Understanding* in 1689 Tyrrell importuned him to make public his earlier effort on natural law as a fitting complement to the larger undertaking.[52] Tyrrell's own *Brief Disquisition of the Law of Nature* (1692), an annotated abridgement and translation of Richard Cumberland's *De Legibus Naturae Disquisitio Philosophica* (1672), followed Locke's argument in the *Essays* closely, sometimes literally. W. Von Leyden, the editor of the *Essays*, suggests that Tyrrell must have had access to the manuscript between 1683 and 1689 when Locke was living in the Netherlands. Tyrrell did oblige Locke by storing some of his Oxford books and papers in

---

[51] Towerson, op. cit. 12; Locke, *Essays on LN*, 139, 203.

[52] Tyrrell to Locke (27 July 1690: iv, no. 1307). Locke found Tyrrell's advice and friendly criticism increasingly irksome. Their friendship cooled considerably during Locke's stay in the Netherlands in the 1680s and never really revived after his return home in 1689: J. H. Gough, 'James Tyrrell: Whig Historian and Friend of Locke', *Historical Journal*, 19 (1976), 581–610.

his home during the philosopher's absence, but what concerns us here is his explanation of man's widespread reluctance to follow the rule of reason.[53] In creating man a 'mixt creature' composed of spirit and matter, said Tyrrell, God recognized that the passions would for ever be in contest with reason, but with the fall of Adam and the 'weakness of reason' as the principal result of that signal event, the Creator was obliged to threaten men with punishments for their surrender to the base appetites and passions.[54] Regrettably, 'the nature of the greatest part of Mankind is so mean and servile, as rather to be terrified by Punishments, then allur'd by Rewards, or governed by the Dictates of Right Reason'. Tyrrell thus established a direct causal link between the sin of Adam and the chaos and predominance of the passions. In making this connection he was utilizing an explanation long established in Christian thought, one taken from Plato by Christians as early as the time of St Paul. If the true nature of man consisted in the faculty of right reason, then it only followed that 'so many violent, wicked and unjust men' who 'make up the greatest part of this Aggregate Body' have chosen to forsake God deliberately.[55] In this setting, a saviour in the person of Christ, whose purpose was to advance and improve upon the natural law through example, precept, and the forgiveness of sins, became imperative. According to Tyrrell, natural law had proved insufficient; traditional religion had once again to fill the gap: men had to be cajoled, then threatened, before they would do that which was in their best interest.

In adopting the ancient concept of natural law, then, medieval Christianity had created a new standard by which men were to be evaluated. To the extent that the standard was missed despite one's best efforts, to that extent one fell short of God's expectations but could expect loving forgiveness. But to the extent that the standard was ignored, to that extent men deserved nothing at all from their Maker, their self-inflicted

---

[53] Cranston, *Locke*, 228, 232, 256; Tyrrell to Locke (20 Jan. 1696: ii, no. 842). W. Von Leyden (*Essays on LN*, 85–8) discusses Tyrrell's borrowings from Locke's work. Tyrrell and Locke later collaborated on a criticism of Edward Stillingfleet's *Mischief of Separation* (1680): see MS Locke c. 34. On Tyrrell and Cumberland see C. Robbins, *The Eighteenth Century Commonwealthman* (New York: Atheneum, 1968), 73–8.

[54] Tyrrell, *Brief Disquisition*, 134, 204.

[55] Ibid. 134, 203–4.

depravity was complete. Locke's 'deeply Puritan pattern of sentiment', shared by Towerson and by Tyrrell, clearly emerges in these early works.[56] He imposed fierce demands upon his fellows, demands which to us seem hopelessly excessive. But by setting these onerous standards of conduct for men, by insisting that given the proper commitment most individuals could come to know God's law and recognize that it was in the best interests of their long-term happiness to obey it, Locke was demonstrating typical Puritan rigour in that most important business of life. The standard was high because the sense of urgency was so great; the 'law enacted by a superior power and implanted in our own heart' presaged great things if only men would work to discover it and govern their own lives accordingly.[57] In the early 1660s Locke expressed no great confidence that most men would—just as the Puritans established their own exceptional standard of behaviour only to concede man's inability to realize it because of the Fall. With the Puritans, however, one at least knew that the quest, although necessary, was in the end futile. Locke believed that the quest could be successful, and to that extent the burden became all the more unsparing, the sense of failure all the more acute: the responsibility upon the individual actor here was total and the philosopher accepted the challenge eagerly. Such was the nature of Locke's 'Puritan' self in the early 1660s. The mould had been shaped by civil disruption, pained memories, and religious disquiet; it would remain unbroken throughout a long and varied career.

[56] The term is John Dunn's (*Locke*, 2).
[57] *Essays on LN*, 111.

3

The Broad-Church Perspective

By 1663 Locke was confronted with the inevitable problem of retaining his Christ Church Studentship. At some point in the near future he could expect to be appointed one of the senior Students (Theologi) and thus be required to take holy orders. By October of that year he had probably already been offered a living; by 1666, at any rate, he seems to have received a number of offers.[1] In some respects this route seemed the natural one for Locke. His abiding concern with questions of human nature and natural law, together with his vigorous rebuttal of Bagshaw's Nonconformist views and his growing respect for Anglican institutions and traditions, appeared to signal an easy transition into the world of the Church. But still he hesitated. The fact was that Locke, like his new Oxford friend and scientific mentor Robert Boyle, believed that he could best serve the Church of England, best combat superstition and irreligion, best understand God and his purposes for mankind, outside the official Church's institutional structure.

Locke was first introduced to Boyle in 1660 and began to frequent the chemist's High-Street laboratory soon thereafter, engaging in experiments and sharing in the empirical researches that took place there.[2] Boyle (1627–91) was easily the most distinguished of the scientific figures that gathered in the city during the Interregnum and in the years immediately after the Restoration. Like Locke a man of unquestionable piety who

---

[1] Locke to John Parry (c.15 Dec. 1666: i, no. 219); Cranston, *Locke*, 77. In October 1663 Dean John Fell of Christ Church, sub-Dean Dr Edward Pococke, and canon Richard Gardiner signed a certificate attesting to Locke's good conduct and character: Fox Bourne, *Locke*, i. 88. Cranston (op. cit. 74) thinks this was possibly a reference for the Bishop of Oxford.

[2] In a notebook dated 1667 and containing extracts from other authors describing the virtues and attainments of famous scholars and churchmen, Boyle's commentaries figure prominently: MS Locke f. 14. Boyle moved to Oxford in the winter of 1655 and remained there until 1668. See M. A. Stewart, 'Locke's Professional Contacts with Robert Boyle', *Locke Newsletter*, 12 (1981), 20–1; L. T. More, *The Life and Works of Robert Boyle* (New York: Oxford University Press, 1944), 79–82, 124.

knew that 'we, in our lapsed condition, must be under a high obligation to obey the declared will of God', Boyle throughout his adult life was troubled by what he saw as the 'great and deplorable growth of irreligion, especially among those that aspired to pass for wits, and several of them too for philosophers'.[3] The most effective way to counter this trend among men of learning, he thought, was to demonstrate the power and glory of God in his handiwork. The truths of God were manifest in both Scripture and nature, Boyle believed, and he viewed scientific undertakings as a necessary adjunct to his own considerable theological studies. For while salvation was doubtless 'far above the reach of our endeavours, and our deserts', men were nevertheless obliged to study God's admirable workmanship. 'It is the first act of religion,' he wrote, 'and equally obliging in all religions: it is the duty of man, as man; and the homage we pay for the privilege of reason.'[4] Locke's scientific interests would shift more in the direction of medicine after 1663, but Boyle's approach to the science of nature, so clearly Baconian in method and Christian in purport, found an enthusiastic ally in the young college lecturer. That influence was evident in an early essay composed by Locke in collaboration with the London physician Thomas Sydenham in 1669, where he took issue with the rigidity and presumption of scholastic reasoning in all fields of learning:

True knowledge grew first in the world by experience and rational observation, but proud man, not content with the Knowledge he was

---

[3] Robert Boyle, *The Christian Virtuoso*, in *Works*, 6 vols. (London: W. Johnston *et al.*, 1772), v. 508; id., *The Excellency of Theology* (*Works*, iv. 23). Gerald Cragg (*From Puritanism to the Age of Reason* (Cambridge: University Press, 1950), 113) said that the scientist 'found in his work a sense of what can only be described as a religious vocation'. Here men discovered 'a new (international) means of expressing religious zeal which had hitherto found an outlet through more conventional religious channels'. See also M. Hunter, *Science and Society in Restoration England* (New York: Cambridge University Press, 1981), ch. 1; R. Westfall, *Science and Religion in Seventeenth Century England* (Ann Arbor, Mich.: University of Michigan Press, 1973), ch. 2.

[4] Boyle, *Occasional Reflections Upon Several Subjects* (*Works*, ii. 360), *Of the Usefulness of Experimental Natural Philosophy* (*Works*, ii. 62). 'He had studied the Scriptures to so good purpose, and with so critical a strictness, that few men whose Profession oblige them chiefly to that sort of learning have gone beyond him in it' (Gilbert Burnet, *A Sermon Preached at the Funeral of the Honourable Robert Boyle* (London: Chiswell, 1692), 24). See also R. M. Hunt, *The Place of Religion in the Science of Robert Boyle* (Pittsburg, Pa.: University Press, 1955). Boyle challenged Thomas Hobbes's rejection of final causality, seeing God not only as the first cause of things, but as ever-present, managing the harmonious system of the universe: Burtt, *Metaphysical Foundations*, 186–99.

capable of, and which was useful to him, would needs penetrate into the hidden causes of things, lay down principles, and establish maxims to himself about the operations of nature, and thus vainly expect that nature, or in truth God should proceed according to those laws which his maxims had prescribed to him.[5]

His early contact with Oxford's empirical scientists taught Locke that science and religion together strengthened Christian belief and that discipline, method, and humility were necessary in the study of both. He would adopt each of these precepts in all his future work, especially in his exploration of the limits of human understanding and in his exegesis of the New Testament; but at this point in his life the world of the cloistered clergyman seemed far removed from the exciting scientific undertakings going on in High Street.

In November 1663 Locke wrote to John Strachey, his friend since boyhood and now a well-to-do landowner, for advice in the matter of taking holy orders and received the answer that he was doubtless looking for all along. 'I have alwaies looked on you as one of a higher head then to take covert under a Cottage,' said Strachey, 'and in my opinion the best Country Parsonage is noe more.'[6] Bolstered by this advice, Locke continued upon the path of irresolution for another three years, tutoring undergraduates and pursuing his medical interests, fortunate in not being pressed by the college to make an immediate decision.

As a college tutor at Christ Church during these years Locke was responsible not only for the academic progress of his charges, but for their moral well-being as well. The seventeenth-century tutor stood *in loco parentis* at Oxford, overseeing

---

[5] 'De Arte Medica', printed in Dewhurst, *Locke*, 39. Locke returned to the attack in the *Essay* (4. 12. 1–6). The schoolmen, said Bacon, 'having subtle and strong capacities, abundance of leisure, and but small variety of reading . . . with infinite agitation of wit, spin out of a small quantity of matter, those laborious webs of learning which are extant in their books' (Sir Francis Bacon, *The Advancement of Learning*, ed. J. Devey (New York: P. F. Collier and Son, 1905), 57). See Paulo Rossi (*Francis Bacon: From Magic to Science* (Chicago: University Press, 1968), 22, 32, 35) for Bacon's views on the collaborative nature of science. Collaborative efforts bespoke humility, as opposed to the perceived arrogance of the Renaissance alchemical and magical traditions where one man's inspiration took the place of systematic enquiry. This pride Bacon took to be the occasion of man's fall (Rossi, 162). See also G. A. J. Rogers, 'Boyle, Locke and Reason', *Journal of the History of Ideas*, 27 (1966), 205–16. Christopher Hill argues that Bacon sought to reverse one consequence of the Fall, namely man's loss of mastery over nature, with his new scientific method (*The Intellectual Origins of the English Revolution* (Oxford: Clarendon Press, 1965), 89).

[6] Strachey to Locke (18 Nov. 1663: i, no. 163).

expenditure, religious training, and conduct. In an age when many students entered the university at fourteen and fifteen years of age (Locke was an exception matriculating at twenty), the responsibilities of the tutor were immense. Locke's tenure appears to have been a successful one, however. There are numerous extant letters from parents of his students expressing their thanks and their trust in Locke's learning and piety, and in all of the correspondence the second quality is identified as being the more important one.[7] When one particular student was transferred from Locke's care to Cambridge University, both parent and pupil wrote to express their warm appreciation of his efforts, the former praising Locke's character and the student at first protesting and later lamenting his removal from Oxford and Locke.[8] His duty as a role model and teacher of sound religious principles Locke never forgot, going so far as to advise his students even after they had left the university community. John Alford was one who received such advice: Locke wrote warning him of the moral pitfalls awaiting him beyond the gates of Christ Church. 'I have not yet quite parted with you,' he said after Alford's exit, 'and though you have put off your gowne, and taken leave of the University, you are not yet got beyond my affection or concernment for you.'[9] Solid virtue and pure religion must be maintained at all costs, he warned, especially in the face of enormous temptation. He told Alford that real satisfaction could only be found in true knowledge and godly living, and that if he could be of any assistance in helping to improve upon the 'notions' that Alford had learned while at Christ Church, then the former student would find his old tutor more than willing to oblige him.

One of the books familiar to Locke before 1660 which

[7] George Berkeley to Locke (27 July 1662: i, no. 136); Henry Townsend to Locke (29 July 1662: i, no. 138); Robert Pickering to Locke (19 Sept. 1662: i, no. 144); Thomas Harborne to Locke (20 Jan. 1663: i, no 154); William Owen to Locke (26 Dec. 1663: i, no. 164); Anne Alford to Locke (23 May 1665: i, no. 171); Henry Flower to Locke (3 Aug. 1665: i, no. 174). Curtis (*Oxford and Cambridge*, 79–81, 107–14) discusses the tutor's duties in more detail. We know little about Locke's own tutor Thomas Cole, but evidently his influence on Locke was not significant: see Mathews, *Calamy Revised*, 125.

[8] George Berkeley to Locke (27 July 1662: i, no. 136); Charles Berkeley to Locke (*c*.17 Aug. 1662: i, no. 140); Charles Berkeley to Locke (Sept./Oct. 1662: i, no. 147).

[9] Locke to John Alford (12 June 1666: i, no. 200). Alford went on to become MP from Midhurst. See M. G. Mason, 'John Locke's Experience of Education and its Bearing on his Educational Thought', *Journal of Educational Administration and History*, 3 (1971), 2.

expressed sentiments on pedagogy that the tutor might have found useful was written by one of his superiors, the Dean of Christ Church from 1648 to 1650 and again in 1659, Dr Edward Reynolds.[10] In his *Treatise of the Passions and Faculties of the Soule of Man*, Reynolds argued that while the major intellectual differences which existed between individuals were due principally to the wide variety of bodily tempers and dispositions observable amongst them, proper education could lessen the dependence on the body to the point where 'the toughest, and most unbended Natures by early and prudent discipline may be much Rectified'. The basic cast of an individual's personality and temperament could not be overturned, counselled Reynolds, but much could be done nevertheless with proper tuition. This expression of moderate environmentalism would later become a hallmark of Locke's *Thoughts concerning Education* and the even better-known *Essay concerning Human Understanding*, and he was undoubtedly already thinking in terms of establishing good habits when he wrote to Alford warning against the pernicious influence of contrary 'notions'.[11]

Reynolds's major purpose in his *Treatise* was not to develop a specific reform of pedagogy, however, but to review the soul's condition in light of the fall of Adam. Here too Locke could discover much that would find expression in the *Two Tracts* and *Essays on the Law of Nature*, for Reynolds interpreted the essential result of the Fall to be the eclipse of reason by the naturally unruly passions and affections. In the state of innocence man possessed an exact constitution, he said, one free from all bodily distempers and where the passions were in natural subordination to the understanding. But in our lapsed state the understanding (as Locke had argued similarly in his letter of

---

[10] MS Locke e. 6: Reynolds's work appears in a list of books under the heading 'Lemmata' completed by Locke before 1660. Reynolds was a member of the Westminster Assembly of Divines in 1643 and vicar of St Lawrence Jewry from 1645 until 1662, where, according to a hostile Wood (*Athenae*, iii. 1083–6), he 'flattered Oliver and his gang'. He became Bishop of Norwich in 1661.

[11] Edward Reynolds, *A Treatise of the Passions and Faculties of the Soule of Man* (London: Robert Bustock, 1640), 11. The same advice is contained in his sermons: 'The foundation of an honourable and comfortable Age, are laid in the Minority of Children; if they be not kept streight at first, the Tree will be crooked incurably at the last' (*Works* (London: Thomas Newcomb, 1679), 883). In *Thoughts on Ed.* (206–7, 325), Locke takes account of tempers, dispositions, and native propensities. The environmentalism of the *Essay* is perhaps best expressed in 2. 1. 2.

20 October 1659 to Thomas Westrowe) no longer had that clearness of apprehension, that keen discernment, to judge of things 'according to their naked and naturall truth, but according as it finds them beare in the Fancie those impressions of Pleasure, which are most agreeable to corrupted Nature'.[12] Reynolds attempted to chart a difficult middle course (as did Locke) between the ethical rationalists and the voluntarists by insisting that all sin was both a violation of 'a perpetuall Law' and 'an unalterable Will'. He believed that although the struggle between reason and appetite was unremitting because of the Fall, all 'by the mercy of God' might be restored again. 'Right Knowledge', with divine assistance, could guide the soul back to God, but that perfection of knowledge depended upon clearness of apprehension, solidity of judgement, and strength of memory—all very human attributes which would eventually find their way into Locke's *Essay concerning Human Understanding*.[13]

Another work read and much approved by Locke, a book which soon became a staple of late seventeenth-century Christian literature, was Richard Allestree's *Whole Duty of Man*.[14] Allestree was a 1640 graduate of Christ Church, where his college tutor had been Locke's old master Richard Busby. A staunch Royalist, he had fought on the King's side during the Civil War, and at the Restoration in 1660 was made a canon of Christ Church; three years later, he was appointed Professor of Divinity. The *Whole Duty of Man* upheld with great force the connection between man's disordered understanding and the

---

[12] Reynolds, *Treatise*, 65. See also *The Sinfulness of Sin* (*Works*, 44); *The Reign of Sin* (*Works*, 110); 'Self-Denial' (Sermon 3, *Works*, 801). As discussed in ch. 1 above, the position outlined here is essentially the Thomist one adopted by Richard Hooker and confirmed by most divines, Anglican and Puritan, throughout the seventeenth century.

[13] Reynolds, *Treatise*, 132, 448, 452; Locke, *Essay*, 2. 9–11, 4. 14. See also M. Johnson, *Locke on Freedom*, 84.

[14] Richard Allestree, *The Practice of Christian Graces, or the Whole Duty of Man* (London: T. Garthwait, 1659): Locke possessed a copy in 1660 (MS Locke f. 11, fol. 12). James Axtell (*Thoughts on Ed.*, 197, n. 2) says that Locke recommended it to his students. He lent a copy of the work to Lady Masham as late as 1695: MS Locke f. 10, fol. 279. He also recommended the work to the clergyman Richard King in 1703: *Works*, x. 306. Allestree's authorship is sometimes questioned: the British Library catalogue identifies him as the author, while the *Dictionary of Anonymous and Pseudonymous Literature*, ed. J. Kennedy *et al.*, 6 vols. (London: Oliver and Boyd, 1932), i. 143, says that while authorship is not absolutely certain, the preponderance of evidence is in favour of Allestree.

fall of Adam: 'we being born after his image . . . are become both Ignorant in discerning what we ought to do, and weak and unable to the doing of it, having a backwardness to all good, and an aptness, and readiness to all evil'. But like Reynolds, the author emphatically denied that all was predestined as the Puritans so firmly held; rather men can and will be recovered upon Christ's forgiveness and their own repentance, 'the hearty, honest endeavour of obeying the whole Will of God'. The rest of the work reads like a handbook of practical Christian morality, covering everything from proper worship to temperance in drinking. For the seventeenth-century educator convinced of the transforming power of education, the *Whole Duty of Man* provided a convenient didactic text, relevant for the Oxford scholar and the Pensford farmer alike, providing guidance for fallen humanity and hope in conjunction with Christ's saving grace.[15]

Locke was elected Censor of Moral Philosophy for the 1664 academic year, and in that post he engaged his students in a discussion of natural law along the lines detailed in the recently published *Essays on the Law of Nature*. At the conclusion of twelve months in that office he decided to take his leave of the university, at least for a while, and accepted an appointment as secretary to Sir Walter Vane on a diplomatic mission to Cleves. The mission itself was a failure from a diplomatic point of view, and the details need not concern us here. The four-month trip abroad, Locke's first, was far more important in helping to redirect his position on the weighty issue of religious toleration. For the appointment itself was made during the brief parliament that Charles II had called while at Oxford in the autumn of 1665. The principal purpose of the session was to vote funds for the war against the Dutch; but the Cavalier majority managed to introduce and pass the last of those penal laws known collectively as the Clarendon Code, just when Locke was beginning to rethink the overall efficacy of that type of coercive legislation.[16] Once in Cleves he discovered, much to his pleasant

---

[15] Allestree, *Whole Duty of Man*, ix–xi, 1; *DNB* i. 324–5. The book was immensely popular throughout the late seventeenth and eighteenth centuries, reaching a 28th edition by 1790: see C. J. Stranks, *Anglican Devotion* (London: SCM Press, 1961), 125.

[16] The Five Mile Act prevented dissenting clergy and schoolmasters from coming within five miles of any city or corporate town, or of the parish where they had taught or

surprise, just the sort of practical accommodation in religion that he had indicated in his controversy with Bagshaw was necessary for him to support toleration. He wrote to Boyle back at Oxford that the Calvinists, Lutherans, and Catholics in the town 'permit one another to chose their way to heaven'. This fortunate situation he thought was due in part to the power of the magistrate there, Frederick William, Elector of Brandenburg; but it also seemed to reflect 'the prudence and good nature of the people, who (as I find by enquiry) entertain different opinions, without any secret hatred or rancour'. Most of the residents, it appeared, were a good deal more interested in making money ('the great cry is ends of gold and silver') than in troubling themselves over the state of their neighbour's soul. Locke by no means applauded this single-minded pursuit of wealth—in fact he regretted the paucity of scientific knowledge evident there—but at least the society as a whole seemed a good deal less polarized than the England of his youth. Even the hated Catholics took on a new and civil demeanour in this unique place, the Catholic clergy behaving better than 'our brethren the Calvinists'.[17] Toleration was beginning to seem less than the mortal threat to the stability of the State that it previously had for Locke; at any rate, he was now acquiring solid empirical evidence in support of the proposition.

After arriving home in February 1666, Locke made the decision not to pursue a diplomatic career, even though another offer was immediately forthcoming.[18] He returned to his Christ Church rooms and continued with his medical studies. During the summer he was introduced to Anthony Ashley Cooper, later first earl of Shaftesbury, and it was through the influence of Ashley Cooper that Locke finally resolved the problem of his

preached. The parliamentary Acts known collectively as the Clarendon Code are printed in A. Browning, ed., *English Historical Documents, 1660–1714* (London: Eyre and Spottiswoode, 1953), 375–86. See also G. R. Cragg, *Puritanism in the Period of the Great Persecution, 1660–1688* (Cambridge: University Press, 1957), 1–30; G. N. Clark, *The Later Stuarts* (Oxford: Clarendon Press, 1934), 19–21; Ogg, *England in Reign of Charles II*, 207; C. F. Mullett, 'Toleration and Persecution in England, 1660–1689', *Church History*, 18 (1949), 18–43. Locke's appointment was probably facilitated by his friend William Godolphin, secretary to Sir Henry Bennet, Secretary of State: Fox Bourne, *Locke*, i. 97.

[17] Locke to Boyle (12 Dec. 1665: i, no. 175); Locke to Strachey (*c.* 26 Dec. 1666: i, no. 180).

[18] Locke to Strachey (22 and 28 Feb. 1666: i, nos. 186, 187).

Studentship. After preparing to petition the faculty to allow him to forgo some of the requirements necessary for the MD degree, thereby enabling him to qualify for one of the medical Studentships, Locke abandoned that course and secured a royal dispensation which allowed him to hold his Student's position without taking holy orders. All of these developments occurred directly after Locke's meetings with Ashley Cooper in the summer, and as the future earl's friend and Secretary of State Sir William Morris signed the royal dispensation, there is little doubt that the fortuitous 1666 encounter was beneficial to Locke. The following Easter, his Studentship now secure, Locke removed to London and joined Ashley Cooper's household. And as Shaftesbury the Privy Councillor had long been an opponent of the Clarendon Code on the practical grounds that persecution ultimately undermined the strength and material prosperity of the nation by forcing its most industrious citizens to emigrate, the atmosphere at his Exeter House residence proved conducive to Locke's own re-evaluation of toleration. He devoted considerable time during that first year in London to the problem, writing to Boyle of his neglect of chemistry 'though I find my fingers still itch to be at it', and at length produced an essay that represented a fundamental break with his previous position on the issue—a break in which Locke, for the first time, placed the magistrate and his subjects on the same level in their ability to discern the dictates of God's moral law, thus attaching greater consequence to subjective religious convictions than (as he had previously done) to the mere temporal benefits which might result from obedience to enforced conformity.[19]

According to Locke in this work of 1667, the magistrate remained a necessary fixture in society because men would never live 'peaceably and quietly together', would never refrain from 'fraud and violence' without some superior power equipped to preserve 'the good, preservation and peace of men in that society over which he is set'.[20] But that had now become

---

[19] Locke to Boyle (12 Nov. 1667: i, no. 228); K. H. D. Haley, *The First Earl of Shaftesbury* (Oxford: Clarendon Press, 1968), 202–3; A. A. Seaton, *The Theory of Toleration Under the Later Stuarts* (Cambridge: University Press, 1911), 237–42. Locke wrote four drafts of the piece, one of which is printed in Fox Bourne, *Locke*, i. 174–94.

[20] Ibid. i. 174. Locke returned to this theme in his *Epistola de Tolerantia* (1689), where he observed that most individuals 'prefer to enjoy the fruits of other men's labours rather than work to provide for themselves' (ed. Gough and Klibansky, 125).

the sole function of the magistrate and he must no longer impose upon the consciences of men where the maintenance of any speculative opinion (for example, belief in the Trinity, purgatory, or transubstantiation) or mode of worship did not interfere with the peaceful functioning of the State. Locke granted that it was still the political sovereign who remained the arbiter of what actions constituted a threat to peace and security; but in now denying the magistrate any power to enjoin individual belief so long as the manner of worshipping God chosen by a subject did not promote civil disturbance, Locke was reversing his previous estimation of Stuart sagacity in religious matters. The difference between monarchs and subjects 'in respect of the King of kings', is at best minimal, said Locke, and the magistrate 'having no more certain or more infallible knowledge of the way to attain [salvation] than I myself, where we are both equally inquirers, both equally subjects', it was necessary that each individual follow his own conscience.[21] In 1667, 'the way to salvation not being any forced exterior performance, but the voluntary and secret choice of the mind', Locke found the imposition of religious beliefs and practices more apt to create secretly hostile hypocrites than loyal, peaceful, and prosperous subjects. To a certain extent he accepted Shaftesbury's utilitarian argument for toleration, but it is clear that the basis of his plea in 1667 went deeper than that, went to the roots of his convictions about human nature, convictions now applicable to royalty no less than to rogues.[22] It was simply, in Locke's revised judgement, no longer within the purview of the magistrate's trust to concern himself with the religious opinions of his subjects. More importantly, coercion undermined the individual's obligation before God to work towards genuine religious conviction. The issue really concerned one's eternal prospects, and with the stakes so high 'no consideration could be sufficient to force a man from, or to, that which he was fully persuaded was the way to infinite happiness or infinite misery'. Should the magistrate 'force me to a wrong religion', he wrote in obvious reference to his larger priorities, 'he can make me no reparation in the other

---

[21] Fox Bourne, op. cit. i. 177, 180.

[22] Ibid. i. 177. This conviction was reiterated in his later *Third Letter on Toleration*, where he wrote (*Works*, vi. 459) that the magistrate 'is as much subject as other men to that corruption of human nature'.

world'. Locke had by no means forgotten the experience of the 1640s and 1650s, when godliness often meant the imposition of one group's particular beliefs upon the entire nation; and he continued to draw the line on toleration whenever force was envisioned by anyone to 'convert' an opponent. 'This, indeed,' he said, 'often happens; but 'tis not the fault of the worship but the men, and is not the consequence of this or that form of devotion, but the product of depraved ambitious human nature', and it was the duty of the magistrate to prevent this situation from ever developing.[23]

The defence of toleration by Locke, then, by no means altered his basic assumptions about human nature. While at one level it might appear as if he had come some distance in the direction of Bagshaw's position, still the rationale for toleration forwarded by Locke was a negative one: the king simply possessed no special access to God's infinite will; his job was to maintain the peace in a world where the very necessity of government bespoke the depravity of men. Bagshaw, at least when writing his defence of toleration in 1660, had approached the whole issue from a more affirmative point of view, emphasizing instead the absolute right of individuals to exercise Christian freedom in areas of indifference. Locke was still very much concerned with civil order, with preserving the peace at all costs; but by 1667 that goal no longer seemed best realized by imposing upon the consciences of dissenters. Better to let men pursue their own way to heaven, he thought, so long as each individual allowed his neighbour the same basic privilege. The magistrate's assignment was to see that they did. And given Locke's estimation of human nature, this one duty would be more than a full-time job for any Stuart sovereign. Locke never attacked the absolute necessity of strong government, from this point in his life on he

---

[23] Fox Bourne, op. cit. i. 176, 177, 178: cf. Dunn, *Political Thought*, 33–7. Locke's changed view on toleration was given further articulation the following year when as secretary to the Lords Proprietors of Carolina, he contributed to the composition of the Fundamental Constitutions of Carolina. There it was agreed that toleration should be observed so long as every prospective settler to the new colony acknowledged a God and publicly worshipped the same. The settlers in Carolina after 1669, not surprisingly, ignored this and all the other provisions of the Fundamental Constitutions (*Works*, x. 193–5); C. M. Andrews, *The Colonial Period of American History*, 4 vols. (New Haven: Yale University Press, 1934–8), iii. 212–27.

sought to confine that strength to areas where it was most appropriate and productive.

In the year following the composition of this piece on toleration, Locke made the acquaintance of the Cambridge divine Dr Benjamin Whichcote.[24] Late in his life he would strongly recommend Whichcote's sermons, along with those of Archbishop Tillotson and Isaac Barrow, as 'masterpieces' of instruction in morality, and in 1668 Whichcote's words both reaffirmed Locke's view of reason first outlined in the *Essays on the Law of Nature* and provided some instructive ideas on the nature of sin in the aftermath of the Fall.[25] Whichcote was born in 1609 and attended Sir Walter Mildmay's Puritan Emmanuel College, Cambridge, where his tutor was an orthodox Calvinist by the name of Anthony Tuckney. After graduating MA in 1633 he was elected a Fellow of the college, ordained a minister in the Church of England, and appointed Sunday lecturer at Trinity Church, Cambridge, where he continued to serve for some twenty years. In 1644 Whichcote was chosen Provost of King's College despite his refusal to take the Covenant, and by 1650 he had become Vice-Chancellor of the University—only to be ejected from both positions at the Restoration. He complied with the Act of Uniformity, however, and by 1662 was appointed curate of St Anne's Blackfriars, where he remained until the church was destroyed in the Great Fire. His return to the capital in 1668 was occasioned by the offer of the curacy of St Lawrence Jewry after it was vacated by John Wilkins upon his appointment as Bishop of Chester.[26]

Whichcote's sermons at Cambridge and in London had a good deal to recommend them to anyone interested in seeking to steer clear of the polemical quarrels which had engaged and distracted Anglican churchmen and their Puritan critics since the middle of the sixteenth century. To avoid division over the meaning of each and every troublesome passage in Scripture,

---

[24] Cranston (*Locke*, 124) says Locke became a member of Whichcote's congregation. The clergyman had been appointed vicar of St Lawrence Jewry in 1668 but since the church had to be rebuilt, he preached regularly for the next seven years at the Guildhall Chapel: *DNB* xxi. 3.

[25] Locke to Revd Richard King (25 Aug. 1703: *Works*, x. 306).

[26] J. D. Roberts, *From Puritanism to Platonism in Seventeenth Century England* (The Hague: Nijhoff, 1968), ch. 1; J. Tulloch, *Rational Theology and Christian Philosophy in England*, 2 vols. (Edinburgh: Blackwood, 1872), ii. 47–50; E. A. George, *Seventeenth Century Men of Latitude* (New York: Scribner's Sons, 1908), 69–85; *DNB* xxi. 1–3.

Whichcote abandoned the ideals of Puritanism in a number of respects and instead worked to establish a set of broad fundamental principles upon which all reasonable Christians could agree. Comprehension of as many believers as possible within the Church, based on the essentials of Scripture as interpreted by reason, was his starting-point. In addition, he adamantly refused to accept the Puritan notion of God's inscrutable will. Faith must be reasonable, thought Whichcote, and it was inconceivable that God would impose upon humanity duties the reasons for which they barely understood. Most modern scholars view Whichcote as the spiritual father of the Cambridge Platonists (he was, for example, John Smith's tutor at Cambridge), and his faith in the reasonableness of religion is regarded by many of these scholars as the single most important identifying characteristic of the Cambridge school. And rightly so; for in fact Whichcote believed that in the state of man's innocence, natural religion or the religion of reason was completely sufficient to direct him towards moral maturity and eternal happiness. He placed great emphasis upon man's power to act in accordance with reason because, like Locke in the *Essays*, he adopted the Aritotelian-Thomist definition of man as a rational creature, one whose unique defining characteristic was the ability, and hence the obligation, to exercise his reason and to discover God's eternal law in the nature of things.[27] 'It is the proper Work of Reason in Man', Whichcote affirmed, 'to find God out in his Works, and to follow him in his Ways. It is the proper Employment of our Intellectual Faculties, to be conversant about God, to conceive aright of him; and then to resemble and imitate him.'[28] Whichcote's evaluation of human nature, then, was considerably more hopeful than the Puritan vision dominant at Emmanuel College. In fact he believed that 'Man, as Man, is Averse to what is Evil and Wicked; for Evil is unnatural, and Good is connatural, to Man.'[29] As a preacher, he

---

[27] V. J. Bourke, *St Thomas and the Greek Moralists* (Milwaukee, Wis.: Marquette University Press, 1947), 22, 24–5; W. Jaeger, *Humanism and Theology* (Milwaukee, Wis.: Marquette University Press, 1943), 17; Gilson, *Christian Philosophy in Middle Ages*, 379–81.

[28] *Select Sermons of Dr. Whichcote* (London: A. and J. Churchill, 1699), 69: see also p. 110, where he says: 'Mind and Understanding in Man, is given on purpose, that man should search after God, and acknowledge him.'

[29] *Moral and Religious Aphorisms*, ed. Samuel Slater (London: J. Payne, 1753), Aphorism No. 42. The work is unpaginated.

restored free will and placed the choice of a godly life within the hands of a species whose souls were closer to God than they were to their own bodies. In Whichcote's view, a loving and compassionate Creator stood ready to forgive men so long as they obeyed the law of their own nature and worked to reject all that was opposite to eternal reason.[30]

Yet despite this very unpuritan definition of human nature, the censure of enthusiasm in religion, the emphasis on free will and a compassionate, reasonable deity who makes religion more a matter of personal ethics than one of ritual observance and niggling bibliolatry, one must be careful in distinguishing between what Whichcote saw as man's essential nature as it proceeded from the hands of God and what it had become in the period since the Fall. Indeed, it is misleading to insist that the Platonists 'almost overlooked evil' and maintained an 'unwillingness so much as to mention original sin'.[31] 'We are to declare the Nature of Man', Whichcote advised, 'not from what it is, by Defection and Apostasy; but from what God made it: What it was, and what it should be.' He and the other members of the Cambridge group, when treating the question of human nature, were discussing an ideal that was perhaps realizable, but one certainly no longer extant due to Adam's sin in Paradise. As Douglas Bush has remarked, the Platonist's optimism 'was held very firmly in check by a Christian consciousness of human frailty and sin and the need for grace, and was very different from the scientific and sentimental optimism which was soon to submerge it'.[32] Locke remained an enthusiastic backer of Whichcote not simply because he rejected predestination and spoke out in support of the minimal creed and because he chided religious enthusiasts and exalted reason, but also due to the fact that the Platonist had faced up to the harsh realities of apostate man with courage and was willing to stand by what seemed to be the only practical solution to the age-old problem.

There is, it must be said, a fundamental tension in Whichcote,

---

[30] *Select Sermons*, 109.

[31] C. Patrides, ed., *The Cambridge Platonists* (Cambridge, Mass.: Harvard University Press, 1971), 38. See also P. M. Davenport, *Moral Divinity with a Tincture of Christ?: An Interpretation of the Theology of Benjamin Whichcote* (Nijmegen: n.p., 1972), 57, where he says that for Whichcote man's nature was 'tilted delicately but definitely heavenward'.

[32] Whichcote, *Moral and Religious Aphorisms*, no. 228; D. Bush, *Paradise Lost in Our Time* (Gloucester, Mass.: P. Smith, 1957), 3.

one that Locke would espy for himself and resolve to his own satisfaction in the later *Essay concerning Human Understanding*. The problem lay in the fact that Whichcote, like virtually every other religious thinker of the seventeenth century, could not find it within himself to abandon the idea of innate moral knowledge—principles of right and wrong woven by God into the very texture of human nature. For to deny this assumption, it was thought by most responsible commentators, would be to undermine the objective and eternal nature of morality itself.[33] Hobbes had already done as much in his universally excoriated *Leviathan*, and Whichcote was certainly not one to do anything that in his mind might smack of the Hobbesian heresy. So for him natural religion—God's eternal law—was born with everyone, constituted 'the very Temper and Complexion of Man's Soul, in the moment of his creation', this 'Law written in the Heart of Man', or 'Truths of first Inscription', having been given by virtue of mankind's status as God's special earthly creation.[34] By obeying the rule of reason men imitated their Creator, ennobled themselves, established order and good government here on earth, and merited salvation hereafter in heaven. But while insisting upon the existence of 'Truths of first Inscription', special touchstones which by definition made revelation superfluous, Whichcote reminded his audience that they could only fulfil their duty to God 'as we come to the use of reason and understanding'. Because he believed that man was born only with faculties 'which without use and improvement, signify little', Whichcote classified those who avoided serious intellectual discipline and education as coming 'hardly under the rank of men'.[35] His doctrine of innate ideas was qualified by

---

[33] J. Yolton, *John Locke and the Way of Ideas* (Oxford: Clarendon Press, 1956), 26–48. See ch. 4 below for a further discussion.

[34] Whichcote, *Select Sermons*, 7, 8, 38. The influence of Hobbes in the later seventeenth century is discussed by Q. Skinner, 'The Ideological Context of Hobbes's Political Thought', *Historical Journal*, 7 (1966), 286–317; S. Mintz, *The Hunting of Leviathan: Seventeenth Century Reactions to the Materialism and Moral Philosophy of Thomas Hobbes* (Cambridge: University Press, 1962). Wood thought that Leviathan had 'corrupted the gentry of the nation, hath infused ill principles into them, atheism' (*Life and Times*, ii. 472). He was more charitable in the *Athenae Oxonienses* (iii, 1206–18). Pepys attested to the Leviathan's popularity in 1668: *The Diary of Samuel Pepys*, ed. R. Latham and W. Matthews, 11 vols. (Berkeley, Calif.: University of California Press, 1970–83), ix. 298.

[35] 'The Difference of Times, with Respect to Religion', Discourse no. 11 in *Works*, 4 vols. (Aberdeen: J. Chalmers, 1751), i. 37; 'The Justice of One Man Towards Another' (Discourse 29: *Works*, ii. 64). This argument was developed by Locke in the *Essay*, 2. 1. 1–8. Recall also his earlier statement in the *Essays on LN*, 143.

the proviso that no one could understand the law within themselves without first having come into the possession of a fully mature, working faculty of reason. In other words, mankind was born with only a potential for making moral decisions.[36] Now Locke, we should observe, was only a couple of years away from questioning the whole argument for innateness. To him the facts of experience more and more belied the assertions of its most strident defenders, and Whichcote, though always clinging to innateness, fully recognized the problems that it invariably created.

For Whichcote the answer to the dilemma of innate ideas that no one seemed to obey, even those of liberal education, lay in the consequences of the Fall. While he rarely referred to the Adam story in his sermons, he was more than sensitive to the historical reality of an affront to God so great that divine revelation must now provide men with a second source of knowledge of their moral obligations: 'Man being out of the way of Creation, by his Defection from God, is recovered by revelation.' God's revelation was the 'Soul's Cure' in the present state of 'Degeneracy and Apostasy', he believed, providing new incentives, offering more direct rewards, but most important of all, making us mindful of 'our ruinous and necessitous Condition', our 'contracted Impotency and great Deformity by our Fall', our 'self-contracted Misery'.[37] It was of course a gratuitous help from God, this revelation, proving beyond a shadow of a doubt his benevolent nature and giving hope for the eventual salvation of all. And man's free will remained intact in the fallen state, although Whichcote made it very clear that the first movement towards obedience under the Gospel must be preceded by the help of God's saving grace. In other words, God was the first cause of all good actions performed by fallen man; he must not only countenance our reform but enable us to proceed in it. This was precisely the position of Aquinas, as was Whichcote's further observation that once God began the process of reconciliation, the sinner, if he were sincere in repudiating sin or the promptings of his irrational side, would receive God's

[36] Roberts, *Puritanism to Platonism*, 93.
[37] *Select Sermons*, 6, 15, 48, 57. On p. 331 he mentions Adam's fall directly. See also 'The Justice of One Man Towards Another', *Works*, ii. 63.

assisting grace in abundance, this grace helping to maintain the reformed in their efforts to obey the dictates of reason.[38]

Locke doubtless learned much from Whichcote. Here for the first time was a popular teacher and pulpit preacher who clearly articulated what to Locke was a more sensible view of the Fall of man, one that retained its Scriptural basis while insisting that reform, though troublesome and terribly demanding, was at least within the purview of frail mankind.[39] In the *Two Tracts* and in the *Essays on the Law of Nature* Locke had expressed doubt as to whether men would ever live rationally; now Whichcote was promising divine assistance to those who at least put forward their best efforts in that direction. Whichcote did have some doubts of his own on the issue, for while it was 'natural' for a man 'in respect of the Principles of God's Creation in him, to live in Regard, Reverence, and Observance of Diety; to govern himself according to the rule of Sobriety and Temperance; to live in Love; and to carry himself well in God's family', still he recognized that mankind was unique amongst God's creation in its singular efforts to live in opposition to the 'Principle it was created in'.[40] This, for the Platonist, was the real essence of the Fall. Human nature was basically good, the core of that nature, reason, being positively god-like. But human nature and humans in the flesh were two very different entities in the mind of Whichcote, as they were in the mind of John Locke. Whichcote's optimism lay in his belief not only that human nature might be realized by men in the flesh, but also that God had become a willing and active partner in the undertaking. In fact, to Whichcote, it appeared that even more than the children of Adam themselves—woefully affected as they had been by the Fall—the Creator longed for the restoration of fallen man. That fact too, sadly enough, bespoke the awful effects of the Fall for the Cambridge Platonist.

---

[38] 'The Prayer . . . used by Dr Whichcote before Sermon' in *Works*, iv. 442, where he says that 'we are in nothing self-sufficient'; 'The Conversion of a Sinner' (Discourse 12: i. 209); 'The Arguments by which Men should be Persuaded to Reconcile Unto God' (Discourse no. 46; ii. 340). On Aquinas see Passmore, *Perfectibility of Man*, 17.

[39] Bishop Burnet praised Whichcote's effectiveness as a teacher, describing him as a man of 'rare temper, very mild and obliging' (Gilbert Burnet, *History of His Own Time*, 4 vols. (London: R. H. Evans, 1809), i. 261).

[40] *Select Sermons*, 39, 60; 'The Joy which the Righteous have in God' (Discourse 4: *Works*, i. 70).

There were other areas where the views of Locke and Whichcote coincided. As a proponent of free will, Whichcote strongly affirmed the powerful formative influence of custom, tradition, and education. His Christian point of departure here was Proverbs 22: 6,[41] and his belief in the infinite malleability of man enabled him to face even the worst possible assessment of human nature with confidence and equanimity: 'For even though the worst that can be said, prove true; that man is bankrupt, and hath suffered shipwreck, is confused in his principles, marred and spoiled by his apostasy, defection, delinquency, and consenting to iniquity . . . yet all this malady may be cured, and his condition is recoverable.'[42] The recovery was to be achieved through Christian education, the power of which was virtually unlimited. 'By Use, Custom, and Practice', Whichcote asserted, 'Men come to be Any thing; though never so Irrational and Unnatural.'[43] Locke, we know, had already behind him a good deal of experience as a college tutor and was at this time engaged in overseeing the instruction of the future second earl of Shaftesbury. He, too, would come to write in approving terms of the remedial capacity of good education; but he was never to become quite as confident in its overall potential as Whichcote seems to have been.

There also existed mutual agreement between Locke and Whichcote on the obligation under which each person lay to enquire after religious knowledge on his own. Their emphasis upon the sufficiency of reason to discover what is natural and to receive what is supernatural fortified what had always been one of the animating principles of the Protestant Reformation— critical self-enquiry. To rely on others for our religious precepts was, for Whichcote, to follow in the steps of the Roman Catholics; and given the fact that in affairs of temporal concern few men were credulous enough to accept the opinions of others, how could we abdicate responsibility in this our special employment? 'The first work of religion', he insisted, 'is to judge and perceive, and this is a work of skill; and therefore, for us to be unawakened and careless, not to employ our highest faculties

---

[41] 'Train up the child in the way he should go: and even when he is old, he will not depart from it.'

[42] 'The True Valuation of a Man' (Discourse 18: *Works*, i. 286).

[43] *Moral and Religious Aphorisms*, no. 194.

in this work, is irrational and unaccountable, unworthy of an intelligent agent.'[44] No one could be deemed religious by another man's knowledge. And where God had not declared his will in terms easily recognizable by rational beings, then it was best for all to exercise charity and restraint. These ideas Locke accepted wholeheartedly in the years after 1667; in fact, most would appear in his *Essay concerning Human Understanding* of 1689 in terms virtually identical to Whichcote's.[45] When he recommended the sermons as 'masterpieces', then, Locke was also passing judgement on his own firmly held ideas.

In his efforts to clarify what he took to be the essentials of the Christian faith, to transcend creedal squabbling and to broaden the basis of the Church of England, Whichcote was continuing a movement within the Church that had begun earlier in the seventeenth century, one which emerged in response to the rise of late sixteenth-century dogmatic Protestantism. The nub of Reformation theology, we know, centred on its understanding of man's depraved nature. But the very power by which men could discern their fallen condition and dependence upon God's grace presupposed the exercise and influence of critical reason. In the early stages of the Reformation the spirit of free enquiry based on reason—the spirit of Erasmus, Tyndale, and Colet—was applied to the search through Scripture with the full expectation that subjective certainty—Holy Writ as interpreted by conscience—would promptly yield a solid, indisputable rule of faith. Erasmus was to the end of his life sceptical of man's ability to agree upon one standard of true religious knowledge by this method and instead accepted the decisions of the Roman Church as best fitted for belief and practice. The religious anarchy that historical hindsight sees in Luther's argument was of course wholly unexpected by the early reformers. Behind their trenchant deprecation of human nature lay an assurance that consensus could be established concerning those beliefs that were necessary for salvation if only right-thinking Christians (or in Calvin's case 'saved' Christians) committed themselves to a diligent study of the Bible. Unhappily, the initial spirit of enquiry had almost immediately given rise to a prolonged

---

[44] 'The Danger of Unfaithfulness to God' (Discourse 9: *Works*, i. 149, 153, 151).
[45] *Essay*, 1. 4. 12, 23; 3. 9. 23.

period of bitter controversy and doctrinal confrontation. Each respective Reformed Church found itself putting together its own inviolable code of orthodoxy, an exclusive confessional dogma. And while this unfortunate development by no means annulled the obligation that each Christian read and study Scripture on his own, it none the less delimited the compass of that study and increasingly defined acceptable interpretations in light of each particular Church's own articles. By 1600 the primacy of Scripture and the rationalizing tendencies of the early Reformation were being eclipsed by the rigid confessions of the various denominations. The result was a crisis of certainty in religion, a disturbing sense of increased doubt and scepticism as to what, if anything at all, constituted the universal criteria of religious faith.[46]

Whichcote's theology was one answer to this growing dilemma, and Locke was fully cognizant of that fact. Lord Herbert of Cherbury had really begun the English rationalizing movement in 1624 with his *De Veritate*. The only escape from the discouraging creedal acrimony, he thought, was to transcend the warfare over dogma and explore the common foundations of all religion, to simplify in order to purify. Mankind possessed certain common notions, he said, those familiar innate ideas by which all men must govern their lives. That there is a supreme being, that he must be worshipped, that the essence of divine worship consists of regulating one's passions, that repentance is necessary, and that there is a life after death—such were the tenets of Lord Herbert's natural religion, one where conduct was plainly of greater importance than agreement on the minutiae of specific doctrinal articles.[47]

The English movement received further support from across the Channel after 1600 as a growing number of anti-Calvinist

---

[46] R. Popkin, *The History of Scepticism from Erasmus to Spinoza* (London: University of California Press, 1979), 4–16; H. G. Van Leeuwen, *The Problem of Certainty in English Thought, 1630–1690* (The Hague: Nijhoff, 1970), xii–xiii; Shapiro, *Probability and Certainty*, 74–8.

[47] B. Willey, *The Seventeenth Century Background* (London: Chatto and Windus, 1934), 127–30; D. P. Walker, *The Ancient Theology: Studies in Christian Platonism from the Fifteenth to the Eighteenth Century* (Ithaca, NY: Cornell University Press, 1972), 164–93. Ernst Cassirer (*The Platonic Renaissance in England*, trans. J. P. Pettegrove (New York: Nelson, 1953), 34) maintains that the Cambridge group consciously imitated Colet, Erasmus, and More in their plea for a non-sectarian Christianity.

Dutch theologians, led by a professor of theology at Leiden University, Jacob Arminius (*c*.1560–1609), assaulted the twin dogmas of predestination and Christ's limited atonement. These Remonstrants, or Arminians as they came to be called after the death of their leader, concentrated their greatest energies upon winning toleration for themselves and overturning what they took to be the arrogance and Antinomianism inherent in Calvinism. The first goal was secured by 1630; but the second suffered a major set-back when in 1619 a special assembly of the Dutch Reformed Church meeting in the city of Dort condemned the Arminian position, identifying it with the Pelagian heresy and stripping the accused clergy of their official positions within the Church.[48] The doctrine of the Remonstrants was first fully articulated by Arminius' successor Simon Episcopius, and its early influence in England resulted from the work of John Hales, Regius Professor of Greek at Oxford and a spectator at the 1619 Synod of Dort. Locke was familiar with Hales's work by 1667; in the 1680s he would himself befriend the leading Remonstrants in Amsterdam and establish an immense respect for both their religious commitment and their spirit of dedicated self-enquiry.[49] Hales's revulsion at the high-handed methods employed by the orthodox at Dort in order to maintain their own special vision of the Gospel message impelled him to rethink the argument that attempted to justify doctrinal uniformity; ultimately he found himself siding with the Arminians. Back in England he befriended others similarly distressed over the inflexible dogmatism of and heightened acrimony between the Laudian establishment and its Puritan opponents. Most

[48] C. Bangs, *Arminius: A Study in the Dutch Reformation* (Nashville, Tenn.: Abington Press, 1973), 332–5; P. Geys, *The Netherlands in the Seventeenth Century, 1609–1648* (London: Benn, 1961), 70–83; P. J. Blok, *History of the People of the Netherlands*, trans. R. Putnam, 5 vols. (New York: Putnam's Sons, 1898–1912), iii. 398–435; Tulloch, *Rational Theology*, i. 11–20. The Arminian emphasis on free will had never been entirely extinguished in England after the Reformation, but the indigenous free-willers constituted a distinct minority throughout the sixteenth century: O. T. Thompson, 'The Freewillers in the English Reformation', *Church History*, 37 (1968), 271–80.

[49] MS Locke f. 14, fol. 16. Ralph Cudworth's daughter Damaris Masham, in whose home Locke spent much of the last fifteen years of his life, wrote to the Remonstrant Philippus van Limborch in 1704: 'I imagine that the sentiments that he [Locke] found in vogue amongst you in Holland pleased him far more, and seemed to him far more responsible, than anything that he used to hear from English theologians.' The letter is printed in A. C. Fraser's edition of Locke's *Essay concerning Human Understanding*, 2 vols. (Oxford: University Press, 1894), i. xxxvi.

influential among Hales's new friends was William Chill-
ingworth, author of *The Religion of Protestants a Safe Way to
Salvation* and a member of a small theological group that met
during the 1630s at the home (Great Tew in Oxfordshire) of
Lucius Cary, Lord Falkland. The Tew Circle became engaged
in an attempt to identify what to them represented the few
essentials of Christian doctrine necessary for salvation under the
Gospel and upon which all Christians could immediately agree.
'For consider of all the liturgies that are or ever have been,' said
Hales in a work written for Chillingworth, 'and remove from
them whatsoever is scandalous to any party, and leave nothing
but what all agree on; and the event shall be, that the public
service and honour of God shall no ways suffer.' To load religion
with a surfeit of public forms and creedal tenets 'is the most
sovereign way to perpetuate schism unto the world's end'.[50]
Even Holy Scripture was abbreviated by the Tew members,
only those things 'plainly revealed' to men of understanding
being regarded as necessary parts of true belief.[51]

In minimizing the centrality of right doctrine to Christianity,
the Broad-Churchmen placed increased emphasis on proper
moral conduct, deeming this the most essential element of
Christ's message to mankind. Certainty on doctrine was for ever
elusive, they claimed, neither Pope, Church Fathers, nor
Scripture as interpreted by conscience having any absolute
claim to infallibility. According to Hales, 'Many deceive
themselves, whilst they argue from their faith to their works,
whereas they ought out of their works conclude their faith.'[52]

---

[50] 'A Tract Concerning Schism and Schismatics' (1636), in *The Works of the Ever
Memorable Mr John Hales of Eaton*, 3 vols. (Glasgow: R. and A. Foulis, 1765), i. 127. On
the Tew Circle see Shapiro, *Probability and Certainty*, 80–7; Wormald, *Clarendon*, 243–56.
McAdoo, *Spirit of Anglicanism*, 13–14, stresses the connection between Hooker's
theological method and that employed by the Tew Circle. On Hales in particular see J.
H. Elson, *John Hales of Eaton* (New York: King's Crown Press, 1948). John Aubrey (*Brief
Lives*, ed. Andrew Clark, 2 vols. (Oxford: Clarendon Press, 1898), i. 150) called Falkland
'the first Socinian in England', but Clarendon (*History of Rebellion*, vii. 217–34) is much
more sympathetic towards him.

[51] William Chillingworth, *The Religion of Protestants a Safe Way to Salvation* (1638), in
Works, 3 vols. (Oxford: University Press, 1838), i. 230. In a journal entry for
26 Apr. 1680 Locke recorded payment for Chillingworth's Works: MS Locke f. 4,
fol. 95. In 1693 and again in 1703 he recommended Chillingworth as the best teacher of
'right reasoning': *Thoughts on Ed.* 296; ibid., 'Some Thoughts Concerning Reading and
Study for a Gentleman' (1703), 399.

[52] Hales, 'Of St Peter's Fall', (*Works*, i. 212).

Their conclusions were not arrived at light-heartedly, but only after long personal search for some infallible rule of faith. Chillingworth's enquiry had taken him first into Roman Catholicism and a brief period of study at the Jesuit seminary of Douai in northern France before bringing him back into the Anglican fold by 1634. He began *The Religion of Protestants* in an atmosphere deeply influenced by Renaissance humanism and with the encouragement of Lord Falkland, Hales, and the other members of the group.[53] The spirit of enquiry and moderation characteristic of Chillingworth's treatise disappeared during the years of civil war in England, but re-emerged after 1660 under new leadership and changed circumstances.

One of the difficulties facing reformers after 1660 was that doctrinal liberals of whatever stripe were more often than not tarred with the infamous brush of Socinianism, an Arian movement whose leader, Faustus Socinus, was born (1539) in Siena, Italy but removed to the more tolerant environs of Cracow, Poland in the wake of persecution by the Italian Inquisition. His antitrinitarian views, based upon what he conceived to be the metaphysical impossibility involved in the orthodox proposition of three Persons in one substance, were combined with a steadfast biblicism that acknowledged the coequal role of reason in religion, and with a second, and even more damnable heresy in the eyes of the orthodox: the denial of Christ's satisfaction for the sins of mankind. Socinus nullified the Atonement on the grounds that any propitiation for sin not directly involving and obligating the sinner in effect lessened the awful nature of every act of disobedience to God. In addition, the very notion of atonement carried with it, thought Socinus, the implication that the Creator could not forgive without Christ's sacrificial act, that God was after all not omnipotent. Alternatively he maintained that the work of Christ (Socinus accepted the supernatural birth and miracles of Jesus) was to make an impression not upon God by substituting himself in the place of actual sinners, but rather to awaken men to the heinous nature of their transgressions. Socinus, like the fourth-century monk Pelagius, attempted to make the attainment of salvation

[53] R. R. Orr, *Reason and Authority: The Thought of William Chillingworth* (Oxford: Clarendon Press, 1967), 37.

more difficult by emphasizing free will and the absolute responsibility of each individual to follow Christ's example. The real nature of Christ's pilgrimage on earth, in the mind of this reformer, was to amplify human consciousness of the majestic will of God, to add new urgency and prophetic cogency to the divine message.[54]

Socinus died in 1607 but before his passing the Racovian Catechism, so named after the city of its publication (Rakow) and containing the substance of Socinian ideas, was printed in Poland and subsequently translated into German (1608), Latin (1608), and English (1609). And while the forces of the Counter-Reformation were at last able to stamp out the last vestiges of toleration in Poland by the mid-seventeenth century, many of the Socinian exiles found refuge in Holland and managed to spread their unique ideas across the Channel. The most controversial elements of the Socinian creed found little active support either in Holland or England, but its more general rationalizing tendencies and emphasis upon behaviour received a warmer reception.[55] The Tew Circle before 1640, the Latitudinarian wing of the Church of England, and the Cambridge Platonists after 1660 could be, and often were, accused of Socinianism by critics who drew little distinction between the Socinian ethos in general and specific Socinian doctrines. Thus anyone engaged in attempting to mediate the dispute between rigid Anglicanism and dogmatic Puritanism often found themselves devoting a large portion of their energies to defending their own orthodoxy.[56]

One of the earliest avowed Socinians in England was a schoolmaster from Gloucester by the name of John Biddle. His *Twelve Arguments Against the Deity of the Holy Ghost* (1647) and other minor works earned for the author both imprisonment and eventual banishment to the Scilly Isles. Among Biddle's few supporters in London, however, was the merchant and

---

[54] D. M. Cory, *Faustus Socinus* (Boston: Beacon Press, 1932), 86–103; McGiffert, *Protestant Thought*, 110–11; *Encyclopedia of Religion and Ethics*, 1917 edn., article on 'Socinianism'.

[55] J. H. McLachlan, *Socinianism in Seventeenth-Century England* (Oxford: University Press, 1951), 54–86, 143. The Racovian Catechism was ordered to be burnt in 1614 but copies of the 1609 edition are in the Bodleian and British Libraries. By 1674 the Bodleian catalogue contained sixty Socinian works, twenty by Socinus alone: ibid., 120–1.

[56] Such was to be Locke's situation in the 1690s.

philanthropist Thomas Firmin. Firmin had first befriended Biddle in 1655, was impressed by his religiosity, and by 1670 his Lombard-Street residence had become the meeting ground for a number of Broad-Church divines and future Anglican leaders like John Tillotson and Edward Fowler, as well as Benjamin Whichcote. John Locke also frequented Firmin's home (the merchant was a close friend of the first earl of Shaftesbury) and it is likely that he first made the acquaintance of these rationalizing churchmen under Firmin's roof.[57] During the 1670s Locke came to share with them not only their desire for toleration, but also the doctrine of the minimal creed and the argument that conduct lay at the heart of Christianity. 'Noe man can say he loves God who loves not his neighbour', he wrote in 1675, and 'Noe man can love his neighbour who loves not his Country: 'Tis the greatest charity to preserve the Laws and rights of the nation, whereof we are. A Good man is a charitable man, is to give to every man his due, From the King upon the throne, to the Begger in the streete.'[58] The old emphasis upon civil peace and social order, always a central component of Locke's political philosophy, was now beginning to emerge, under the influence of Latitudinarian and Platonist morality, as an important part of his Christianity. On the simplicity of God's law, he concluded that 'Whatsoever carrys any excellency with it and includes not imperfection it must needs make of the idea of [the] law of god'.[59] He lamented the state of present Protestantism as one that had lost the original vigour first acquired during the sixteenth-century struggle against 'Romish Fopperies', accused the 'Great Clergy' of seeking their own interests over those of universal Protestantism, and warned against increasing sectarianism as the bane of Reformed teaching.[60]

---

[57] On Biddle's life and work see W. Turner, *Lives of Eminent Unitarians*, 2 vols. (London: Unitarian Association, 1840), i. 23–56; Cranston, *Locke*, 126–7; Fox Bourne, *Locke*, i. 309–10. Locke owned several of Biddle's works by 1680: MS Locke f. 4, fols. 10–11. Firmin's ideas are discussed in R. Wallace, *Antitrinitarian Biography*, 3 vols. (London: E. T. Whitfield, 1850), iii. 372–89. See also G. Burnet's favourable assessment in *History*, iii. 292.

[58] 'Philanthropy or the Christian Philosophers', MS Locke c. 27, fol. 30. His new view on toleration, first expressed in the 1667 essay, reappeared in a commonplace book of 1679: MS Locke d. 1, fol. 125, under the heading 'Toleratio'.

[59] MS Locke f. 4, fol. 145.

[60] MS Locke c. 27, fol. 30.

Locke also endorsed the Broad-Church criticism of religious sceptics who had made much of the fact that Protestant efforts to discover a clear standard of true knowledge in Scripture had come to naught. Catholics had attempted to take advantage of the Protestant dilemma by pushing Erasmus's position to the extreme of pure fideism, or total faith in the wisdom of the Church without the intervention of reason, while atheists simply pointed out that the whole rule-of-faith controversy added additional credibility to their own admittedly radical alternative. Locke and the liberal churchmen argued that an absolute rule of faith in every particular was unnecessary, and that probable knowledge, knowledged based upon the best evidence available, was more than adequate to establish the validity of Christian revelation. If sceptics questioned the truths of religion simply because those truths could not be demonstrably proven, said Locke, 'If all things must stand or fall by the measure of our understandings, and that denid to be wherein we find inextricable difficultys there will very little remain in the world, and we shall scarce leave our selves soe much as bodys soules or understandings.' Mankind possessed probable evidence in support of such things as the existence of God, the immortality of the soul, and the necessity for repentance, and since most of our daily actions were based on no better knowledge, it would be arrogance and pride 'to doubt of a god because he is above our narrow understandings'.[61] The future Latitudinarian Archbishop of Canterbury, John Tillotson, a friend of Locke and a popular Tuesday-afternoon lecturer at Whichcote's St Lawrence Jewry, agreed entirely with this analysis. For Tillotson the man who took 'a pleasure and a pride in unravelling almost all the received principles of both religion and reason' betrayed his depravity in the most conspicuous manner. It was the 'strength of men's lusts, and the power of vicious inclinations' that biased the understanding in the direction of atheism and pointed up the practical consequences of the first sin.[62]

Locke, then, discovered much that was admirable in the

---

[61] Journal entry (8 Feb. 1677). Excerpts from Locke's journal are printed in *Early Draft*, 89. See Chillingworth's preface to his *Religion of Protestants* (*Works*, i. 3) for another example of the argument from probable evidence.

[62] John Tillotson, 'The Wisdom of Being Religious', in *Works*, ed. T. Birch, 10 vols. (London: J. F. Dove, 1820), i. 332, 369.

Broad-Church perspective. The appeal to reason in religion was supported by the discoveries of seventeenth-century science, where the new cosmology and advancing physics seemed to place mankind in an orderly, rational universe. Reason was fast uncovering the secrets of the physical world, and there was a growing sense of confidence that its application in the realm of theology could do the same for religion. By demonstrating the consonance of rational religion with revelation the liberal churchmen could, they thought, vindicate Christianity in the eyes of its enlightened critics and also buttress their central argument that the truths of the faith were few and easily apprehended by all believers. A comprehensive Church possessed of a theology in no way opposed to the temper of the scientific mind seemed to devout Christians like Locke the best of all possible alternatives to the often violent by-products of conflicting belief that had been the hallmark of much of the century.

A good deal has been written about the Platonists and the Latitudinarians. And most of the literature has properly focused on the break with Calvinism which the movement for comprehension and the minimal creed signalled. There is no questioning the fact that Restoration liberal churchmen, in recalling and refining the doctrines of Lord Herbert, the Remonstrants, Socinus, and the Great Tew Circle, were first and foremost concerned to put an end to the divisions within the Protestant community by moving away from intellectualized religion in favour of practical morality and ethical conduct. Ralph Cudworth's well-known sermon before the House of Commons in the spring before Locke was admitted to nearby Westminster School encapsulates the overriding goal of the movement. 'Ink and paper', he submitted, 'can never make us Christians, can never beget a new nature, a living principle in us; can never form Christ, or any true notions of spiritual things, in our hearts.' Accusing the Puritans of the very arrogance they so much condemned in men not of their own opinion on the matter of predestination, he warned that 'We have no warrant in Scripture to peep into these hidden roles and volumes of eternity, and to make it our first thing that we do, when we come to Christ, to spell out our names in the stars.' It was behaviour in this life, said Cudworth, not one's adherence to fine-spun doctrines, that really mattered before God: 'Let nothing be esteemed of greater confidence and concernment to thee than what thou doest and actest, how thou livest.'[63] The focus on behaviour, although surely apt to stir up bitter memories of the Pelagian heresy and the abuses of late medieval Catholicism, appeared crucial to the anti-Calvinists if Protestantism were not to make an absolute mockery of Christian teaching with its increasing sectarianism and escalating mutual recrimination. As Locke would later note in his journal, 'the great disputes that have been and are still in the several churches have been for the most part about their own inventions and not about things ordaind by God himself, or necessary to salvation'.[64]

Thus a new spirit was beginning to inform much of Restoration theology, despite the harshness of the Clarendon Code and the failure of Shaftesbury's efforts to legislate toleration. Locke's friends among the Latitudinarians became popular and influential preachers in London, and after the Revolution of 1688 dominated the episcopal bench. Many had been taught by the Cambridge men: Tillotson was called upon to deliver Whichcote's funeral sermon and Simon Patrick fulfilled the same function upon the death of John Smith.[65] And while Platonists like Cudworth, Henry More, and John Smith were more emphatic about the mind–body distinction than were Latitudinarian churchmen such as Tillotson, Patrick, Edward Fowler, and Isaac Barrow, both groups identified

[63] 'Sermon Preached Before the Honourable House of Commons at Westminster' (March 1647), in *Works of Ralph Cudworth*, 4 vols. (Oxford: D. A. Talboys, 1829), i. 297, 300, 343. Cudworth's role as Master of Christ's College, Cambridge is discussed by M. Nicholson, 'Christ's College and the Latitude Men', *Modern Philology*, 27 (1929), 35–53. See also Passmore, *Ralph Cudworth*, 80. Identical sentiments were expressed by the Platonist John Smith in his 'Discourse Concerning the True Way or Method of Attaining to Divine Knowledge', in *Select Discourses of John Smith* (London: F. Flesher, 1660), 9.

[64] MS Locke f. 8, fol. 97. Although he seems never to have met Cudworth, Locke, as indicated in note 49 above, spent most of his last years as the guest of Cudworth's daughter, Damaris Masham.

[65] A. Lichtenstein, *Henry More: The Rational Theology of a Cambridge Platonist* (Cambridge, Mass.: Harvard University Press, 1962), 26; Cragg, *Puritanism to Age of Reason*, 63; Simon Patrick 'A Sermon Preached at the Funeral of Mr. John Smith', in *Select Discourses of John Smith* (London: F. Flesher, 1660), 519. Tillotson attended Clare College (1647–54) while Cudworth was Master there. He was associated with Whichcote as Tuesday-afternoon lecturer at St Lawrence Jewry from 1663: L. G. Locke, *Tillotson: A Study in Seventeenth Century Literature* (Copenhagen: Rosenkilde and Bagger, 1954), 21, 35.

reason in man as being truly god-like and stressed the need for rational control over the iniquitous passions. Both were in essential agreement with the analysis of human nature first put forward by the spiritual mentor of the Platonists, Benjamin Whichcote. Because of these tendencies, late seventeenth-century theology has often been viewed as simply another episode in the protracted struggle between Pelagianism and Augustinianism. The liberal theologians of Restoration England allegedly went beyond the Christian dispute and reintroduced the idea of teleological perfection as understood by the Greeks, a perfection worked by men alone and synonymous with the mastery of the intellect over the debilitating attractions of sense. Theology seemed useful to these men, according to the allegations, only in so far as it reinforced this basic idea, and practical morality became the sum and substance, the only real business of organized religion.[66]

Surely, given the sharp break with Puritan ideas on so many fronts after 1660—the flight from dogma and the abandonment of predestination being chief among them—the charge against the moderate churchmen seems at least fairly plausible. But we must remember that these men considered themselves to be reformers whose guiding purpose was to make the Christian faith more meaningful and exacting to a Protestant world clearly tottering—in their minds anyway—under the oppressive weight of stultifying doctrine. Their deep concern with casuistical divinity and rigorism, continuing a tradition begun by Puritans like William Perkins and Richard Baxter, bespoke their refusal to separate morality from Christian faith: true belief, they held, must issue in godly conduct.[67] While never acknowledging him directly, these theologians found much that was appropriate to their special circumstances in the views of Pelagius, in particular his call for strict individual responsibility and his emphasis upon unmitigated guilt for even the smallest of sins. But their rehabilitation of free will did not carry with it any easy guarantee that all men would be saved. As Chillingworth

---

[66] See, for example, Allison, *Rise of Moralism*, 192; H. Davies, *Worship and Theology in England: From Andrewes to Baxter and Fox, 1603–1690* (Princeton, NJ: University Press, 1975), 184; Cragg, op. cit. 29.

[67] T. Wood, *English Casuistical Divinity During the Seventeenth Century* (London: SPCK, 1952), 34, 35, 118; McAdoo, *Structure of Caroline Moral Theology*, 64–97.

warned, 'repentance is not so ordinary a thing, nor of so easy dispatch, as most mistake it, who conceive it to be nothing more, but true sorrow for sin passed, with true intention to forsake it'.[68] Nor did they endorse, and this was true for Locke as well, the Semi-Pelagian notion recently revived by Socinus that the first movement towards repentance began with the sinner. This claim went well beyond the pale for the Broad-Churchman because it diminished the seriousness of the first sin and freed mankind from its dependent status.[69] We must read these Restoration theologians, friends of Locke and influential pulpit preachers, not only in light of their break with some important elements of the Puritan past, or with regard to the points of contact between their ideas and Pelagian-Socinian-Deistic notions, but in full view of their total theology, of their areas of continuity with the orthodox past, and, most importantly, of their steadfast adherence to the larger Christian view of man and his place in God's creation.

Perhaps the best evidence of the orthodoxy of the Broad-Church divines, and of Locke, is to be found in the writings of the one man who ostensibly represented the antithesis of liberalizing Christianity—and whose major work remains to this day the most influential seventeenth-century statement on the Fall and its consequences for man—the former Latin Secretary for the Commonwealth government and disillusioned defender of righteous regicide, the Puritan poet Milton.

Actually, Milton's Puritanism, if in truth the appellation is at all appropriate, extended little beyond an intense disdain for Church of England discipline, civil interference in matters of opinion and religious practice, and perceived monarchical tyranny. In his strict biblicism he represented that which was best in a long Protestant tradition, and in *Paradise Lost* he

---

[68] 'Against Punishing Crimes with Death' (*Works*, iii. 473).

[69] Chillingworth insisted that the emphasis upon conduct in no way meant that by good works, 'which is the error of the papists', one merited salvation: Sermon 1 in *Works*, iii. 28. See also Sermon 4 (iii. 130), where he condemns Socinus for denying the meritorious death and sacrifice of Christ. Jeremy Taylor, another member of the Tew Circle, said that 'It is not a good life that justifies a man before God, but it is faith in the special promises' (*Unum Necessarium; or, The Doctrine and Practice of Repentance*, in *The Whole Works of the Right Reverend Jeremy Taylor*, ed. Reginald Heber, 15 vols. (London: Ogle, Duncan, and Co., 1822), viii, (p. cclxvi). I cannot agree with Cranston's statement (*Locke*, 126) that Locke and the later Latitudinarians were 'more deserving' of the Socinian label.

exhibited the same spirit of high seriousness and moral urgency about the problem of original sin evident in the writings of his Anglican and Puritan contemporaries. That this champion of the Puritan Commonwealth found much that was unpalatable in Calvinist doctrine is no surprise given his unyielding insistence upon the primacy of the moral agent in the great scheme of salvation. Dual predestination, where a few are chosen and the rest sentenced to hell, he rejected outright, for he believed that the doctrine had to do with salvation solely, not damnation. This was not to say, however, that Adam's sin was in any way inevitable by virtue of God's foreknowledge of all things. For the Creator had made men perfect, thought Milton, and that perfection lay in the exercise of right reason. Adam had sinned, had rejected reason, of his own free will:

> They therefore as to right belongd,
> So were created, nor can justly accuse
> Thir maker, or thir making, or their Fate,
> As if predestination over-rul'd
> Thir will, dispos'd by absolute Decree
> Or high foreknowledge; they themselves decreed
> Thir own revolt, not I: if I foreknew,
> Foreknowledge had no influence on their fault,
> Which had no less prov'd certain unforeknown.[70]

Yet despite the fall of Adam and his repudiation of God's sovereignty, Milton continued to insist, like the liberal divines, that man's free will remained intact and his faculty of right reason, though greatly attenuated, was still of sufficient strength to win God's favour. And that favour—eternal salvation—was open 'to all who heartily believe and continue in their belief . . . and that thus the general decree of election becomes personally

---

[70] Milton, *Paradise Lost*, iii. 111–19, in *Works*, ed. F. A. Paterson, 18 vols. (New York: Columbia University Press, 1931–8), ii. 81; id., *De Doctrina Christiana* (*Works*, xv. 91, 97); E. Smith, *Some Versions of the Fall* (Chatham: W. and T. Macay, Ltd., 1973), 26; F. E. Hutchinson, *Milton and the English Mind* (New York: Macmillan, 1948), 175; D. M. Hamlet, *One Greater Man: Justice and Damnation in Paradise Lost* (Lewisburg, Pa.: Bucknell University Press, 1973), 82–4. On Milton's ambivalence over Adam's transgression see A. Lovejoy, 'Milton and the Paradox of the Fortunate Fall', in his *Essays in the History of Ideas*, 277–95. Dewey Wallace (*Puritans and Predestination*, 132) places Milton amongst a group he calls 'sectarian Arminians' who questioned the implications of predestination for morality, while Douglas Bush (*Paradise Lost in Our Time*, 36–9) finds in the concept of 'right reason' the firmest bond between Milton and the Platonists.

applicable to each particular believer, and is ratified to all who remain steadfast in the faith'. Milton's synergism suggests that there was a good deal more of the humanist, of the Broad-Churchman, in the author who set out to justify the ways of God to men than there was of the unbending Puritan. How else could he have suggested the following picture of a forgiving Deity?

> Man shall not quite be lost, but sav'd who will
> Yet not of will in him, but grace in me
> Freely voutsaft; once more I will renew
> His lapsed powers, though forfeit and enthrall'd
> By sin to foul exorbitant desires;
> Upheld by me, yet once more shall he stand
> On even ground against his mortal foe,
> By me upheld, that he may know how frail
> His fall'n condition is, and to me ow
> All his deliv'rance, and to none but me.[71]

Milton's God was Whichcote's God—and Locke's God, because he 'desires not the death of any one, but the salvation of all'. He hates nothing which constitutes his own handiwork and has 'omitted nothing which might suffice for universal salvation'. Adam's fall was at bottom the product of the surrender of reason to the peccant appetites. It was now up to men, aided of course by the infusion of prevenient grace, to remedy the effects of their lapsed condition, to become members of the Elect. After all,

> Why should not Man,
> Retaining still Divine similitude
> In part, from such deformities be free,
> And for his Makers Image sake exempt?[72]

We can recall that one of the essential facets of Christian anthropology since the time of Paul involved a primal transgression on the part of Adam and Eve in the Garden, followed by expulsion from Paradise, the infection of sinfulness, and the loss of immortality. We also know that Paul rejected the

---

[71] Milton, *De Doctrina Christiana* (*Works*, xv. 107); *Paradise Lost*, iii. 173–82 (ed. cit. ii. 83–4).

[72] *De Doctrina Christiana*, 103; *Paradise Lost*, xi. 511–14 (ed. cit. ii. 364). 'Paradise Lost', writes Christopher Hill, 'appeared at exactly the time of Arminianism's victory', while Locke 'summed up a secularized Arminian Puritanism' (*Milton and the English Revolution* (London: Faber, 1977), 277).

classical notion of a pristine soul imprisoned within a corrupt body ever struggling to free itself and reunite with its spiritual Creator. Although, as we have seen in the case of Whichcote, the anti-Calvinists grounded their Christian ethics on the cultivation of reason and control over the sensual appetites, they remained within the camp of Pauline orthodoxy by refusing to entertain the notion that man's rational faculties had been left unimpaired by the Fall. The very fact that reason could do so little without the enabling force of God's grace made this abundantly clear. Ralph Cudworth went so far as to argue that knowledge, which the classical mind had assumed to be synonymous with virtue, was actually of little advantage to mankind. In fact, he considered it 'a piece of that corruption, that runneth through human nature, that we naturally prize truth more than goodness, knowledge more than holiness'. The Latitudinarian divine Simon Patrick, while not as extreme, expressed a commonly held opinion when he said that our use of 'bare natural reason' in searching out the rule of faith must at all times be accompanied by the guidance of God's helping grace. And John Tillotson, in speaking of the education of children years before his appointment to the See of Canterbury, observed that while good example and the early inculcation of proper habits could work significant change in the minds of young Christians, all of whom were 'naturally inclin'd to that which is evil', still one must implore God's 'powerful Assistance and Blessing; without which, all that we can do will prove ineffectual'.[73] Locke himself wrote in the 1680s that men must in charity 'pray god for the assistance of his spirit for the enlightening of our understandings and subdueing our corruptions that soe we may perform unto him a reasonable and acceptable service and shew our faith by our works'.[74] Here was combined the liberal emphasis on conduct together with a plea

---

[73] Cudworth, *Works*, i. 307; Simon Patrick, 'A Sermon Preached on St. Mark's Day', in *The Works of Simon Patrick*, ed. A. Taylor, 9 vols. (Oxford: University Press, 1858), viii. 186; Tillotson, 'Of the Education of Children' (*Works*, iii. 526, 538). See also Tillotson's 'Of the Difficulty of Reforming Vicious Habits' and 'The Necessity of Supernatural Grace' (*Works*, ii. 512; viii. 486). Cudworth spoke of 'the renewing spirit of Christ' in 'The Christian's Victory' (*Works*, iv. 368). Patrick's background (he was a friend of Whichcote and Smith) is treated by M. Jacob, *The Newtonians and the English Revolution* (Ithaca, NY: Cornell University Press, 1976), 43–5.

[74] 'Pacifick Christians' (MS Locke c. 27, fol. 80).

for God's assistance in guiding men towards eternal salvation, assistance which was deemed imperative if the sin of Adam were ever to be excused.

The anti-Calvinists never forgot that Christianity had historically viewed man and his nature in terms of weakness and debility born of pride. Isaac Barrow, one of the divines whom Locke met through Shaftesbury and whose sermons he recommended to his nephew Richard King for instruction in 'a larger view of the parts of morality', thought it of utmost importance that all Christians be made 'sensible of our weakness, our vileness, our wretchedness':

For how low was that our fall, from which we could not be raised without such a depression of God's only Son! How great is that impotency, which did need such a succor to relieve it! How abominable must be that iniquity, which might not be expiated without so costly a sacrifice!

Barrow thought it 'madness for us to be conceited of any worth in ourselves, to confide in any merit of our works, to glory in anything belonging to us'. The great magnitude of the Fall for this Broad-Churchman was confirmed by the fact that divine forgiveness necessitated the sacrifice of God's only son. 'Would the son of God', asked Barrow, 'have so Emptied, and abused himself for nothing? Would he have endured such pains and ignominies for a trifle?'[75]

Barrow's sinewy language here was by no means exceptional. His identification with the liberal divines of the Restoration period was the product of his 'plain style', the didactic nature of his sermons, and his conviction that to eternal salvation in heaven, 'if we please, by obedience to his holy laws we may certainly enter'.[76] But his unflinching avowal of man's sinful nature and helplessness without the atoning sacrifice of Christ

[75] Isaac Barrow, 'Upon the Passion of our Blessed Saviour' (1677), in *The Theological Works of Isaac Barrow*, ed. A. Napier, 9 vols. (Cambridge: University Press, 1859), i. 135–6. Statements like this one make the charge of Socinianism against the Latitudinarians all the more implausible. Tillotson edited Barrow's theological works after his death in 1677 at the age of forty-seven. Locke seems to have first met Barrow at Shaftesbury's home in London. See P. H. Osmond, *Isaac Barrow: His Life and Time* (London: SPCK, 1944), 204; *DNB* i. 1224.

[76] Barrow, 'Of the Goodness of God', in *Works*, iii. 508. On the 'plain style' of the Latitudinarians, see I. Simon, ed., *Three Restoration Divines: Barrow, South, Tillotson* (Paris; n.p., 1952), Introd.

was just as much a part of Broad-Church belief. To suggest that
these men avoided discussing grace and original sin is simply
unwarranted.[77] Edward Fowler, another friend of Locke's in
London and after 1691 Bishop of Gloucester, while indicating
that Christians were blessed in having divine revelation to set
before them their duties in clear language where the ancients
had to rely completely upon frail reason, deplored the fact that
'Beastly intemperance and uncleanness of all sorts, the most
sordid covetousness, wretched injustice, oppressions, and cruel-
ties' still distinguished most Christian nations. The fault, he
believed, lay in the fact that depraved men would not take the
time or expend the necessary effort to consider the Gospel rule.
This was precisely Locke's position before entering Shaftesbury's home, and he reiterated it more than once in his journal
during the 1670s.[78] For Fowler the 'Generality of Christians',
'woefully lost to all true goodness', confirmed the reality of
mankind's apostasy. He made no specific mention of the Adam
story, but in affirming that 'There is no [more] heinous monster
in nature as a Reasonable Creature living in Contradiction to
the Dictates of his Understanding, trampling under-foot the
eternal laws of Righteousness, and opposing himself to the
known will of the Great Sovereign of the World', he was
expressing a common Broad-Church theme. The Latitudinarian rector of Bath and champion of the new science Joseph
Glanvill perhaps best summed up the feelings of his peers when
he wrote that 'we are not now like the Creatures we were made,
but have lost both our Makers image, and our own. And
possibly the beasts are not much inferior to us, then we are to our
ancient selves: a proud affecting to be like Gods, having made us
unlike Men.'[79]

One of the books which Locke had read during the period
when he was re-examining his ideas on religious toleration was
written by another important member of the Tew Circle,

---

[77] The claim is made by Shapiro, *Probability and Certainty*, 87.

[78] Edward Fowler, *The Design of Christianity* (London: Tyler and Holt, 1671), 168,
171; Locke, journal entries (8 Feb. 1677, 17 June 1679) printed in *Early Draft*, 88, 112.
Tillotson held the same opinion: see, for example, 'Of the Inward Peace and Pleasure
Which Attends Religion' and 'The Unprofitableness of Sin' (*Works*, ii. 97–8, vii. 299).

[79] Edward Fowler, *Libertas Evangelica* (London: R. Norton, 1680), 104, 168; Joseph
Glanvill, *Scepsis Scientifica: or Confessed Ignorance, the Way to Science* (London: E. Cotes,
1665), 5.

Jeremy Taylor. His *Discourse of the Liberty of Prophesying* (1647) took the offensive against the opponents of the minimal creed by charging those who would impose their doctrines upon the conscience of others with a form of arrogance and pride reminiscent of the first sin, implementing a devious stratagem of Satan designed to extirpate piety and practical duty. The sole requirement for salvation, according to Taylor, was that men believe in Jesus Christ crucified and live their lives accordingly.[80] This, he held, had been the position of the Church during the first four centuries, and could be proved conclusively be a serious study of the early Church Fathers.

Taylor had graduated from Oxford in 1630 and was brought to the attention of William Laud in 1634.[81] After preaching before the Archbishop at Lambeth Palace in that year, he was elected a Fellow of All Souls College and at length was made a personal chaplain first of Laud and then of Charles II, all before he had reached the age of twenty-five. It was no surprise, then, when his first book, *Episcopacy Asserted* (1642), adopted for its theme the divine institution and necessity of bishops within the Church of England. The king was so taken by the performance that he had the degree of DD conferred on Taylor by Royal decree. But like so many other aspiring churchmen of that day, Taylor's fortunes were to change drastically with the defeat of the Royalists. Taking up residence in Wales after 1645, he turned to school teaching and, with the patronage of a local landowner, betook himself to writing the *Liberty of Prophesying* as

---

[80] Taylor, *A Discourse of the Liberty of Prophesying*, in *Works*, ix. 443–5. This simple faith was exactly that set forward by Locke in his *Reasonableness of Christianity* (1695). Cranston says that Locke first read the *Liberty of Prophesying* in 1667 but does not give a reference. In his account-book from Westminster School Locke recorded 'Docto Tailers works' among his possessions. Taylor's name appears again in Locke's account-book from Christ Church for the year 1661 and in a manuscript entry of 1667: MS Locke f. 11, fols. 24, 70; f. 14, fol. 8. However, only one work of Taylor's appears in Locke's final library catalogue: P. Laslett and J. Harrison, eds., *The Library of John Locke* (Oxford: Clarendon Press, 1971), 244. See especially sect. 16 of *Liberty*, entitled 'Whether it be lawful for a Prince to Give Toleration to Several Religions', and sect. 14 (p. 213), where Taylor, like Locke in the essay on toleration, concedes that the magistrate must possess strong coercive powers lest society degenerate into 'perpetual confusion'.

[81] For all of his imperiousness on matters of ceremony and outward forms, Laud was exceptionally liberal in his patronage of young men like Hales (Laud's chaplain), Taylor, and Chillingworth (Laud's godson), all of whom differed with him on theological matters: see H. Trevor-Roper, *Archbishop Laud, 1573–1645* (London: Macmillan, 1940), 280, 337–8.

a practical means of settling the differences then dividing English Christians.[82]

Like his friends at Tew and the Restoration Broad-Church-men, Taylor had a good deal to say about the results of the Fall, free will, and the role of grace in the drama of salvation. And although his reaction to Augustinianism originated, as H. R. McAdoo argues, 'from within the liberality which he shared with Chillingworth, Grotius, and the Cambridge Platonists', his readiness to address and evaluate the Adam story directly precipitated a controversy the likes of which Taylor had so much deprecated in the *Liberty of Prophesying*. The work in question was his *Unum Necessarium* (1655), intended by Taylor as more a devotional treatise than a ground-breaking exposition of the Paradise story and its consequences. Nevertheless, he immediately found himself under attack by a host of Anglican and Presbyterian divines for allegedly emasculating the import of the Thirty-Nine Articles.[83] Adam was created mortal in the Garden of Eden, said Taylor, subject to the same evil inclinations and obnoxious appetites which so troubled contemporary Englishmen. Only in Paradise there was 'a tree appointed to be the cure of diseases and a conservatory of life'. When the first man freely repudiated God's single injunction, his punishment was the withdrawal of the promise of immortality. Men were now subject to the necessity of dying and all the 'affections of mortality—concupiscence, selfishness, sickness, and passion. But human nature was left unaltered by the Fall, said Taylor; God had not taken from us any of our 'natural perfections' such as the use of reason and the power to transcend the transient attractions of sense. 'And this is all,' he maintained; 'as natural death by his sin became a curse, so our natural imperfection became natural corruption, and that is original sin.'[84] The 'afflictions of the fall' did not disqualify men

---

[82] C. J. Stranks, *The Life and Writings of Jeremy Taylor* (London: SPCK, 1952), 41–68. On Taylor's devotional works in particular, see id., *Anglican Devotion*, 64–95.

[83] McAdoo, *Spirit of Anglicanism*, 77; H. R. Williamson, *Jeremy Taylor* (London: D. Dobson Ltd., 1951), 84–95.

[84] Taylor, *Unum Necessarium*, in *Works*, ix. 9, 11, 12. Taylor's interpretation of the Fall story was actually first intimated in his history of the life of Christ, the first such work in English of its kind: *The Great Exemplar of Sanctity and Holy Life* (1649) (*Works*, ii. pref., p. xxxii). See also 'The Deceitfulness of the Heart' (*Works*, v. 495), about which an otherwise hostile modern commentator writes: 'It would be preposterous to accuse

from salvation, as God took into consideration the weakness of the present state and asked only that everyone endeavour to the best of his abilities to obey the law.[85]

At bottom Taylor was not saying anything here that had not already been implied by the anti-Calvinists since the days of Lord Herbert. 'We all naturally have great weaknesses', he explained, 'and an imperfect constitution, apt to be weary, loving variety, ignorantly making false measures of good and evil', but in spite of this 'we are not by Adam's sin made necessarily and naturally vicious'. He made it perfectly clear that it was not a good life that justified man before God, that only the satisfaction of Christ's death and the power of his enabling grace in conjunction with repentance could accomplish that. His treatment of the Fall was of a piece with his stern view of Christian duty. 'We are taught ways', he said in reference to the teachings of Catholics and Calvinists, 'of going to heaven without foresaking our sins; of repentance without restitution, of being in charity without hearty forgiveness, and without love.'[86] In response he believed it imperative for everyone to re-examine the Pauline proof-text on original sin, Romans 5:12, and to read that text not in light of St Augustine's glosses upon it but as St Paul first understood it.[87] Taylor's own exegesis—the straightforward manner in which he drew out the implications of the Broad-Church perspective on the Fall—while largely unacceptable to a generation still committed to the letter of the law as put forward in the Thirty-Nine Articles, embodied the emerging liberal spirit within the Church, one heartily endorsed by Locke throughout the rest of his life.

Jeremy Taylor went on to become Bishop of Down and Conner after the Restoration, despite his controversial writings on original sin. But the views he offered were not forgotten by the Broad-Churchmen. In fact, his contention that by the Fall

Taylor of Pelagianism on the basis of this great sermon' (Allison, *Rise of Moralism*, 93). Taylor returned to the defence of his interpretation after the first wave of criticism in *Deus Justificatus* (1656) (*Works*, ix. 317).

[85] This was similar to Tillotson's position in 'The Distinguishing Characteristics of a Good and a Bad Man' (*Works*, ii. 141).

[86] Taylor, *Unum Necessarium* (*Works*, viii. 262, 290; ix. 44, 59, 80); id., *A Short Catechism* (*Works*, xv. 14); id., 'The Christian Conquest over the Body of Sin' (*Works*, vi. 249, 250).

[87] Id., *Deus Justificatus*, Epistle Dedicatory (*Works*, ix. 312). Locke would undertake just such an examination of St Paul's epistles in the 1690s.

man had forfeited only 'those supernatural assistances'[88] which God had offered Adam in Paradise was taken up by John Locke early in the 1690s; and like Taylor he approached the issue not out of any hopes of lessening man's burden of sin and dependence, but rather in order to make the gravity of that condition more obvious and the case for reform more pressing. In a manuscript fragment entitled 'Homo ante et post lapsum', Locke outlined what he took to be Adam's condition before the Fall in terms strikingly similar to Taylor's.[89] 'Man was made mortal,' Locke wrote, 'put into a possession of the whole world, where in the full use of the creatures there was scarce room for any irregular desires but instinct and reason carried him the same way and being neither capable of covitousness or ambition when he had already the free use of all things he could scarce sin.' In the state of Paradise, God set for man one 'probationary law' whereby he was refused the nourishment of one particular fruit. The punishment for violating this prohibition was natural death, the loss of immortality. The fact that Adam could not keep this easy compact with God indicated that 'man made mortal' in Paradise, as Taylor had argued, had a natural inclination to forbidden things. How else explain the transgression? With Adam's disobedience 'now he and in him all his posterity were under a necessity of dying and thus sin enterd into the world and death by sin'. After the great sin our first parents, explained Locke, recognizing the seriousness of their actions and reluctant to face their Maker, turned their minds away from God and towards the pleasures of this life; 'and when private possession and labour which now the curse on earth had made necessary, by degrees made a distinction of conditions it gave room for covetousness, pride and ambition, which by fashon and example spread the corruption which has so prevailed over mankind'.[90] The Fall had been the occasion for God's withdrawing his promise of immortality without the necessity of dying. Under the second covenant, reasoned Locke, the Creator has generously offered to man a new opportunity for eternal

---

[88] Taylor, 'A Further Explication of the Doctrine of Original Sin' (*Works*, viii. 78).

[89] MS Locke c. 28, fol. 113.

[90] In the *Unum Necessarium* (*Works*, viii. 259) Taylor said that as men contracted new and more numerous relations outside Paradise, they increasingly 'hindered one another', their faculties 'became disordered', and their will 'became perverse'.

salvation, but not before a lifetime of trial and the death of the body. The terms of the second covenant were by definition much more exacting than Adam's probationary law in Paradise, but the sons of Adam, endowed with reason and free will, and able to secure Christ's saving grace, could still aspire to the greatest of Christian rewards.

Locke never published his interpretation of the Adam story. By the mid-1690s he was already under attack for his denial of innate ideas of morality; the unwarranted charges of Socinianism (and even atheism) were beginning to surface, and the philosopher, always loathing the controversy that surrounded his work, decided to keep his views to himself. Still, the Lockean analysis of the Fall, for all its unorthodoxy, remained within the larger framework of the Broad-Church perspective. By seeing as results of the Fall not the complete depravity of humankind, the necessity of sinning, and the futility of moral endeavour, but rather the many natural infirmities consequent to mortality—the unruliness of the passions, the impairment of reason, the shortness and inconsistency of judgement, the preoccupation with sensual satisfaction—the Broad-Churchmen were able to prescribe solutions to the problem of depravity through the encouragement of a godly life. 'The commandments are instanced in things against our natural inclinations,' cautioned Taylor, 'and are restraints upon our appetite; and although a man may do it in single instances, yet to act a part of perpetual violence and preternatural contentions, is too hard and severe an expectation, and the often unavoidable failings of men will shew how impossible it is.'[91] All were enjoined to obey the commands of God and all were promised the assistance of heavenly grace in the undertaking. Perfect obedience was now impossible, of course, but that fact would be taken into consideration on the day of judgement. If, as it has often been suggested, the Broad-Churchmen—the Tew Circle, the Cambridge Platonists, and the Latitudinarians—prepared the groundwork for late seventeenth- and early eighteenth-century Deism—the religion of Shaftesbury, Tyndale, and Toland—then that preparation was wholly inadvert. For while these

---

[91] Taylor, op. cit. 266. Tillotson said that 'a man must offer great force and violence to himself' in order to overcome 'the corruption of our nature' and 'vicious habits' ('The Difficulties of a Christian Life Considered', in *Works*, vi. 165).

thinkers were deeply concerned with practical morality, with the actual behaviour of believing Christians, they also understood, better than did the exponents of Deism, the full meaning of Christ's coming, of his life and death. The Deists, after all, tended to cheapen the significance of the latter event; John Locke and the men who met to discuss religion at Thomas Firmin's did just the opposite. As part of their undertaking, Locke and his associates laboured to fully illuminate the nature of the Fall. To mitigate its severity, they knew, meant to lessen the significance of Christ's sacrifice. The Deists, it can be said, willingly accepted that lessening; the Broad-Churchmen, John Locke included, adamantly refused to countenance the crucial diminution.

4

Creating the Moral Agent

WE have already seen that Christianity, in opposition both to what it considered to be the errors of the classical view of man, and to the Pelagian belief that individuals might perfect themselves through the exercise of free will and the help of right education, uniformly considered man and his nature in terms of his weakness and limitations, his dependent status under an all-powerful Creator. The cultivation of humility and an acceptance of one's finite capacity, the recognition of sinfulness and rebellion at the centre of human personality, the attempt to set a precise measure of man's ability in order that everyone might better serve their Maker—such had been the on-going and onerous task of the faith since its inception.[1] And such in a very real sense was the task of John Locke in his most important work, the product of some twenty years of thought and energy, composed during what was still very much an age of faith: *An Essay concerning Human Understanding.* 'If by this Enquiry into the Nature of the Understanding', he said at the outset of the book which evolved from discussions on morality held at Shaftesbury's home in 1671, but only completed in 1688, 'I can discover the Powers thereof; how far they reach; to what things they are in any Degree proportionate; and where they fail us, I suppose it may be of use, to prevail with the busy Mind of Man, to be more cautious in meddling with things exceeding its comprehension; to stop, when it is at the utmost Extent of its Tether; and to sit down in a quiet Ignorance of those Things, which, upon Examination, are found to be beyond the reach of our Capacities.'[2] Locke had taken on in the famous *Essay* a simple

[1] See ch. 1 above. See also Hoopes, *Right Reason in the English Renaissance*, 64–5.

[2] *Essay*, 1. 1. 4. As to the origins of the *Essay*, Locke tells the reader in the Epistle that it was begun after a meeting with some friends in his room (presumably at Exeter House). James Tyrrell was there and remembered the discussion to have centred on 'the principles of morality and revealed religion' (see Cranston, *Locke*, 141). Locke began two drafts of the work in 1671: B. Rand, ed., *An Essay concerning the Understanding, Knowledge, Opinion and Assent* (Cambridge, Mass.: Harvard University Press, 1931) and *Early Draft.*

yet demanding Christian task: he would oblige men to probe the compass of their own minds, to recognize the boundaries of their meagre intellectual vision, and to shift their interests and energies accordingly in a more appropriate direction, one where their abilities might yield a more substantial return. He wanted men to realize that they had been created 'not to know all things, but those which concern our Conduct'. And he hoped that the resulting knowledge of 'Our short-sightedness and liableness to Error' would serve to check man's 'over-confidence and presumption', would become 'a constant Admonition to us, to spend the days of this our Pilgrimage with Industry and Care, in the search, and following of that way, which might lead us to a State of greater Perfection'.[3]

Locke thus began his enquiry with a moral question, a Christian question: what type of knowledge was really worth having in this life, what type of knowledge could and should men work to acquire? In his own special way, but certainly influenced by his Broad-Church friends, he had set out to check, once and for all with the aid of solid empirical evidence, the centuries-old sin of pride, the sin of Adam in Paradise. For too long now men had sought to 'let loose our Thoughts into the vast Ocean of Being, as if all that boundless Extent, were the natural, and undoubted Possession of our Understandings, wherein there was nothing exempt from its Decisions, or that escaped its Comprehension'.[4] Not only would he dispose of this special piece of arrogance, this unrestrained hubris, but in the process of its demolition the author would also seek to elaborate upon the troubling nature of men whose boundless curiosity was combined with an unwillingness or lack of resolve to pursue the greater moral good even when they recognized and acknowledged it. In the end, the message which he delivered on the

---

[3] *Essay*, 1. 1. 6; 4. 14. 2. In his journal for 8 Feb. 1677 Locke wrote that the 'main concernment' of man is to know what those actions are that he is to doe what those are he is to avoid what law he is to live by here and still be jugd by hereafter' (entry printed in *Early Draft*, 88). This particular journal was begun by Locke in 1675 on his departure for France. It has been edited and published by James Lough as *Locke's Travels in France* (Cambridge: University Press, 1954).

[4] *Essay*, 1. 1. 7. Lovejoy discussed this late seventeenth- and early eighteenth-century attack on human presumption in 'Pride in Eighteenth Century Thought' in *Essays in the History of Ideas*, 62–8; id., *Great Chain of Being*, 8–9. It appears prominently in Pope: 'Know then thyself! Presume not God to scan!/The proper study of mankind is man' (*Essay on Man*, ed. M. Mack (London: Methuen, 1970)), Epistle II, ll. 1–2.

problematic question of mankind's potential for good was, not surprisingly, a deeply depressing one, an almost Augustinian one. The *Essay* reaffirmed many of Locke's most inelastic convictions.

Now, plainly, this interpretation of the *Essay* and its place in the history of ideas has not always been accepted. The *Essay* has often been viewed, for instance, in the context of the broader scientific movement of the seventeenth century.[5] The well-known under-labourer image which Locke set for himself in the Epistle to the Reader, coupled with references to his scientific friends—Robert Boyle, Thomas Sydenham, and 'the incomparable Mr. Newton'[6]—gives the reader the impression that Locke's undertaking was designed first and foremost to provide educated Englishmen with a new and radical epistemological foundation for the burgeoning natural sciences of the day, the growth of interest in which was, perhaps, best symbolized by the chartering in 1660 of the Royal Society. And for those interested in Locke's educational thought, the *Essay*'s treatment of the *tabula rasa*, where the author depicted the mind of man at birth 'to be, as we say, white Paper, void of all Characters, without any ideas', has represented the starting-point of an eighteenth-century movement to eradicate the last remnants of the old notion of Christian depravity, what the historian Carl Becker once described as 'a black spreading cloud which for centuries had depressed the human spirit'.[7] According to this influential school of thought, the significance of the *tabula-rasa* concept lay in the fact that 'simply by exposing children to salutary influences and shielding them from unsavory ones, it would be possible to rear moral giants and perfect citizens. Education would become merely a matter of determining what experiences a child should be exposed to and eliminating all deleterious experiential influences.'[8] The human mind, previously thought to contain certain innate ideas, and human nature itself, previously believed to be somehow fatally flawed, had supposedly been revealed by Locke to be nothing more than the product of its environment. Theoretically the educator was now

---

[5] John Colman (*Locke's Moral Philosophy*, 1–4), discusses this popular perspective.

[6] *Essay*, Epistle to the Reader, p. 10.

[7] *Essay*, 2. 1. 2; Carl Becker, *The Heavenly City of the Eighteenth Century Philosophers* (New Haven, Conn.: Yale University Press, 1932), 64–5.

[8] Quoting W. S. and M. L. Sahakian, *John Locke*, 53.

free to mould the child's mind in accordance with the laws of nature, to advance man's knowledge and potential for good, and to remake society for the better in a world grown wise in the ways of God.[9]

Neither of these explanations, however, fully illuminate the author's larger purpose in the *Essay*. On the one hand, while there is no denying that Locke cared a great deal about the many practical advances being made in such fields as medicine, chemistry, and physics during the seventeenth century (his own activities while at Oxford in the 1650s and 1660s attests to that), he made it emphatically clear that he expected very little progress to be made towards a verifiable science of nature.[10] Men would forever want adequate ideas of the precise make-up or real essence of those minute bodies existing outside us in nature. By our senses we are able only 'to know, and distinguish things; and to examine them so far, as to apply them to our Uses, and several ways to accommodate the Exigencies of this Life'. But our 'dull and weak' faculties prevented 'a perfect, clear, and adequate knowledge of them'.[11] In rejecting the search for truths beyond the pale of human understanding, in admitting that 'the great Fabrick of the Universe, and every part thereof, further exceeds the Capacity and Comprehension of the most inquisitive and intelligent Man', Locke echoed the Christian condemnation of man's refusal to accept his creatureliness.[12] St Paul's

---

[9] It is within this context that the *Essay* has been viewed by many twentieth-century social scientists. Marvin Harris (*The Rise of Anthropological Theory* (New York: Cornell University Press, 1968), 11), for example, says that the book 'was the midwife of all those modern behavioral disciplines, including psychology, sociology, and cultural anthropology, which stress the relationship between conditioning environment and human thought and actions'.

[10] His suspicions were long-standing. See journal entry for 29 July 1676: 'There are difficultys about matter and motion so great that I believe the wit of man will never be able to resolve' (*Early Draft*, 81); Locke to Edward Clarke (29 Jan. 1686: ii, no. 844). See also Romanell, *Locke and Medicine*, 19.

[11] *Essay*, 2. 23. 12; 4. 3. 26. R. I. Aaron, 'The Limits of Locke's Rationalism', in *Seventeenth Century Studies Presented to Sir Herbert Grierson* (Oxford: Clarendon Press, 1938), 301–2. M. White, *Science and Sentiment in America* (New York: Oxford University Press, 1972), 17–19; J. Yolton, 'The Science of Nature', in *John Locke: Problems and Perspectives*, ed. J. Yolton (Cambridge: University Press, 1969), 186–7.

[12] *Essay*, 3. 6. 9. Tillotson expressed similar sentiments as early as 1664: 'No less wisdom and understanding than that which made the World and contrived this vast and regular frame of Nature can thoroughly understand the Philosophy of it, and comprehend so vast a design' (*Works*, i. 317). Willey (*Seventeenth Century Background*, 273) notes the parallels between the language used by Locke and John Milton on the subject of man's limited intellectual abilities.

lament in Romans 1:22—'Professing themselves to be wise, they became fools'—parallels Locke's estimation of the metaphysicians of his own day, idly explaining all creation from the starting point of a priori innate maxims. Mankind's position in the hierarchy of creation or great chain of being was for Locke less than flattering, there probably being 'far more Species of Creatures above us, than there are beneath; we being in degrees of Perfection much more remote from the infinite Being of GOD, than we are from the lowest state of Being, and that which approaches nearest to nothing'.[13] The attack on intellectual presumption was unswerving throughout, but the *Essay*'s circumscription of man's intellectual powers in this area in no way impugned his ability to successfully investigate and manage life's most important work—Christian conduct. For however short their knowledge of the world around them, 'it yet secures their great Concernments, that they have light enough to lead them to the knowledge of their Maker, and the sight of their own Duties'. Moral knowledge was both 'the proper Science' and the 'greatest interest' of mankind.[14] The *Essay*, he hoped, would make a contribution, however small, to the advancement of that science.

On the other hand, the puissant lure of the *tabula-rasa* concept has often led to an over-emphasis on the environmentalist aspects of Locke's thought, with a consequent underestimation of those elements which suggest that the mind is much more than a passive receptacle upon which sensory data is inscribed, and to a neglect of other equally important elements which help to clarify his understanding of original sin and its consequences

[13] *Essay*, 3. 6. 12: see also 4. 12. 12, where he says 'That we should not take doubtful Systems, for complete Sciences; nor unintelligible Notions, for scientifical Demonstrations'. Attacking the contemporary practice of teaching science by forwarding allegedly innate propositions, Locke observed: 'He that shall consider, how little general Maxims, precarious Principles, and Hypotheses laid down at Pleasure, have promoted true Knowledge, or helped to satisfy the Enquiries of rational Men after real Improvements . . . will think, we have Reason to thank those, who in this latter Age have taken another Course, and have trod out to us, though not an easier way to learned Ignorance, yet a surer way to profitable Knowledge.'

[14] Ibid. 1. 1. 2, 5; 4. 12. 11; D. E. Leary, 'The Intentions and Heritage of Descartes and Locke: Toward a Recognition of the Moral Basis of Modern Psychology', *Journal of General Psychology*, 102 (1980), 289–91. Richard Ashcraft ('Faith and Knowledge in Locke's Philosophy' in *Locke: Problems and Perspectives*, ed. Yolton, 198) says 'Locke wrote the *Essay concerning Human Understanding* in order to secure the great ends of religion and morality.' R. S. Woolhouse (*John Locke* (Brighton: Harvester Press, 1983), 7–14) discusses the Essay's connection with seventeenth-century scepticism.

for Adam's posterity. Actually, there was nothing further from Locke's mind than to suggest that all men were initially equal and that subsequent differences were due solely to their individual educational experiences. Nor did he ever embrace the Pelagian claim that 'Everything good, and everything evil, on account of which we are either laudable or blameworthy, is not born with us but done by us.'[15] He insisted that 'We have our Understandings no less different than our Palates'[16] and described in detail how and why most men would throughout their lives ignore the call of reason and the importunities of education. The learning process, as he later said in *Some Thoughts concerning Education*, was in reality a long-term struggle to teach the child 'to get a mastery of his Inclinations, and submit his Appetite to Reason'.[17] And for the vast majority who continued to live their days outside the province of reason, who refused to live up to their nature as rational beings, well, Locke did not hedge about their fate. That fate was of course worse than simple annihilation, for Locke was a believing Christian who, as we discovered earlier, found the basis of the moral order in the decrees of a Creator possessed of the absolute power to reward and to punish.[18] It involved, rather, the real possibility of infinite misery imposed by a God whose every call for reform, calls like the one contained in Locke's *Essay*, had been impudently turned aside by those who would deliberately follow in the steps of the archetypal man.[19]

[15] N. G. Petryszak, 'Tabula Rasa: Its Origins and Implications', *Journal of the History of the Behavioral Sciences*, 17 (1981), 19–21; F. Musgrove, 'Two Educational Controversies in the Eighteenth Century: Nature and Nurture: Private and Public Education', *Paedegogica Historica*, 2 (1962), 84; J. G. Mason, 'A Critical Interpretation of the Educational Thought of John Locke', (Univ. of Nottingham Ph. D. thesis, 1960), 4, 40.

[16] *Essay*, Epistle to the Reader, 8: again at 4. 20. 5. This outlook was a Broad-Church commonplace: see, for example, Taylor, *Liberty of Prophesying* (*Works*, viii. 99).

[17] *Thoughts on Ed.* 134.

[18] D. Gauthier, 'Why Ought one Obey God? Reflections on Hobbes and Locke', *Canadian Journal of Philosophy*, 7 (1977), 429–43.

[19] Both H. McLachlan (*The Religious Opinions of Milton, Locke and Newton* (Manchester: University Press, 1941), 94), and D. P. Walker (*The Decline of Hell: Seventeenth Century Discussions of Eternal Torment* (Chicago: University Press, 1964), 93) deny that Locke believed in eternal torment. But in some brief undated notes Locke indicated that 'It is also evident that the power that made a man exist here in a state capable of pleasure and pain can as well make him exist again after he has lost all sense and perception by death [?or] he that has made him exist can bring him back up to a state of sensibility and continue in it capable of pleasure or pain as long as he pleases' (MS Locke c. 28, fol. 139). In 1676 he wrote that 'infinite misery' will certainly overtake the atheist (journal, 29 July 1676 in *Early Draft*, 82). See also Locke's *Epistola de Tolerantia*, 123.

In order to better appreciate the full significance of Locke's *Essay*, we must look again at what he had to say about the process by which (he believed) men acquire knowledge, the nature of that knowledge or his 'way of ideas', and some of the problems that inevitably arose in the search after knowledge. In this way we can best identify some of the inadequacies of the long-accepted argument which places the work at the forefront of Enlightenment environmentalism and the eighteenth-century repudiation of Christian depravity.

What was the 'Original, Certainty and Extent of humane Knowledge'[20] for Locke, and how did his reflections on this matter influence his view of man's nature? As the *tabula-rasa* concept, adumbrations of which can be found as early as 1664 in the *Essays on the Law of Nature*, suggests, Locke argued that the mind at birth was devoid of all innate principles or primary notions, including—and this was of greatest concern to his contemporaries—innate practical principles or moral ideas. Rather, the basis of all knowledge was sensation and reflection. 'Our observation', he indicated, 'employed either about external, sensible Objects; or about the internal Operations of our Minds, perceived and reflected on by our selves, is that, which supplies our Understandings with all the materials of thinking.'[21] Sensation involved the power of objects existing outside us 'to operate after a peculiar manner',[22] producing within our minds all those secondary qualities which form the building-blocks of knowledge. Reflection, on the other hand, involved the active participation of the mind. Once sense

---

[20] *Essay*, 1. 2. 1.

[21] Ibid. 2. 1. 2; cf. *Essays on LN*, 132–245.

[22] *Essay*, 2. 8. 23. Locke declined to examine the material or physical foundations of sensation, or 'by what Motions of our Spirits, or Alterations of our Bodies, we come to have any Sensation by our Organs, or any Ideas in our Understandings'. But as bk. 2 unfolds, it became obvious that a total neglect of the question would make impossible any scientific enquiry into the origins of knowledge. Thus the author found himself engaging in 'Physical Enquiries a little father than, perhaps, I intended'. Objects produce ideas in our minds, he said with singular lack of precision, 'by impulse'. Insensible corporeal particles coming from the object impinge upon the senses, and then 'tis evident, that some motion must be thence continued by our Nerves, or animal Spirits, by some parts of our Bodies, to the Brains or the seat of Sensation, there to produce in our Minds the particular Ideas we have of them' (*Essay*, 1. 1. 2; 2. 8. 12, 13, 22). See also 'Remarks Upon Some of Mr. Norris's Books' (*Works*, x. 248); J. Yolton, 'Locke's Concept of Experience', in *Locke and Berkeley: A Collection of Critical Essays*, ed. C. B. Martin and D. M. Armstrong (Notre Dame, Ind.: University Press, 1968), 41–2.

impressions are received, the mind, if it will, is able to reflect upon them, sorting and arranging in the hope of producing clear and distinct ideas. The mind can then arrive at knowledge by acting upon these ideas, establishing the 'connection and agreement, or disagreement and repugnancy' that exists between them.[23] According to this analysis, our knowledge could never extend beyond our ideas as presented to us by the objects of nature, the exact composition of the primary qualities that produce ideas in us being for ever beyond our ken. It was this fact which effectively precluded, for Locke, the establishment of a verifiable science of nature.

The author's denial of innate ideas occasioned a flurry of criticism which continued unabated until his death. The quarrel is instructive for us in that Locke's intentions, greatly misunderstood even by some of his closest friends,[24] probably best reveal the fierce demands which he placed on his fellow Christians to know and to live by the unalterable moral law. They were Broad-Church demands, Latitudinarian demands, by virtue of their intense rigour and insistence that one was justly condemned by failing to mind the call. John Yolton has shown how the belief in innate ideas, and especially innate moral ideas, was avidly defended by virtually all Locke's contemporaries who believed that these self-evident truths were absolutely necessary for the stability of morality and religion. Only in this way, they thought, could morality be given an objective foundation, could a crisis in the epistemology of morals be avoided; to deny innate moral ideas seemed to smack of Hobbesian relativism, and this the seventeenth century refused to tolerate. As Thomas Burnet wrote in a published letter to Locke, 'This I am sure of, that the Distinction, suppose of Gratitude and Ingratitude, Fidelity and Infidelity, Justice and Injustice, and such others, is as sudden without any Ratiocination, . . . 'Tis not like a Theorem, which we come to know by the help of precedent Demonstrations and Postulatums, but it rises as quick as any of our Passions, or as Laughter at the sight of a ridiculous Accident or Object.'[25] The

---

[23] *Essay*, 4. 1. 2; D. Greenlee, 'Locke and the Controversy over Innate Ideas', *Journal of the History of Ideas*, 38 (1977), 251.

[24] In particular Anthony Ashley Cooper, third earl of Shaftesbury: see ch. 7 below.

[25] Thomas Burnet, *Remarks Upon an Essay concerning Human Understanding in a Letter Addressed to the Author* (London: M. Wotton, 1697), 5. Burnet penned two additional

idea of innateness was maintained in either one of two forms. A naive form held that God had implanted principles of right and wrong in man at birth while a more sophisticated version intimated that although men were not born with completed ideas of morality, 'such knowledge was implicit in the soul and merely required experience to elicit awareness of it'.[26] But Locke, after surveying the religious and moral literature of the seventeenth century, and doubtless recalling the Civil War experience, saw no constructive reason to continue the charade of innate ideas in the face of so much countervailing evidence. He observed 'that if different Men of different Sects should go about to give us a List of those innate practical Principles, they would set down only such as suited their distinct Hypotheses, and were fit to support the Doctrines of their particular Schools or Churches'.[27] This complete lack of consensus over religious and moral questions had always deeply disturbed him. For Locke there did of course exist an eternal rule of right and wrong, one in fact similar in content to the putative innate law; but the contents of that law had to be discovered via the light of reason working upon the data furnished by sense experience. The process whereby men conclude the promulgation of a rule of law—the law of reason—from the idea of an omnipotent and wise Creator who designed the machine-like world we perceive with loving kindness, required the sort of firm dedication to the way of rational self-enquiry that could only be realized through proper education.[28] In abolishing innate moral ideas, then,

responses to the *Essay*. In his *Third Remarks Upon an Essay concerning Human Understanding* (London: M. Wotton, 1699), 4, he appealed to the natural conscience as the means by which one immediately distinguished moral right from wrong and based his contention, as did many moralists of the day, on Rom. 2: 14–15: 'For when the Gentiles, who have not the law, do by nature those things that are of the law, these having not the law, are a law unto themselves: Who show the work of the law within their hearts'. On Burnet, who was Master of the Charterhouse from 1685 until his death in 1715, see *DNB* iii. 408–10 and S. A. Grave, *Locke and Burnet* (East Freemantle: Westover Press, 1981), 1–5. Locke replied to Burnet's first *Remarks* indirectly, appending an unfriendly rebuttal to a published letter addressed to Edward Stillingfleet (*Works*, iv. 186–9). Locke criticized Burnet's *Third Remarks* in the margins of his copy: see N. Porter, 'Marginalia Lockeana', *New Englander and Yale Review*, 11 (1887), 33–49.

[26] Yolton, *Locke and Way of Ideas*, 39–40; cf. Woolhouse, *Locke*, 29–31.

[27] *Essay*, 1. 3. 14.

[28] He first outlined the process in the eighth of his *Essays on LN* and published them in the *Essay*, 4. 9, 10. For a discussion see J. Yolton, *John Locke and the Compass of the Human Understanding* (Cambridge: University Press, 1970), 174–5; W. Von Leyden, 'John Locke and Natural Law', *Philosophy*, 31 (1956), 29–30.

Locke made the place of education central, indeed absolutely imperative, to the life of the civilized Christian community. Moral principles required 'Reasoning and Discourse, and some Exercise of the Mind, to discover the certainty of their Truth'. And it was these moral principles, once discovered, which served as a 'curb and restraint' on a whole cluster of innate tendencies, tendencies guaranteed to 'carry men to the over-turning of all Morality' if not properly controlled.[29] Innateness, according to Locke, represented the easy way out for those who cared little for extended and (so he thought) obligatory intellectual effort. It 'eased the lazy from the pains of search, and stopped the enquiry of the doubtful', but that would not be good enough come the day of judgement.[30] Since men were born without a sense of right and wrong, but were required by God to know and obey his laws none the less, education took on an almost life-and-death importance in Locke's mind. For if the tutor failed to develop the rational faculties of the child so that each could discover for himself the laws of morality, and if the tutor had not prepared the child to implement what he had discovered in order to counteract the innate impulse to overturn all morality, then that pupil's prospects for eternal bliss in the next life would not be very propitious. The Lockean educator was faced with a daunting task.

Locke also explained that the mind had two different ways of perceiving the agreement or disagreement between its ideas. The most reliable means to acquire knowledge, he said, was by intuition—a sort of flash of insight where the mind establishes the correct relation between its ideas immediately upon reflection. As Richard Aaron has pointed out, intuition is infallible, it is the power to know with absolute certainty. Unfortunately, while 'this kind of Knowledge is the clearest, and most certain, that humane frailty is capable of', it is not always

---

[29] *Essay*, 1. 3. 1, 13. One example of this innate tendency towards evil was given by Locke in a letter to Edward Clarke. All children love dominion over others, he said, 'and this is the first originall of all vitious habits that are ordinary and natural' (Locke to Clarke, 29 Apr. 1687: iii, no. 929).

[30] *Essay*, 1. 4. 24. In a chapter added to the fourth edition of the *Essay* (1700) Locke chided those who founded their convictions on what they perceived to be immediate revelation from God. Religious enthusiasts avoided 'the tedious and not always successful Labour of strict Reasoning' in order to flatter their own 'Laziness, Ignorance and Vanity' (op. cit. 4. 19. 5, 8).

within our reach.[31] The alternative avenue to knowledge Locke called demonstration. Here the mind cannot so easily put together some of its ideas, but must rely upon the intervention of intermediate ideas to discover the proper relationship. The mind must employ its various innate powers in this case,[32] utilizing the intermediate ideas to prove the agreement or disagreement between any two others. And here is where the problems begin for frail human beings. For, according to Locke:

> This knowledge by intervening Proofs, though it be certain, yet the evidence of it is not altogether so clear and bright, nor the assent so ready, as in intuitive Knowledge. For though in Demonstration, the Mind does at last perceive the Agreement or Disagreement of the Ideas it considers; yet 'tis not without pains and attention. There must be more than one transient view to find it. A steddy application and pursuit is required to this Discovery.[33]

Those who would rely upon demonstrative knowledge must first of all possess a strong and reliable memory. All of the intermediate ideas employed in demonstration must be intuitively perceived to be correct, while each step in the process must 'be carried exactly in the Mind'. Demonstration usually involved a long train of proofs and it was the memory, said Locke, that must precisely retain and then recall these proofs. But because the memory often failed at this juncture, 'it comes to pass, that this is more imperfect than intuitive Knowledge, and Men often embrace Falshoods for Demonstrations'.[34]

---

[31] *Essay*, 4. 2. 1; R. I. Aaron, *Locke*, 221.

[32] Some of Locke's critics accused him of denying innate faculties or powers along with innate ideas. John Yolton says that there existed 'a general tendency throughout the seventeenth century and the early years of the eighteenth to interpret Locke as advocating a simple sensationalism' (*Locke and Way of Ideas*, 86). See also S. Lamprecht, *The Moral and Political Philosophy of John Locke* (New York: Russell and Russell, 1962), 72.

[33] *Essay*, 4. 2. 4.

[34] Ibid. 2. 10. 2; 4. 2. 7. Here again, as in the case of the origins of sensation, Locke failed to examine the possible physical origins of the memory's frailty and decay. This was a serious business for the author, since if our memories fail us, 'All the rest of our Faculties are in great measure useless' (2. 10. 8). Without a strong, reliable memory men would be confined in all their thoughts to present objects. While admitting that in every mind 'there seems to be a constant decay of all our Ideas, even those which are struck deepest', he was unsure 'How much the Constitution of our Bodies and the make of our animal Spirits, are concerned in this'. Nevertheless it did seem probable 'that the Constitution of the body does sometimes influence the Memory' (2. 10. 5). Later (*Thoughts on Ed.* 286), he admitted 'that the strength of the Memory is owing to a happy Constitution, and not to any habitual Improvement got by Exercise'.

Demonstrative knowledge also required the active engagement of various of the mind's other innate faculties or powers. The faculty of discernment, when it is properly developed, enabled men to distinguish between the numerous sensations which enter into the mind and to arrive at those clear and distinct ideas which all knowledge depends upon. Comparing ideas, abstracting from particular ideas to create general names, and composing many simple ideas in order to generate a complex one, all of these important faculties, 'if wanting, or out of order, produce suitable defects in Men's Understanding and Knowledge'.[35] Therefore whenever men failed to exercise thoroughness, caution, and patience in searching after demonstrative knowledge, their ideas were likely to be confused and without solid foundation. The whole learning process was then closely intertwined with the God-given powers of the mind, and thus constituted a much more complicated and delicate enterprise than that which was implied by the *tabula-rasa* concept. And although Locke continued to believe that every person 'was capable of knowing several truths', including (most importantly) moral truths, they were not to be secured without considerable personal effort. The individual who willingly devoted constant attention to the operations of his mind would surely be rewarded with clear ideas and certain knowledge, but the laggard would remain in a state of darkness and moral torpor (not to mention mortal peril to his soul), for ever resigned to acquiring his guiding principles in a gratuitous fashion from the designing and the depraved.[36]

In addition to the fact that the acquisition of knowledge was a much more complex and difficult process than the *tabula-rasa* concept might initially suggest, Locke also concluded from his investigations that our ability to procure actual knowledge in this our temporal state was extremely limited. It was so restricted, in fact, that any person who would assent to nothing that fell short of knowledge 'would be sure of nothing, in this World, but of perishing quickly'.[37] In spite of his careful

---

[35] *Essay*, 2. 11. 2, 4–12.

[36] Ibid. 1. 2. 5. Locke criticized 'those who affected to be Masters and Teachers' for insisting upon innate ideas only to dupe their followers, 'In which posture of blind Credulity, they might be more easily governed by, and made useful to some sort of men, who had the skill and office to principle and guide them' (1. 4. 24).

[37] Ibid. 4. 11. 10.

procedural guidelines for searching out knowledge, he resolved that for the most part men must be content with less than certainty. Normally, they must exercise their minds to judge of the probability of any proposition. And probability was nothing more than belief or judgement, or, as the author defined it, 'The admitting or receiving any Proposition for true, upon Arguments or Proofs that are found to persuade us to receive it as true, without certain Knowledge that it is so'.[38] With his discussion of probability Locke arrived at that point in the *Essay* where he considers how the mind, using its reasoning, judging, and discerning powers, begins to perform an even more crucial role in the learning process than demonstrative knowledge required. Accurate judgement based on the information provided by the powers of the mind working with sense data was crucial at this stage. In the first edition Locke seemed to suggest that the mind's conclusions follow immediately (and automatically) from what we first perceive to be the greater good; but in the second and subsequent editions, recoiling from the determinist tendency of this position, he altered his view and insisted that men have the ability to refrain from acting until they have fully considered the relative merits of each specific proposition or course of action. In this consisted man's freedom and his chief duty. 'That in this state of Ignorance', Locke said, 'we short-sighted Creatures might not mistake true felicity, we are endowed with a power to suspend any particular desire, and keep it from determining the will, and engaging us in action.' To withhold judgement, to forbear 'a too hasty compliance with our desires' until we explore 'the good or evil of what we are going to do' was for Locke the highest perfection of human nature possible and all that God required of Adam's descendants.[39]

Now this was surely a tall order for even the best of men to fulfil, and it was on the shoulders of the educator that the heaviest burden fell. For when Locke, in the *Essay*, came to examine the springs of action, when he sought to discover what

---

[38] Ibid. 4. 15. 3.

[39] Ibid. 2. 21. 50, 53, 47. John Passmore ('Locke and the Ethics of Belief', *Proceedings of the British Academy*, 64 (1978), 198) writes that for Locke 'Our duty . . . is to hold ourselves back from choosing, or from believing, until we have considered the situation fully; people who do not do this can properly be blamed.' See also W. C. Swabey, *Ethical Theory from Hobbes to Kant* (New York: Greenwood Press, 1969), 38–9; Parry, *Locke*, 24–5.

it was that actually motivated men and gave impetus to the will, he fell back upon a theory of ethical hedonism which had first appeared in some journal entries written while he was living and travelling in France during the 1670s; and, as we shall see presently, according to this theory the educational process provided the sole means by which the worst aspects of that ethical hedonism might be avoided. His friendship with François Bernier, a follower of the French Epicurean Pierre Gassendi, probably influenced the unfolding of his thought in this direction, although it is obvious that Locke never felt entirely comfortable with the rationalist strain of his *Essays on the Law of Nature*—where men seemed at times to be obliged more by their own apprehension of the good as the product of God's perdurable reason than by the threat of punishment and the lure of reward.[40] The rationalist or intellectualist standpoint, we recall, found one of its staunchest defenders in the Platonist Ralph Cudworth, and to the extent that it presumed the ground of obligation to rest in the eternal order of things and in mankind's recognition of that order, the theory left room for a good measure of confidence in human nature.[41] It seemed to imply that men would, once arrived at the use of mature reason, obey the moral law on the basis of its very reasonableness, thereby making Christian sanctions unnecessary (or at least less necessary) as a motive to godly behaviour. Whatever Cudworth's own intentions might have been, the theory lessened the significance of the Fall by equating virtue with reason and evil with ignorance, by returning to the Platonic conception of a human nature in which error was the result of an uninformed intellect rather than a wilfully disobedient one.

According to Locke's hedonistic theory, the will of man was always impelled by some particular uneasiness, some perception of absent pleasure or happiness. Nature had implanted within each individual an instinctual desire for happiness and an equal

---

[40] E. A. Driscoll, 'The Influence of Gassendi on Locke's Hedonism', *International Philosophical Quarterly*, 12 (1972), 91–4. The first appearance of Locke's ethical hedonism occurs in a shorthand journal entry for 16 July 1676 printed in *Essays on LN*, 265–72.

[41] Ralph Cudworth, *The True Intellectual System of the Universe*, ed. Thomas Birch, 2 vols. (New York: Gould and Newman, 1838), ii. 357. Locke actually recommended Cudworth's *True Intellectual System* for the student, but as a history of natural philosophy, not a treatise on ethics: *Thoughts on Ed.* 305. See also J. Martineau, *Types of Ethical Theory*, 2 vols. (Oxford: Clarendon Press, 1885), ii. 400–2.

aversion to pain and misery; and most men, forever mistaking where their true pleasure and happiness lay, spent their days in an endless unthinking round of seeking to placate successive uneasinesses—'pursuing trifles'—all to the neglect of God's eternal law. At any moment in their lives men are found to be motivated solely by what appears in their minds to be a necessary part of their immediate happiness, usually the transient exigencies of the flesh.[42] In one blunt yet potent sentence, Locke summed up what for him represented a fundamental disengagement from one of the original goals of the *Essay*—the hope that having been shown the limits of their power to know, men might then live as humble, tolerant, and peaceful Christians: 'But yet upon a stricter enquiry,' he revealed, 'that good, the greater good, though apprehended and acknowledged to be so, does not determine the will, until our desire, raised proportionable to it, makes us uneasy in the want of it.' Men would never hunger after righteousness until they had been made to feel uneasy at its absence, until they had learned to desire virtuous living as a means to greater personal pleasure. 'Change but a Man's view of these things; let him see, that Virtue and Religion are necessary to his Happiness', and the selfish individualism that lay at the base of Locke's ethical hedonism would be rendered harmless. But fail to raise a man's desires to this elevated plane, fail to convince him that the immediate pursuit of temporal wants in preference to the far-removed pleasures of the next life will ultimately destroy his chances of enjoying those celestial pleasures—fail to do this, and one fails in that most elemental task of rational beings. Anyone 'that will not be so far a rational Creature, as to reflect seriously upon infinite Happiness and Misery, must needs condemn himself, as not making that use of his Understanding he should.' Indeed, this very freedom to reflect illustrated man's fallen state: for as Raymond Polin has observed, 'The first manifestation of

---

[42] *Essay*, 2. 21. 38; 1. 3. 3; Mabbott, *Locke*, 103; M. Johnson, *Locke on Freedom*, 147; P. Kraus, 'Locke's Negative Hedonism', *Locke Newsletter*, 15 (1984), 53–5. In *Thoughts on Ed.* 149 Locke described the 'Propensity to indulge Corporeal and present Pleasure' as the root of 'all Vitious Actions, and the Irregularities of Life'. Aristotle thought that most men would mistakenly identify the chief good as immediate pleasure, 'and hence they are content with the life of sensual enjoyment' (*Nicomachean Ethics*, i. 5). And Chillingworth defined sin as 'preferring a low, inconstant, changeable good, before another more worthy and of greater excellency and perfection' (*Works*, iii. 104).

human freedom is the disruption of man's natural determination by the good and the abandonment of his judgement to the pressures of his passions. Liberty is therefore, first of all, the mark of man's imperfection and pravity.'[43]

The sombre implications of what Locke was saying here, and in some other short papers written about this time, are obvious.[44] In their constant efforts to flee from pain and secure happiness, men are naturally caught up in the crush of concerns that affect them directly in the here and now. All absent good, no matter how great it might be, and despite the fact that reasonable men might acknowledge that goodness, will not impel a man's will to action unless he can be convinced that attainment of the absent good is integrally necessary to his long-term happiness. 'How many are to be found', Locke asked, 'that have had lively representations set before their minds of the unspeakable joys of Heaven, which they acknowledge both possible and probable too, who yet would be content to take up with their happiness here?' Although the mind might have the power to suspend the execution of all its desires until it has considered the relative merits of each of them, 'it is natural, as I have said, that the greatest, and most pressing should determine the will to the next action'. But he recognized that all too often the greatest desire in most men was far from being consonant with the greatest good.[45]

Locke was, of course, not alone in declaring for this troublesome ethical theory. Some variety of hedonism had always been a part of Christian thought, despite its more

---

[43] *Essay*, 2. 21. 35, 60, 70; MS Locke c. 28, fol. 114. R. Polin, 'Locke's Conception of Freedom' in *Locke: Problems and Perspectives*, ed. Yolton, 3; S. B. Drury, ('John Locke, Natural Law and Innate Ideas', *Dialogue*, 19 (1950), 540) says that Locke 'was in search of a theory compatible with man's fallen nature' when he developed his hedonistic ethics. See also I. A. Snook, 'John Locke's Moral Theory of Education', *Educational Theory*, 20 (1976), 364; Colman, *Locke's Moral Philosophy*, 48.

[44] 'Of Ethic in General', MS Locke, c. 28, fols. 146–54; 'Thus I Think', ibid. c. 28, fols. 143–5; 'Ethica', ibid. c. 42, fol. 224.

[45] *Essay*, 2. 21. 37, 47. Rebuking those who would excuse their immoral actions with the claim that the passions were too strong for human reason to check, Locke wrote: 'Nor let any one say, he cannot govern his Passions, nor hinder them from breaking out, and carrying him into action, for what he can do before a Prince, or a great Man, he can do alone, or in the presence of God, if he will' (*Essay*, 2. 21. 53). And in *Thoughts on Ed.* 138 he made 'the great Principle and Foundation of all Virtue and Worth' the ability of man 'to deny himself his own Desires, cross his own Inclinations, and purely follow what Reason directs as best, tho' the Appetite lean the other way'. Sin, in other words, was the deliberate choice of a free moral agent.

distasteful aspects. In Locke's day, the Latitudinarian divines were most insistent upon its overall validity. Like Locke they recognized that because men were rarely led by reason alone, supernatural sanctions were necessary in order to curb their base instincts and passions. Tillotson conceded that 'To be sure, love is the noblest and most generous principle of obedience, but fear commonly takes the first and fastest hold of us'; and few churchmen of the age were apt to disagree. Earlier in the century, Chillingworth had written that 'the expectations of those glorious rewards which are laid up in heaven, are sufficient, even to any reasonable man, to derelish unto him the vain, unsatisfying pleasures of this world'.[46] Most Christians could live comfortably with this theory because it provided them with additional evidence of man's fallen nature while underscoring the personal quality of God's sovereignty. But ethical hedonism was open to the charge, formerly levelled by Cudworth and soon to be renewed by Locke's friend and student Anthony Ashley Cooper, that men acted in accordance with the moral law for selfish reasons alone and not out of any love for their Maker.[47] How could one honestly associate a theory which seemed to make morality a purely mercenary thing with a religious system that decried selfishness and greed as two of the worst offences conceivable? Locke's ethical hedonism, then, underscored his previous observations on man's essential nature. By 1689 he had abandoned whatever hopes he might have entertained in the past that men would automatically follow God's law once the intrinsic reasonableness of that law was discovered. From then on, when he spoke of the fully rational man he meant that person who understood that his own selfish interests, pleasure, and personal happiness were best served by obeying the law of God. The rational man obeyed that law, in other words, for his own reasons, not for God's. One

---

[46] Tillotson, 'The Distinguishing Character of a Good and a Bad Man' (*Works*, ii. 143). Preaching before the Commons in 1678 he said that the intrinsic goodness of religion was only likely to impress 'the minds of serious and considerate men' (*Works*, ii. 212). Chillingworth, Sermon 9 (*Works*, iii. 260). See in addition Isaac Barrow, 'Of Self-Love in General' (*Works*, iv. 86); Jeremy Taylor, *Ductor Dubitantium* (*Works*, xii. 231).

[47] Cudworth, *Treatise*, 18; id., *True Intellectual System*, ii. 357; Anthony Ashley Cooper, *An Essay on the Freedom of Wit and Humour* in *Characteristics of Men, Manners, Times*, ed. J. M. Robertson, 2 vols. (New York: Bobbs-Merrill, 1964), i. 66.

acceded to the law in order to avoid the fate of Adam, not because one was in any sense better than he.

Given this state of affairs, the task at hand clearly involved habituating men to both a dread of eternal punishment and a selfish craving for transcendent reward. In a manuscript fragment of 1693, Locke wrote that men must be made alive to virtue, must be made to 'tast' it: 'To do this one must consider what is each mans particular disease, what is the pleasure that possesses him. Over that general discourses will never get a mastery. But by all the prevalencys of friendship all the arts of persuasion he is to be brought to live the contrary course.' And the arts of persuasion remained the province of the educator.[48] To teach the child to suspend his base and peccant desires, to bring him to prefer a distant pleasure to a more accessible one, to overturn the natural bent of his mind—to make him rational, a 'Person' who accepts responsibility for his actions—such was the job of the educator; and a more important assignment would be difficult, in Locke's view, to identify. For, as he warned in another important work published soon after the *Essay*, 'To turn him loose to an unrestrain'd Liberty, before he has Reason to guide him' is only 'to thrust him out amongst Brutes, and abandon him to a state as wretched, and as much beneath that of a Man, as theirs'.[49]

In his popular *Thoughts concerning Education*, first published in 1693 but originally composed during the 1680s in the form of letters to his friend Edward Clarke advising him on the upbringing of his eldest son, Locke stated that 'Vertue is harder to be got, than a knowledge of the World; and if lost in a Young Man is seldom recovered.' His description of the child whose mind had not been made 'pliant to Reason', who had not had habits of virtue 'woven into the very Principles of his Nature', was a familiar one to seventeenth-century moralists and writers

[48] MS Locke c. 28, fol. 113. In 1679 he wrote that 'All men have a stock of love laid up in them by nature wch they cannot forbeare to bestow on something or other. We should there fore take care to choose fit and worthy objects of our love lest like women that want children the proper objects of their affection, we grow fond of litle dogs and monkys' (ibid. d. 1, fol. 25).

[49] *Two Treatises*, 2. 6. 63. For Locke 'Person' is 'a Forensick Term appropriating Actions and their Merit' (*Essay*, 2. 27. 26). For a discussion of this important concept in Locke's thought see Yolton, *Locke: An Introduction*, 17–32; Tully, *Discourse on Property*, 106–11.

on education. In fact, there is very little in the work to suggest
that the author was breaking new and controversial ground in
the area of educational theory. The call for sweeping curricular
reforms, the emphasis upon practical training for the gentleman
as opposed to the scholar, and the desire for a more efficient
teaching methodology (especially in language training)—all of
these things had been on the minds of reformers since at least the
1620s, receiving particular attention during the civil-war years
when the little circle led by Samuel Hartlib turned to
Parliament as the hoped-for engine of change.[50]

Even concepts commonly attributed to Locke like the *tabula
rasa* and the determinative power of good habits—concepts
which have much engaged the attention of scholars searching
for the foundation-stones of eighteenth-century environmentalism—even these were widely discussed and debated by writers
traditionally thought of as much closer than Locke to the
traditional Christian perspective on man's essential nature. In
two of the books that Locke set his undergraduates at Christ
Church in the 1660s, Richard Allestree's *Whole Duty of Man* and
The Gentleman's Calling, both the transforming power of
education and the consequences of original sin are discussed in a
manner similar to Locke's own treatment of the same issues.
Referring to Romans 9:21, Allestree declared that 'Mens minds
are naturally of the same Clay', and that 'Education is the
Potters hand and the wheel that forms them into Vessels of
honor or dishonor.' None the less, all men, being born after the
image of Adam, with a 'backwardness to all good, and an
aptness, and readiness to all evil', have not their wills under the
control of reason prior to experiencing the steadying hand of the
enlightened pedagogue.[51] Jean Gailhard expressed exactly the

[50] Locke, *Thoughts on Ed.* 138, 146, 166; G. H. Turnbull, *Samuel Hartlib: A Sketch of His
Life* (Oxford: University Press, 1920); id., 'The Visit of Comenius to England in 1641',
Notes and Queries, 196 (1951), 137–40; H. Trevor-Roper, 'Three Foreigners: The
Philosophers of the Puritan Revolution', in his *The Crisis of the Seventeenth Century* (New
York: Harper and Row, 1968), 237–93; V. Salmon, 'Problems of Language Teaching:
A Discussion among Hartlib's Friends', *Modern Language Review*, 59 (1954), 13–24; J.
O'Brien, 'Commonwealth Schemes for the Advancement of Learning', *British Journal of
Educational Studies*, 16 (1968), 30–42; F. Watson, 'The State and Education during the
Commonwealth', *English Historical Review*, 15 (1900), 58–72; W. A. L. Vincent, *The State
and School Education in England and Wales, 1640–1660* (London: n.p., 1958).

[51] Locke, *Thoughts on Ed.* 114–15, 244. Locke, of course, said that in composing
Thoughts on Ed. he had considered his subject 'only as white Paper, or Wax, to be

same sentiments in a work of 1678. 'The nature of Youth for the most part is like Wax by the fire', he wrote; but care must be taken lest the child be drawn into evil practices, 'for the inward principle being naturally corrupt, namely, the mind darkened, and so unable to discern true from false, the will and affections deprav'd and prone to evil, if these natural dispositions be strengthened' all would be beyond repair. And Obadiah Walker, a Catholic convert and co-author with Allestree of a sharply Augustinian commentary on the Epistles of St Paul, believed that although there remained within everyone 'some what of that pravity derived to us from our first parents, inclining us as much, if not more, to evil, then to good', still the power of custom and good habits inculcated early could modify a man's nature for the better. These men shared with Locke the Broad-Church understanding of the consequences of the Fall: a natural proneness to evil which could and ultimately must be checked through the forces of moral education.[52] It was for this reason, and this reason alone, that the instilling of Christian virtue was consistently placed first upon the educational agenda in virtually all of the courtesy books, Locke's included, throughout the seventeenth century.[53]

---

moulded and fashioned as one pleases' (op. cit. 325). Richard Allestree, *Whole Duty of Man*, 9; id., *The Gentleman's Calling* (London: T. Garthwait, 1660), 13. Rom. 9:21: 'Hath not the potter power over the clay, of the same lump to make one vessel unto honour, and another unto dishonour?' Locke's emphasis in *Thoughts on Ed.* on the importance of good habits, the power of example, warnings against maidservants, and the need for a well-trained tutor were anticipated by Erasmus, who took them from Quintilian: see R. R. Bolger, *The Classical Heritage and its Beneficiaries* (Cambridge: University Press, 1954), 338.

[52] Jean Gailhard, *The Complete Gentleman: or Directions for the Education of Youth* (London: Thomas Newcombe, 1678), 4, 9; Obadiah Walker, *Of Education, Especially of a Young Gentleman* (Oxford: n.p., 1673), 19 (Walker's book was very popular, a sixth edition being published before 1700); Richard Allestree, Obadiah Walker, and Abraham Woodhead, *A Paraphrase and Annotations Upon the Epistles of St Paul* (Oxford: At the Theatre, 1675), 3, 4. On the Broad-Church divines and education, see Taylor, *Unum Necessarium* (*Works*, viii. 469; ibid. ix. 61, 120, 172). Tillotson, 'Of the Education of Children' (*Works*, iii. 483–547) is a work strikingly similar to Locke's *Thoughts on Ed.*

[53] Gilbert Burnet, '*Thoughts on Education*' (1668), in *Bishop Burnet as Educationist*, ed. J. Clarke (Aberdeen: University Press, 1914), 9, 37, 68; Stephen Penton, *The Guardian's Instruction* (London: n.p., 1688), 6, 12; Denis Grenville, *Counsel and Directions Divine and Moral* (London: Robert Clavell, 1685), 5; William Darrell, *A Gentleman Instructed* (London: E. Evets, 1704), 44–7; William Ramesey, *The Gentleman's Companion* (London: n.p., 1676), Epistle Dedicatory; Richard Lingard, *A Letter of Advice to a Young Gentleman (1670)*, ed. F. Erb (New York: McAuliffe and Booth, 1907), 5; Clement Ellis, *The Gentle*

What I am suggesting here is that Locke's supposedly novel emphasis upon the malleable nature of human personality and the efficacy of systematic education to engender rational behaviour was not unique for its time, and in no respect undermined his deeper belief, widely shared by so many of his contemporaries, that in Adam's fall all men had inherited a penchant for irrational behaviour which constituted the essential feature of human mortality and was in fact the root of all sin. Milton's conviction that the goal of education was 'to repair the ruines of our first Parents by requiring us to know God aright, and out of that Knowledge to love him, to imitate him, to be like him, as we may the neerest by possessing our souls of true vertues' was Locke's conviction as well. The philosopher's language: 'Teach him to get a Mastery over his Inclinations, and submit his Appetite to Reason', plainly lacks the strict theological impress rightly associated with all things Puritan, and to that extent we can draw a distinction, albeit a small one, between the two men. Further than this we cannot go.[54] To argue as some have done that Locke believed men at birth to possess no nature at all, no predisposition for either good or evil, is to obscure what the author assumes throughout both the *Essay* and *Some Thoughts concerning Education*: that without education into morality men would never become what they had been fitted by God to be; they would in effect deny God's sovereignty, and would remain sinners by choice.[55] 'Our first Actions', he

Sinner (Oxford: Henry Hall, 1660), 101–5, 129; Francis Brokesby, *Of Education* (London: John Hartley, 1701), 12; Richard Brathwait, *The English Gentleman* (London: I. Dawson, 1641), Epistle Dedicatory. For a general overview see G. L. Braur, *The Education of a Gentleman: Theories of Gentlemanly Education in England, 1660–1775* (New York: Bookman Associates, 1959), ch. 1.

[54] *Thoughts on Ed.* 314; John Milton, *Of Education* (*Works*, iv. 277). On Locke's position here recall 'Homo ante et post lapsum' (MS Locke c. 28, fol. 113): there were no 'irregular desires' in Paradise, reason and instinct carrying men to the free use of all that they required without greed or ambition. After the Fall 'covitousness, pride and ambition' prevailed, thereby introducing the 'curse' of private possessions and labour. The 'root of all evil' in men was connected with their turning away from God and towards the things of this world. In the *Essay* (3. 9. 23) Locke described Christ on earth as being subject 'to all the frailties and Inconveniences of humane Nature, Sin excepted', thereby making the reality of sin one of the constants of human nature. Peter Laslett (*Library of John Locke*, eds. Laslett and Harrison, 26, (n. 1) says Locke probably did not see Milton's *Of Education* until 1694.

[55] Cf. Passmore, 'Malleability of Man', 23; Ezell, 'Locke's Images of Childhood', 149. Hans Aarsleff ('The State of Nature and the Nature of Man in Locke', in *John Locke:*

stated emphatically, 'being guided more by Self-love, than Reason or Reflection, 'tis no wonder that in Children they should be very apt to deviate from the just measures of Right and Wrong: which are in the Mind the Result of improved Reason and serious Meditation.'[56] Education was there to help realize man's essential nature as it could be; what that nature was at birth for Locke—well, that was another matter entirely.

If then we look at Locke's discussion of the limits of the human understanding—the innate and variable powers of the mind, the difficulties encountered in the knowing and judging process, the implications of a hedonistic ethic, the countless number of passions, tempers, and dispositions that so disturb the smooth functioning of the mind and hamper the efforts of the educator—if we look at these constants of the human personality and set them against the popular environmentalist interpretation of the *tabula rasa*, it becomes evident that the *Essay* and *Some Thoughts concerning Education* were meant primarily to reaffirm a picture of man in society that, if anything, would make any program for social reform a laborious undertaking at best. There is certainly a reformist tone to the works, and the author continued to believe that at least some individuals could be educated to the point where the faculty of reason would effectively override the attractions of the baser instincts. But Locke's certainty that 'there are very few lovers of Truth for Truth's sake, even amongst those, who perswade themselves that they are so', together with his lifelong social conservatism which unsympathetically assumed that the majority of men, given up to the drudgery of constant labour, could be no more knowing 'than a Pack-horse', placed important restraints on his more sanguine leanings. It was 'almost unavoidable', he thought, that most men would continue to take both their principles and their prejudices from those who were only too eager to furnish them, and thus, worshipping 'the Idols that have been set up in their Minds . . . become zealous Votaries to

Problems and Perspectives, ed. Yolton, 101), while admitting that for Locke man's passionate nature frustrates the operation of reason, nevertheless writes that 'Reason pulls one way and passion the other, but Locke never assumes that mankind at large is wholly dominated by one or the other.' The problem remains: reason does not pull at all until one learns to use it.

[56] *Thoughts on Ed.* 214.

Bulls and Monkeys; and contend too, fight, and die in defence of their Opinions'.[57] Most men would continue sinners, in other words, sinners in the face of overwhelming and obvious evidence that their course could only steer them directly towards eternal damnation, and sinners despite their God-given power to overturn, at least for themselves, the consequences of Adam's primal transgression. It was becoming clear to Locke that stronger incentives were needed, and needed quickly, if men were to avoid this terrible situation. He was gradually coming round, although he never acknowledged it, to the position of his old critic Thomas Burnet, who had told Locke that 'the illiterate part of Mankind (which is far the greatest part) must have more compendious ways to know their Duty, than by long and obscure Deductions'.[58] Morality might be found out by man through the use of reason alone, but for Locke it was fairly obvious that for all practical purposes it rarely would be. And even then he knew that its discovery did not necessarily oblige men. Only God could do that, and only a Redeemer could make those obligations plain to all. Locke would return after 1693 to a very old solution to the problem, one from which he had fled in the aftermath of the Civil War because of its then divisive and volatile nature, its liability to misunderstanding. There seemed after 1693 no real alternative. In those very early days of what we have come to identify in a more general sense as the Age of Enlightenment, John Locke would return to Scripture to lead men into obedience.

[57] *Essay*, 4. 19. 1, 20. 2; 1. 3. 26.
[58] Burnet, *Remarks*, 4.

5

The Covenant of Faith

WHEN, in 1692, the founder and principal moving force behind the Dublin Philosophical Society voiced his unreserved endorsement of the way of ideas contained in Locke's *Essay*, the author's immediate response was to pen an especially friendly letter thanking the stranger for his approval and support. Thus began what would become one of Locke's closest friendships, a friendship carried on for seven years largely by post across the inhospitable barrier of the Irish Sea. And although they were destined to meet but once, John Locke and William Molyneux shared a corresponding outlook on matters philosophical that served to strengthen both of them in their respective intellectual endeavours for the remainder of their days.[1] When the Dubliner died unexpectedly after returning home from a visit to England in 1698, Locke wrote to Molyneux's younger brother Thomas, saying 'I have lost in your brother, not only an ingenious and learned acquaintance, that all the world esteem'd; but an intimate and sincere friend, whom I truly lov'd, and by whom I was truly loved.'[2] On one matter only, it seems, was Molyneux in the least bit disappointed in Locke. From the very outset of their amicable correspondence, he constantly importuned Locke to fulfil what for him was one of the implicit pledges of the *Essay*: the eventual formulation and publication of a demonstrable science of morality based upon the facts of human nature. 'Good Sir,' he petitioned soon after Locke's first letter, 'Let me Beg of you to turn your thoughts this way. and if so

---

[1] Locke to Molyneux (16 July 1692: iv, no. 1515). On Molyneux see T. Hoppen, *The Common Scientist in the Seventeenth Century: A Study of the Dublin Philosophical Society, 1683–1708* (Charlottesville, Va.: University of Virginia Press, 1970); id., 'The Dublin Philosophical Society and the New Learning in Ireland', *Irish Historical Studies*, 14 (1964), 99–118; P. Kelly, 'Locke and Molyneux: the Anatomy of a Friendship', *Hermathena*, 126 (1979), 99–118; Kippis, *Biographia Britannica*, v. 3123–34; *DNB* xiii. 585–8. Molyneux's praise of the *Essay* appeared in his *Dioptrica Nova* (London: B. Tooke, 1692).

[2] Locke to Thomas Molyneux (27 Oct. 1698: vi, no. 2500).

Young a Freindship as mine have any force; Let me prevail
upon you.' Anxious to foster the emerging goodwill between
himself and his new-found ally, Locke at first responded by
promising not to neglect 'the first leisure I can get to employ
some thoughts that way', but, as first the months and then the
years slipped by, he at length admitted that the task would for
ever elude him. Not to despair, however, for 'Did the world want
a rule, I confess there could be no work so necessary, nor so
commendable': but, happily for all, 'the Gospel contains so
perfect a body of Ethics, that reason may be excused from that
enquiry, since she may find man's duty clearer and easier in
revelation than in herself'.[3]

It was not so clear and easy as might first appear, however.
Locke's final position on the matter of demonstrating morality
through the unaided exercise of reason, his failure to tackle that
which he had always assumed to be within the reach of frail
humanity, necessitated a special return to Scripture, one where
the core elements of the Bible story and its directives regarding
earthly conduct had to be carefully and diligently educed from
the bulky mass of interpretive encumbrances that had grown up
and multiplied over the centuries, distorting and debasing the
original Christian message. He knew fully how much the Bible,
subject as it was to the obscurity and abuse of words which he
had examined in Book Three of the *Essay*, could be misinter-
preted by the casual or the partial reader.[4] If the moral law as it
was promulgated in Scripture were ever to be adequately
known and practised, then it was imperative that the word of
God be made plain to all, that the essence of the faith be
rediscovered and reinstated with a new precision. Locke's
response to the apparent failure of his thirty-year search for an
ethical code based entirely upon the discoveries of reason was an

---

[3] Molyneux to Locke (27 Aug. 1692: iv, no. 1530); Locke to Molyneux (20 Sept.
1692: iv, no. 1538); Locke to Molyneux (5 Apr. 1696: v, no. 2059). Other occasions
when Molyneux asked Locke to write a treatise on morality: 15 Oct. 1692: iv, no. 1544;
2 Mar. 1693: iv, no. 1609; 16 Sept. 1693: iv, no. 1661; 15 Jan. 1695: v, no. 1838;
14 Mar. 1696: v, no. 2038. Molyneux was not the only one of Locke's friends to make the
request: see James Tyrrell to Locke (9 Aug. 1692: iv, no. 1522).

[4] *Essay*, 3. 9, 10; J. T. Moore, 'Locke's Concept of Faith', 89–129; id., 'Locke's
Analysis of Language and the Assent to Scripture', *Journal of the History of Ideas*, 37
(1976), 707–14; id., 'Locke on the Moral Need for Christianity', *Southwestern Journal of
Philosophy*, 1 (1980), 25–30; H. P. Hamlin, 'A Critical Evaluation of John Locke's
Philosophy of Religion' (University of Georgia Ph. D. thesis, 1972), 14.

anonymous little book with a misleading title, *The Reasonableness of Christianity*, a work that quickly won for the author the undeserved but understandable wrath of a clerical establishment already unnerved by his previous denial of innate moral ideas in the *Essay* and now enraged by what appeared to be Locke's open sympathy for the hated antitrinitarians and free-thinking Deists, those unconscionable polluters of minds and promoters of reckless irreligion.[5]

It was regrettable and disappointing to Locke that his brief work on the essentials of Christian belief was almost immediately seen as a first bridge between the Latitudinarian doctrine of the minimal creed and the more extreme deistic conception of the absolute sufficiency of reason in religion. For those individuals who fastened upon this issue alone seemed deliberately to ignore the wider assumptions of the work. The *Reasonableness*, we shall discover, was a book about the failure of reason, not an apotheosis of it; it was about the sinfulness of Adam's posterity and their inability to achieve salvation without the loving intervention and atoning sacrifice of Christ, about the consequences of the Fall, about human depravity, and the means by which it might be excused.

The message of the *Reasonableness* doubtless began to take shape in the author's mind as far back as the 1670s, during those years at Exeter House when he first came into contact with preachers like Whichcote and the Latitudinarian divines who gathered at the London home of Thomas Firmin. There the sole rationale behind the adoption of the minimal creed had been its perceived ability to put an end to the doctrinal squabbling that had so distracted Englishmen for close on a hundred years. At that time, the alternative avenue to God's law, the rule of reason, still seemed within reach for Locke; thus the Scriptural way to truth via the minimal creed, although worth while, was by no means imperative. His ideas were further refined during his five-and-a-half year exile in the Netherlands during the 1680s. Abandoning his chambers at Christ Church in late August 1683, one year after the final disgrace of Shaftesbury for his role in the Exclusion Controversy, Locke took ship and

[5] Takashi Kato ('The *Reasonableness* in the Historical Light of the *Essay*', *Locke Newsletter*, 12 (1981), 45–57), discusses the compensatory nature of Locke's book on religion.

crossed the Channel in early September, staying briefly in Rotterdam and then settling for the winter in Amsterdam.[6] His reasons for fleeing, his biographers tell us, centred on his fear of persecution in the wake of the Rye House Plot and the political executions that followed. Especially disturbing was the conviction of Algernon Sydney, whose Whiggish sympathies and vigorous rebuttal of Sir Robert Filmer's *Patriarcha* were dangerously akin to the views expressed by Locke in his own unpublished reply to the same work.[7] Once in Amsterdam and out of the reach of his political enemies, Locke settled down to begin work on the drafts of the *Essay* that he had first composed some twelve years earlier. The exile, whatever its cost in privileges lost and friends now removed, at least afforded the 51-year-old bachelor an opportunity to bring together his disparate thoughts on a number of philosophical issues which he had previously slighted because of obligations within the Shaftesbury circle.[8]

During that first winter in Amsterdam, Locke met the great-nephew of Simon Episcopius and present leader of the Dutch Remonstrants, Philippus van Limborch, who later recalled:

When Mr. Locke heard from Dr. Guenellon, that I was professor of theology among the remonstrants, he introduced himself to me, and we afterwards had many conversations about religion, in which he acknowledged that he had long attributed to the remonstrants doctrines very different from those which they held, and now that he understood what they really were, he was surprised to find how closely they agreed with many of his own opinions.[9]

---

[6] On Shaftesbury's role during these years, see J. Miller, *Popery and Politics in England* (Cambridge: University Press, 1973), 189–95; id., *James II* (Hove: Wayland Publishers, 1977), 109–19; J. R. Jones, *The First Whigs: The Politics of the Exclusion Crisis, 1678–1683* (Oxford: University Press, 1961); Haley, *First Earl of Shaftesbury*, chs. 23–7.

[7] Cranston, *Locke*, 226–30; Jean Le Clerc, 'The Life and Character of Mr Locke', in *Essay Concerning Human Understanding*, ed. Calkins, p. xxiv. Peter Laslett's introduction to Locke's *Two Treatises* established that the work was written in 1681 to promote the Whig cause, not to justify a revolution (1688) which had already taken place. On the Exclusion Controversy, see J. R. Jones, *Country and Court* (Cambridge: Harvard University Press, 1979), 197–216; David Ogg, *England in Reign of Charles II*, 559–619.

[8] R. L. Colie, 'John Locke in the Republic of Letters', in *Britain and the Netherlands*, ed. J. S. Bromley and E. H. Kossman (London: Chatto and Windus, 1960), 112–13. Locke was expelled from his Christ Church Studentship in November 1684 by royal command: Locke to Thomas Herbert (28 Nov. 1684: ii, no. 797); Thompson, *Christ Church*, 99–104. In a letter written two months after his departure, Locke asks Edward Clarke to send him news of friends in England: Locke to Clarke (21 Nov. 1683: ii, no. 773).

[9] Limborch to Damaris Masham, 10 Nov. 1704. Quoted in Fox Bourne, *Locke*, ii. 6.

Locke's own opinions were, we know, those held by the Broad-Church divines back in England; and at the time that he befriended Limborch the Remonstrant was engaged in writing, at the urging of his own English friends among the Cambridge Platonists, his *Theologia Christiana*, a lengthy exposition of Arminian belief and a work in many respects similar to Locke's later *Reasonableness*. Of the manuscript itself Locke thought very highly, admitting that 'most of my observations in the course of reading were made not so much with the idea of correcting you as of informing myself on points I had decided to consult you about later'.[10]

The *Theologia* examined in exhausting detail the Arminian doctrines of the minimal creed, religious toleration, and the primacy of ethical conduct. Locke warned Limborch of the inevitable hue and cry which these and other ideas would raise amongst the Dutch Calvinists, and advised his friend to 'leave these pugnacious folk to themselves and their concerns'; but surprisingly the book sold rather well, reaching a seventh edition soon after the author's death in 1714 and being translated into English and Dutch.[11] As we observed earlier, the Remonstrants had welcomed the persecuted Polish Socinians into their midst, and as a result were often accused by hostile critics of espousing Socinian doctrines. That charge had no validity where Limborch was concerned, however. He flatly rejected the notion that men could somehow merit salvation on their own without the helping grace of God, upheld the doctrine of the Atonement and insisted upon the certainty of everlasting punishment for impenitent sinners.[12] On the question of original sin, where the radical Socinians repudiated even the mildest formulation of the doctrine, Limborch was more ambiguous. Clearly, he wanted to dissociate himself from the Calvinist

---

[10] Locke to Limborch (26 Sept. 1685: ii, no. 834). According to De Beer, the *Theologia* was not published until May 1686, but in a letter of 21 Sept. 1685 Limborch thanks Locke for his criticisms of portions of the manuscript: Limborch to Locke (21 Sept. 1685: ii, no. 832); and De Beer, *Correspondence of Locke*, ii. 743, n. 2. For Limborch's theological ideas and connection with the Platonists see R. L. Colie, *Light and Enlightenment: A Study of the Cambridge Platonists and Dutch Arminians* (Cambridge: University Press, 1957), 27–31.

[11] Locke to Limborch (1 Oct. 1686: iii, no. 868). Publishing information from De Beer, op. cit. ii. 651.

[12] Limborch, *Theologia Christiana*, trans. William Jones as *A Complete System or Body of Divinity, Both Speculative and Practical, founded on Scripture and Reason*, 2 vols. (London: John Darby, 1713), i. 181, 199, 191, 231, 287; ii. 793.

interpretation. The phrase 'original sin', he said, 'is no where to be met with in Scripture', meaning that men neither sin necessarily because of Adam's fall nor possess any hereditary internal corruption which legitimizes their damnation; and in comments on the difficult Pauline proof-text Romans 5:12, he dismissed the idea that sin was transmitted by Adam to all his descendants. He also attempted to deny what he took to be the 'Schoolmen's' definition—the notion that original sin entailed a complete loss of righteousness—by asserting that 'God does not punish the innocent Posterity of Adam for his Sin.'[13] This, one might think, was surely enough to provoke Locke's friendly warning about the critics lying in wait for another thrust at Socinianism. But Limborch, while objecting to those who went beyond a purely naturalistic explanation of Adam's liability to death, nevertheless admitted 'that Adam did indeed lose his Original Righteousness (as they term it) or rather did fall from a State of Innocence and Integrity into a State of Sin', and consequently 'was made more inclin'd to Evil, and to lust after things unlawful [more] than before'.[14] Something of real significance had been lost by man through the Fall, and the author attempted to convey that message without becoming ensnared in the familiar Calvinist vocabulary. Unfortunately he could only accomplish this by moving dangerously towards the type of dualism that was so alien to St Paul:

And here we freely own that Men are now born less pure than Adam was created, and with some propensity to sin. But this inclination is not to sin properly so call'd, or the Habit of Sin transmitted to them by Adam, but only a natural Inclination of attaining that which is grateful to the Flesh; which is properly owning to the Constitution of the Body, which we derive from our next immediate Parents.[15]

Limborch recognized the possible implications of what he was advancing here, for later he attempted to clarify his position, and demonstrate his Pauline orthodoxy, by adding that the longings of the flesh were clearly under the direction of the intellect. ''Tis the Mind that properly is the Criminal,' he said, 'whilst the Bodily Members are as so many instruments to

---

[13] Ibid. i. 190, 192, 197.
[14] Ibid. i. 190.
[15] Ibid. i. 198.

execute what the Soul resolves upon.' God proscribed certain pleasures of the flesh in order that he might 'try the Readiness of our Obedience'.[16] The understanding, will, and affections were not, as the Calvinists thought, inwardly averse to all moral good. That, said Limborch, would be to deny the wisdom and benevolence of the Creator; it would be designating God the author of sin and thereby mitigating the seriousness of all transgressions. But they were undeniably prone to evil; here began the first motions towards sinful behaviour, and to the extent that one capitulated to these tendencies the pollution of sin became all the more unremitting. Repentance was the corner-stone of Remonstrant doctrine; but 'Repentance presupposes Sin', presumes a distinct habit of living and a mind 'if not altogether, yet in some measure, averse to Virtue, and enslaved to vice'.[17] Locke had no quarrel with this reading of Scripture. Years later he was happy to report that his own efforts to understand 'wherein the Christian faith consists', his work over the winter of 1694–5 on the *Reasonableness of Christianity*, had led him to conclusions identical to those of Limborch, the one theologian 'for whom I am not a heretic'.[18]

The years in Holland would have been a good deal less tolerable, perhaps even dangerous, had it not been for Limborch's friendship. When Locke's name appeared on a list of alleged conspirators against the government of James II in the summer of 1685, it was Limborch who assisted him in securing a safe house where he might avoid arrest and possible extradition. During that winter of confinement (1685–6) Locke continued to work on the manuscript of the *Essay*, and in addition composed a brief paper, dedicated to Limborch, on the familiar subject of religious toleration. Another of Locke's Arminian friends, the professor of philosophy at the Remonstrant Seminary and editor

---

[16] Ibid. ii. 468; i. 199. Part of that obedience entailed the exercise of one's rational faculties in examining all received principles of religion: see Limborch's Introduction to his *History of the Inquisition*, trans. Samuel Chandler, 2 vols. (London: J. Gray, 1731), i. 2.

[17] Limborch, *Theologia Christiana*, ii. 522, 795.

[18] Locke to Limborch (10 May 1695: v, no. 1901). On 26 Oct. 1694 (v, no. 1804) he informed Limborch that the *Theologia* was 'highly esteemed among Anglican theologians'. In 1692 Limborch dedicated his *History of the Inquisition* to Tillotson. Locke had spoken to Tillotson on Limborch's behalf asking for the Archbishop's permission: Limborch to Locke (17 June 1692: iv, no. 1507); Locke to Limborch (30 June 1692: iv, no. 1509).

of the *Bibliothèque universelle et historique*, Jean Le Clerc, observed
in his periodical that there was currently in print such a
profusion of books on toleration 'that people scarcely speak of
anything else'.[19] Locke's composition, largely consistent with his
earlier effort of 1667, did not reach the printer's hand until after
the author had left for home in 1689. Having begun the work at
the suggestion of Limborch, the ever-cautious Locke preferred
to remain aloof from its anonymous publication. And when an
English translation was published in London soon after Locke's
return there, it too was innominate.[20]

In a codicil to his will written just weeks before his death,
Locke denied ever being privy to the English translation of the
Epistola de Tolerantia. But although he did not participate in the
actual translation, he knew fully about the undertaking and did
nothing to prevent it.[21] The translator was a former merchant
living in London named William Popple. Locke had befriended
Popple sometime during the summer after his return to England
in February 1689. By November the two men, together with
Locke's host in Rotterdam during his last two years of exile, the
Quaker merchant and bibliophile Benjamin Furly, were
exchanging ideas on religion.[22] Prior to his own return to
London in 1688 after almost two decades in France, Popple had
written a short treatise, with which Locke was familiar in
Holland, entitled *A Rational Catechism*. Given that his translator
is charged with being a Socinian, that he became Secretary to
Locke's 'Dry Club' (a discussion circle begun by Locke in 1692
and devoted to religious matters), that he befriended both

---

[19] Le Clerc quoted in *Epistola de Tolerantia*, p. xiv. An abridgement of Locke's *Essay*
appeared in Le Clerc's *Bibliothèque universelle et historique* in 1688. On Le Clerc see Colie,
Light and Enlightenment, 31–5; Paul Hazard, *European Mind*, 87.

[20] 'He did not set his Name to it, that he might not be engag'd in any personal
Quarrels, which might possibly have turn'd to his disadvantage, without serving any
ways to the advancement of Truth' (Le Clerc, 'Life and Character', p. xxxi.).

[21] P. King, *The Life of John Locke* (Oxford: University Press, 1829), 266; Locke to
Limborch (10 Sept. 1689: iii, no. 1182).

[22] From the evidence of Locke's journal, it appears that Locke had become a regular
visitor at Popple's home by November of 1689, even lending household items to Mrs
Popple: MS Locke f. 10, fols. 27, 41. Popple was the nephew of the poet Andrew Marvell
and may have been educated under his direction: see C. Robbins, 'Absolute Liberty:
The Life and Thought of William Popple', *William and Mary Quarterly*, 3rd ser. 24 (1967),
190–223. On Furly see W. I. Hull, *Benjamin Furly and Quakerism in Rotterdam* (Lancaster,
Pa.: Lancaster Press, 1941).

Locke's former student and soon-to-be critic Anthony Ashley Cooper and his merchant friend Thomas Firmin, and that, through Locke's influence, he became Secretary to the newly created Board of Trade in 1696, Popple's religious ideas must have been of some interest to the philosopher.[23]

Not surprisingly, Popple's thought is very similar to Limborch's; and in one important respect it anticipates what became the most controversial element of Locke's *Reasonableness of Christianity*. Aside from the more obvious and expected Broad-Church commonplaces—the flight from narrow dogma and creed-making, the emphasis upon Christian practice over theory, the assertion that salvation was possible for all, the plea for toleration, and the argument that natural religion was in all things congruent with the revealed word in Scripture—Popple followed Limborch in rejecting the idea that revelation was unnecessary in an enlightened age. He understandably argued that the discoveries of reason were the product 'of deep Meditation', thereby making natural religion an impossibility for the 'Vulgar sort of People'. But the vulgar were not always alone here. Even the gifted who normally possessed that faculty in full frequently 'do either slip or break the fine-spun Thread of their own Consequences, and stand in need of a stronger Force to subject them unto their Duty'.[24] Beyond this rather harmless failing, Popple insisted, there existed in every man a 'voluntary Negligence', a stubborn streak which led men to eschew reason and which ranked 'amongst the most enormous Corruptions of Humane Nature'. Surprisingly referring to St Augustine for support, he concluded that this wilful 'Corruption into which Mankind has fall'n' made the extra incentives of revealed religion crucial to the maintenance of the moral order.[25]

---

[23] MS Locke c. 25, fols. 56–7, 'Rules for the Dry Club' in Popple's hand. In 1692 Locke gave Popple a copy of his *Third Letter Concerning Toleration* for review: Cranston, *Locke*, 68. The next year he lent Popple a copy of *The Fundamental Constitutions of Carolina*, probably because of the unique provisions for toleration in that document: MS Locke f. 10, fol. 57. On the third earl of Shaftesbury and Popple see MS Locke f. 10, fols. 226, 298, 309–10, 319. Cranston, (*Locke*, 200), accuses Popple of Socinianism. Kliblanski and Gough (eds., *Epistola de Tolerantia*, p. xxii, n. 1) say that Locke read the *Rational Catechism* in 1687.

[24] William Popple, *A Rational Catechism* (London: Andrew Sowle, 1687), 67.

[25] William Popple, *A Discourse of Human Reason* (London: A. Churchill, 1690), 52, 72. De Beer (*Correspondence of Locke*, iv. 36–7) says that Popple was likely to have been the author of this work. Later, in 1695, both Locke and Popple wrote friendly criticisms of

It was this voluntary 'corruption' that made the minimal creed so important to Popple, as it was to Limborch and would be for Locke.[26] Since God in his goodness, said Popple, wanted all men to be saved, he would never have made that salvation contingent upon belief in so many incomprehensible mysteries. The relative importance of articles and creeds was not to be measured 'by the notions of the Learned', but by the capacity of the meanest of Christians. For Popple, belief in Christ who came to save men from the iniquity of their sins, and who was the only Son of God, raised from the dead, constituted the full extent of necessary doctrine. With this belief was required the faithful practice of Christian virtues and a sincere repentance for sins past. Necessary doctrine had to be clear and plain, he thought, lest the majority of men be for ever enslaved to the sin of their own making, sin that was universal in extent and from which no man could be excused on the basis of his own shabby exertions.[27]

Locke's own adoption of the minimal creed in the *Reasonableness of Christianity* was, he tells us, prompted by a careful study of Scripture in which the meaning of each and every word contained therein was taken in its most obvious and direct sense. As he later wrote regarding the study of St Paul's Epistles, 'He that would understand St Paul [and by implication all Biblical authors] right, must understand his Terms, in the Sense he uses them, and not as they are appropriated, by each Man's particular Philosophy, to Conceptions that never enter'd the Mind of the Apostle.'[28] We can trust Locke's veracity here about

the Deist Stephen Nye's forthcoming *Discourse Concerning Natural and Revealed Religion* (London: Jonathan Robinson, 1696). Nye was another member of the Firmin circle. He agreed with Locke and Popple that natural religion was insufficient to lead men to a knowledge and obedience of the moral law, and that the 'degenerate state of the world' necessitated God's first sending Moses and then Christ to restore the injunctions of that law (op. cit. 98). MS Locke c. 27, fols. 92–3.

[26] Limborch to Locke (29 June 1695: v, no. 1919): 'I myself love a simple style that does not depart from the language of the Gospel and does not urge things to be believed other than those which our Lord commands us to believe and which can be understood and believed even by the common people.'

[27] Popple, *Discourse*, 2–3, 84; id., *Rational Catechism*, 72, 92, 104.

[28] Locke, *Reasonableness* (*Works*, vii. 5); id., 'An Essay for the Understanding of St Paul's Epistles, by Consulting St Paul Himself', in *Paraphrase and Notes on the Epistles of St Paul*, ed. A. W. Wainwright (Oxford: Clarendon Press, 1987), 114. Locke's critical approach to the Bible was not new. He was familiar with the work of Richard Simon, and his friend Le Clerc wrote a defence of Simon's *Critical History of the Old Testament* in 1685: MS Locke f. 10, fol. 133; Laslett and Harrison, eds., *Library of Locke*, nos. 2673, 2694; Locke to van Limborch (26 Sept. 1685: ii, no. 834).

the origins of the work, but we should not ignore the fact that at least two of his close friends had already propounded most of the central ideas set forth in it. The result of his search turned up, not unexpectedly, the same single article of belief that Popple had discovered for himself years earlier: faith in Christ as the Messiah, Locke said, was the only belief that one was required to hold in order to qualify as a Christian. He later pointed out that Scripture contained a good deal more than this, that in fact the entire New Testament 'being the declared will and mind of our Lord and Master . . . we are bound to receive as right and truth', but one's designation as a Christian did not require a thorough prior understanding of it. Each Christian was expected both 'to study, and thereby build himself up in our most holy faith; receiving with steadfast belief, and ready obedience, all those things which the Spirit of truth hath therein revealed', and to live a life of good works in accordance with the guidelines best set forth in Matthew 5 and Luke 6, the Sermon on the Mount or Beatitudes; but these were the natural concomitants of true belief in Christ as Messiah, not separate prerequisites to that belief.[29] In Locke's view, God had designated this belief in Christ as Messiah the single essential article because, although desirous of saving all men, the Creator understood fully the consequences of what Locke had only recently come to concede, namely that 'natural religion, in its full extent, was nowhere . . . taken care of, by the force of natural reason': the desiderata of necessary belief had to be narrowed if men were to avoid the punishment which they all deserved. Because it was 'too hard a task for unassisted reason to establish morality in all its parts, upon its true foundation, with a clear and convincing light', the essentials of a saving faith had to be made plain to all. 'The greatest part cannot know,' a chastened Locke observed, 'and therefore they must believe.'[30]

This urgent exegesis, coming as it did from the pen of one already suspected of unorthodoxy, placed the philosopher and his novel ideas well beyond the pale for many of his

---

[29] Locke, *Reasonableness*, 26, 34, 53, 104; id., *First Vindication of the Reasonableness of Christianity* (*Works*, vii. 176); *Second Vindication of the Reasonableness of Christianity* (*Works*, vii. 228, 230–1). Locke referred the reader to Simon Patrick's *Witness to Christianity* for confirmation of the single article. Popple also pointed to the Sermon on the Mount as containing the essence of Christian morality: *Rational Catechism*, 71.

[30] *Reasonableness*, 139, 146.

contemporaries. 'Read John Locke who writ of Human Understanding, and hath had little of it since, and not overmuch then', was the acerbic advice of one John Edwards two years after the initial appearance of the *Reasonableness*.[31] Edwards, Calvinist Doctor of Divinity and embattled controversialist on the side of religious intolerance at a time of increasing forbearance and mutual lenity, was unquestionably Locke's most dogged and unbending critic. In an age when authors were anything but delicate in pointing out the failings of an adversary, John Edwards was positively cruel. 'The seraglio of Otes' was the churchman's description of the quite country estate of Francis and Damaris Masham, located some twenty miles north-east of London, where the elderly Locke was now living.[32] But verbal excesses aside, much of what Edwards had charged against Locke was also of concern to others. The anonymous author of the *Reasonableness*, Edwards opined, seemed strangely silent about the mystery of the Trinity, appeared to question the import of revelation, equivocated on the Atonement, and implied that there were no mysteries to be found in Christianity.[33] These were mendacious indictments on most counts, but certainly not unusual ones in the contentious atmosphere of the 1690s. All hints of unorthodoxy were magnified during that decade because it was in those years that

[31] John Edwards, *A Brief Vindication of the Fundamental Articles of the Christian Faith* (London: n.p., 1697), 4.

[32] MS Locke c. 23, fol. 200: anonymous letter to Locke's bookseller John Churchill. Author identified by Laslett, *Library of Locke*, 8.

[33] John Edwards, *The Socinian Creed* (London: J. Robinson, 1697), 25; id., *Some Thoughts Concerning the Several Causes and Occasions of Atheism* (London: J. Robinson, 1695), 121; id., *Socinianism Unmasked* (London: J. Robinson, 1696), 26. In his *A Free Discourse Concerning Truth and Error* (London: n.p., 1701), 423, Edwards accused Locke of denying innate ideas, questioning the resurrection of the same body, doubting the soul's immateriality, and conceding the possibility of thinking matter. The charge of antitrinitarianism is plausible: Locke was silent on the matter, although an anonymous correspondent requested that he clarify his position (Anonymous to Locke, *c*.2 Sept. 1695: v, no. 1939). In 1690 he had forwarded some antitrinitarian papers of Isaac Newton, at Newton's request, to Jean Le Clerc for anonymous publication. He had doubtless discussed the question of the Trinity with Newton at Oates: F. Manuel, *The Religion of Isaac Newton* (Oxford: Clarendon Press, 1974), 12; Newton to Locke (14 Nov. 1690: iv, no. 1338). Newton eventually asked that the papers be returned to him unpublished. See also Locke's notes 'Adversaria Theologica' printed in King, *Life of Locke*, 336–40, where Locke quoted from John Biddle in weighing the evidence against belief in the Trinity. On Oates see P. Laslett, 'Masham of Otes: The Rise and Fall of an English Family', *History Today*, 3. 8 (1953), 535–43.

the influence of Deism reached its peak, when challenges to all forms of revealed religion became both unrestrained and uninhibited. The most famous, or rather infamous, of the Deist manifestos, John Toland's *Christianity Not Mysterious*, appeared in print soon after the *Reasonableness*. Eagerly adopting Locke's way of ideas in defence of an argument which made human reason sufficient in every endeavour, Toland, in the words of Leslie Stephen, 'gave articulate expression to a widely diffused, but as yet latent, sentiment'.[34] Unhappily for Locke, it was now a case of guilt by association. In the rush of criticism that followed publication, his emphasis upon Christ as redeemer, his insistence on the universality of sin, and his discussion of the all-important covenant of faith were overlooked entirely. Accused of overturning all religion and making man the master of his own salvation in the baneful tradition of Pelagius, Locke found himself engaging in just the sort of factious quarrel over religion that he had always decried and sought to avoid. 'I must confess,' he wrote in his first rebuttal to Edwards's intemperate remarks, 'discourses of this kind, which I met with, spread up and down, at first amazed me; knowing the sincerity of those thoughts, which persuaded me to publish it not without some hope of doing some service to decaying piety, and mistaken and slandered Christianity.'[35] Again, I think we can trust Locke's

[34] L. Stephen, *History of English Thought in the Eighteenth Century*, 2 vols. (New York: Harbinger, 1962), i. 88; John Toland, *Christianity Not Mysterious* (London: n.p., 1696), especially sect. 3, 'Nothing Mysterious or Above Reason in the Gospel'; F. H. Heinemann, 'John Toland and the Age of Enlightenment' *Review of English Studies*, 20 (1944), 125–46. Locke dissociated himself from Toland on more than one occasion: Locke to Molyneux (3 May 1697: vi, no. 2254; 15 June 1697: vi, no. 2277); 'A Letter to the Right Reverend Edward [Stillingfleet], Lord Bishop of Worcester' (*Works*, iv. 177). On the Deists see Stephen, op. cit. i. 76–156; S. C. Pearson, Jr., 'The Religion of John Locke and the Character of His Thought', *Journal of Religion*, 58 (1978), 253–6; G. R. Cragg, *Puritanism to Age of Reason*, 136–55; M. Pattison, 'Tendencies of Religious Thought in England, 1680–1750', in *Essays*, 2 vols. (Oxford: Clarendon Press, 1898), ii. 42–8; J. Redwood, *Reason, Ridicule and Religion: The Age of Enlightenment in England, 1660–1750* (Cambridge, Mass.: Harvard University Press, 1976), 30–48; R. Stromberg, *Religious Liberalism in Eighteenth-Century England* (Oxford: University Press, 1954), 52–87.

[35] Locke, *First Vindication of Reasonableness* (*Works*, vii. 165). That Locke meant to check the rise of Deism is evident from the opening statement in the *Reasonableness* (4–5) where he insists on the necessity of a redeemer. Popple wrote later that 'The *Reasonableness of Christianity*, (however Reasonable a Book it be) has I doubt had little Effect upon those that call themselves Deists in this Age' (Popple to Locke, 16 Jan. 1696: v, no. 2002). On Locke's disagreement with Toland, see J. C. Biddle, 'Locke's Critique of Innate Principles and Toland's Deism', *Journal of the History of Ideas*, 37 (1976), 411–22.

sincerity, especially when we consider, as his immediate critics did not, what he upheld of traditional Christian doctrine as well as what he pulled down.

Locke began the *Reasonableness* on what was, given the unsettled climate of religious opinion, such a controversial note that the potential critic need not have gone much beyond the first few pages (and one suspects that many did not) in order to feel justified in attaching the Socinian label. For he led off with a frontal assault on the Calvinist reading of Romans 5:12 by observing that 'If by death, threatened to Adam, were meant the corruption of human nature in his posterity, it is strange, that the New Testament should not any where take notice of it.' What the first man suffered through the Fall, said Locke, and what he has burdened posterity with ever since, was a loss of 'perfect obedience, which is called justice in the New Testament; though the word, which in the original signifies justice, be translated righteousness'. The privation meant that no one could realistically hope to fulfil the requirements of the Mosaic law of works whereby perfect obedience would be rewarded with salvation as a debt discharged. In other words, as a result of the Fall men could no longer obey the law of God, the law of right reason—the law of their own nature. 'It was such a law', he wrote, 'as the purity of God's nature required, and must be the law of such a creature as man; unless God would have made him a rational creature, and not required him to have lived by the law of reason.'[36] It was also a law that Toland and his fellow Deists insisted was none too onerous, with obedience to that law within easy reach of rational men. Locke, however, while denying that every person inherited some mysterious stain from Adam whereby he must sin necessarily throughout his life, refused to exempt mankind from the need for a redeemer. He was making an argument for the *de facto* pervasiveness of sin, sin that was the product of a voluntary but universal unwillingness to obey God's law.[37] Fortunately, the new covenant of faith, in

[36] Locke, *Reasonableness*, 5, 7, 11.

[37] The pervasiveness was assumed in the *First Letter on Toleration* which he wrote for Limborch in the winter of 1684: 'He who wishes to enlist under the banner of Christ must first of all declare war upon his own vices, his own pride and lust' (*Epistola de Tolerantia*, 59). Locke's attitude had changed little from 1660 when he described Christ's mission 'to redeem men from the slavery of sin and Satan' (*Two Tracts*, 142).

which Christ reconciled repentant sinners to God, afforded all a second chance. Christ had found mankind, said Locke, 'under a corruption of manners and principles', freely came into the world 'to reform the corrupt state of degenerate man', and, with our faith in him as Messiah together with a life of repentance 'God of his free grace' would justify, would count that simple faith for righteousness.[38]

None of this undermined the philosopher's long-standing conviction that it was theoretically possible for men to discover the contents of the moral law without the aid of revelation, even though that had never been accomplished in full. What he was indicating concerned the impossibility of anyone obeying that law completely even if he were successful in discovering it unassisted. The Christian, if he would be saved, must first of all devote himself to a serious study of Scripture, where 'all the duties of morality lie there clear, plain and easy to be understood'.[39] He must then prove his adherence to the one necessary doctrine, belief in Christ, by living a life in accordance with the moral precepts enunciated therein.[40] God did not require perfect obedience under the covenant of faith, said Locke, for 'he knew our make, and the weakness of our constitution too well'; but if men obeyed to the best of their individual and unique abilities, 'he will give us his Spirit to help us to do what, and how we should'.[41] There had never been, nor would there ever be, sinless sons and daughters of Adam. In fact, the very existence of the covenant of faith bespoke the ubiquitous nature of sin. The new covenant, it is true, would excuse that sin, but not before the sinner had pledged obedience, and proved himself obedient, to the moral law as proof of his belief in Christ. The 'all merciful God' may have 'consulted the poor of this world, the bulk of mankind', when he promulgated

---

[38] Locke, *Reasonableness*, 110, 111, 112, 144; *First Vindication* (*Works*, vii. 175); *Second Vindication* (*Works*, vii. 353). The role of unmerited grace appeared earlier in a manuscript outline for one of Locke's discussion groups. Written in 1688 while he was living with the Quaker Benjamin Furly, Locke declared that all men must pray for 'the assistance of his spirit' to enlighten the understanding and subdue 'our corruptions': MS Locke c. 27, fol. 80.

[39] *Reasonableness*, 146–7. See also Locke to Richard King (1700: *Works*, x. 309–11).

[40] *Second Vindication*, 234: 'disobedience to any law of the least consequence, if it carry with it a disowning of the authority that made it, forfeits all'.

[41] *Reasonableness*, 112, 151.

the requirements of the law under the covenant of faith, but he had left those requirements virtually unchanged, the rule of right being 'the same that ever it was', and 'the obligation to observe it is also the same'. Unfeigned and unflagging repentance was for Locke 'as absolute a condition of the covenant of faith; and as necessary to be performed as that [faith]'.[42]

Sinful men, argued Locke, must turn to the plain words of Scripture to learn the precepts of the moral law. In this, Christians were both fortunate and heavily burdened: fortunate because they had been singled out by the Creator to receive the Word as an additional confirmation of the law of nature, with the promise of reward for those who obeyed; but burdened due to the obvious fact that they now had no plausible excuse for disobedience. Touching upon the increasingly debated problem of the fate of those to whom the Gospel message had never been promulgated, Locke rather lamely argued that the light of reason could lead even the heathen to God if properly employed; but one suspects that he was ill at ease with this unlikely scenario.[43] The fact was, in his view, that Christians would be expected to set the standard of godly living because of their access to revelation, and could be sure of a more rigorous accounting at the hands of their Maker in light of their unique status.

Critics like John Edwards would have none of this. Ignoring Locke's protest that he had indeed required more of Christians than belief in one article—that in fact 'our Saviour taught a great many other truths', which, once understood, had to be believed—Edwards remained disturbed by what he perceived to be the deistic tendencies of Locke's single doctrinal tenet.[44] At bottom he believed that Locke was engaged in a devious attempt, reminiscent of the purported Catholic grand design, to keep the bulk of Christians in ignorance about the Bible by suggesting that faith in Christ as Messiah was all that was required of them. How could Locke seriously profess an interest

---

[42] Ibid. 14, 103, 157.

[43] Ibid. 133. Locke was a dedicated reader of travel books. Some 275 titles, or 7.6 per cent of his final library collection consisted of books on geography and exploration: Laslett and Harrison, *Library of Locke*, 18.

[44] Locke, *Second Vindication* (*Works*, vii. 228).

in the salvation of men's souls, he enquired, 'when he puts out their Eyes, when he studies how to nurse them up in Ignorance and Blindness, and thereby to Ruine their Souls for ever'.[45] What was to prevent someone even more reckless in his reading of Scripture from deciding that even this one Lockean article of faith was simply one too many?

In a sense, it was unfortunate that the disagreements between Edwards and Locke were so sharp and that the language used throughout on both sides only served to widen the breach. For their differences, although not to be discounted, overshadowed what were in retrospect many shared ideas, and a substantial measure of agreement on the nature of man which, while of course unacknowledged by the principals, reflected that wider congruence of views shared by Anglicans and Puritans alike throughout the seventeenth century (as discussed in Chapter 1 above). Edwards's eighteenth-century biographer found his works (there were over forty titles) altogether 'too scholastic and calvinistic' for the Age of Enlightenment, and Edwards himself freely admitted his reputation as 'too forward a man', one who lacked modesty when taking up his pen in defence of Calvin's teachings, 'though they be the very same that our excellent Church teaches us'.[46] Yet in spite of his mostly deserved reputation as a misplaced product of another age, a sort of troublesome visitor from the era of the Civil War ready to risk all in defence of some quibble over an obscure passage in Corinthians, Edwards betrayed just enough Puritan trust in the power of reason and in the efficacy of natural religion, just enough confidence in the ability of man to recognize his sorry lot and attempt to do something about it, to make obvious to later, more detached observers a narrowness in the intellectual

[45] Edwards, *Socinianism Unmasked*, 59–60, 61. Edwards's misunderstanding of Locke is discussed by D. G. James, *The Life of Reason: Hobbes, Locke, Bolingbroke* (London: Longman, 1949), 105–6.

[46] Kippis, *Biographia Britannica*, i. 543; Edwards, *Sermons on Special Occasions and Subjects* (London: n.p., 1698), pref.; id., *The Arminian Doctrines Condemn'd by the Holy Scriptures* (London: n.p., 1711), pref. Towards the end of his career he betrayed some misgivings about various of the 'Harsh Passages' that punctuated his polemical writings, but overall he remained unrepentant: 'I should have been much more displeas'd, if I had not with Freedom and Sincerity told the World what my Apprehensions were, and had I not Utter'd Plain Truth' (*Some New Discoveries on the Uncertainty, Deficiency and Corruptions of Human Knowledge and Learning* (London: n.p., 1714), pref.).

'chasm' between himself and Locke neither man would ever have expected.

Edwards, it must be said, was very much a part of that intellectual world still governed by the quasi-magical directives of divine providence, one where the appearance of comets boded extreme natural calamities on earth, where the decay of trade and industry served as a warning and a penalty against what could only be a surfeit of vice throughout the nation, and where Biblical literalism on the matter of the earth's formation and astronomical location highlighted the importance of the human drama in God's overall plan for the universe.[47] But he was also a man who could write with some measure of force both about the argument from design and about the progressive unfolding of religious knowledge in order to convince those who might be leaning in the direction of atheism, and who had all but abandoned revelation, of the wisdom and justice of God from the evidence of the world around them. And he was a man who, very early in his career, could speak of sin as somehow antithetical to man's real nature, as 'rank poison' which 'corrupts and debauches our minds' and effects 'an alienation of man from himself'.[48] Now this was an important concession for anyone as 'Calvinistic' as Edwards to make. And yet he made the point again and again, even during those years of heated controversy with Locke, when the last thing that one might expect from his side was a profession of deep respect for human reason.

During a Commencement sermon at Cambridge in 1699 Edwards described the mind of man as being shaped in 'the very Image and Portraiture of God himself' and asserted that since we are rational creatures 'Religion and Virtue are engrafted in

---

[47] John Edwards, *Cometamantia: A Discourse of Comets* (London: n.p., 1684), 3; id., *Sermons on Special Occasions*, 141; id., *Brief Remarks on Mr. Whiston's New Theory of the Earth* (London: n.p., 1693), 23.

[48] id., *A Demonstration of the Existence of God from the Contemplation of the Visible Structure of the Greater and Lesser World* (London: n.p., 1696); id., *The Plague of the Heart* (Cambridge: n.p., 1665), 4, 6. Bishop Sprat's famous apologia *The History of the Royal Society of London, for the Improving of Natural Knowledge*, ed. J. I. Cope and H. W. Jones (St Louis, Mo.: Washington University Press, 1959) and Joseph Glanvill's *Plus Ultra: or, the Progress and Advancement of Knowledge since the Days of Aristotle* (London: James Collins, 1668) are two of the best contemporary sources which help set the stage for the argument from design. R. S. Crane ('Anglican Apologetics and the Idea of Progress', in *Idea of Humanities*, i. 226–36), discusses Edwards's theory of progress.

our very Nature.'[49] He was speaking here in support of the doctrine of innate ideas, but innate ideas in their dispositional form, where men 'have not the use of Original Notions presently, or in our Infancy or Childhood'. While ostensibly rejecting Lockean epistemology, Edwards's admission that every rational being 'must take some time to act the Man, to exert his Thinking Faculty' before the innate notions of good and evil implanted at birth begin to have any influence, placed him virtually beside his opponent on the question of the need for education into morality. Where for Locke ill-education, custom, and habit were guaranteed to lead the *tabula-rasa* child down the slippery path to perdition, Edwards perceived the same factors as effectively stamping out the early seeds of morality, the innate notions of the god-like rational soul. Locke himself found little point to the claims of the dispositional innatists, so close was their analysis of ideas to his own.[50] Edwards recognized the similarity too, but insisted that it was just as plausible to argue that men have no rational soul for a number of years because they do not exert it as to claim (as Locke did against the proponents of innateness) that they possess no innate notions due to the fact that most of them are not discovered until one reaches maturity and the full use of reason. Edwards could not jettison innate ideas because to do so would be tantamount in his mind to rejecting the divine presence within each man; it would be to 'detract from the Divinity it self, and from the Essential Nature and Guise of Mankind'. Edwards the Calvinist wanted to strengthen the argument for man's reasonable nature, wanted to make sin a voluntary action against 'those Principles of Nature which are implanted in all Men's Breasts, and which all assent to, and cannot be ignorant of'. And while he constantly lectured about original sin and predestination as

---

[49] John Edwards, *The Eternal and Intrinsick Reasons of Good and Evil* (Cambridge: University Press, 1699), 4, 12; id., *Free Discourse*, 39, 51. In a sermon preached before Charles II, Edwards declared that men were obliged by God to improve and cultivate their rational faculties, understanding, and judgement, with the aid 'of our Bodily Senses', by 'Observation and well-grounded Experience' (*Sermons on Special Occasions*, 10).

[50] See Locke's response to James Lowde's *A Discourse Concerning the Nature of Man* (London: Walter Kettilby, 1694), printed in the Nidditch edition of the *Essay* (354–5). See also Locke's criticism of Burnet's theory of dispositional innateness printed in Porter, 'Marginalia Lockeana', 35.

necessary doctrines of the Christian faith, he simultaneously joined hands with his Puritan contemporary across the ocean, Increase Mather, and with his Latitudinarian enemy closer to home, John Locke, in exhorting the depraved to 'strive to enter in at the straight gate'.[51]

Edwards also followed Locke in his treatment of the law of nature, or natural religion: once sufficient in themselves to discover the full law of morality, 'Nature and Reason by the fall of Adam, and by the Evil Habits and Customs of Men' had lost that sufficiency and all now required the special guidance of God in Scripture to assist them in the way of virtue. The apostasy of the first man, he asserted, had corrupted our natural faculties and infused us with 'an inward propensity to what is vicious', but by the special grace of the Holy Spirit we might once again do good in the eyes of the Creator.[52] Edwards thus placed himself squarely on the side of those Puritans who were determined to avoid the Antinomianism inherent in predestinarian theology, and in so doing he shifted to a vision of the Fall where the loss of original righteousness, as opposed to total and irreversible depravity, became the central feature of Adam's unwelcome legacy to humanity. He moved, in other words, towards the Broad-Church vision of John Locke, where men gifted with reason in the image of the Creator, but prone to evil after the fashion of Adam, might even yet enjoy the blessings of eternal life, might still be saved in spite of themselves. The angry exchange with Locke over necessary doctrine obscured this deeper agreement on the nature of man, but this should not prevent our acknowledgement of its existence. To his own discredit Edwards carried on with his offensive long after Locke was in the grave, convinced that there should be no repose, no eternal peace for one who dared question Calvinist formulae, all the while never sensing the true extent of his own movement away from those formulae.

Locke's all-important disagreement with the Deists, and agreement with Edwards—his assumption in the *Reasonableness* that salvation was impossible without the gratuitous saving grace of Christ, combined with the nearly Thomistic view of

---

[51] Quoting Mather, *Awakening Truths*, in *The Puritans*, ed. P. Miller and T. Johnson, 337.

[52] Edwards, *Free Discourse*, 70; id., *Eternal and Intrinsick Reasons*, 5.

man implicit in that assumption—was recognized and applauded by at least one of his readers. The Nonconformist divine and advocate of religious toleration Samuel Bold sided with Locke against Edwards and attempted to allay whatever doubts had emerged regarding the philosopher's orthodoxy.[53] 'You have bin treated very Injuriously, and with detestable Disingenuity', he wrote to Locke after having read the *Second Vindication of the Reasonableness* and then having reflected on Edwards's charges.[54] Bold's own efforts to demonstrate the groundless nature of the attacks against the minimal creed, while rebuffed by Edwards, further illuminate Locke's basic position. For Bold followed Locke in identifying faith in Christ as the one necessary article, in observing that Christians were required to work constantly towards an understanding of all that was revealed in Scripture, and in stressing the gratuitous nature of saving grace and mankind's unending need for that grace. He wrote that

When we are thoroughly sensible that we are Sinners, under the Curse of the Law, and justly obnoxious to the most heavy displeasure and wrath of Almighty God, and that there is no way for our obtaining Peace with Him, Pardon and Salvation, but by Jesus Christ, then our knowing him to be the only, the all-sufficient, and a most compassionate and gracious Saviour of Sinners, will dispose and influence to resign up our selves without reservation to his conduct.[55]

Bold was fully attuned to Locke's purpose in approaching Scripture without preconceptions, as the common people 'who were principally concerned in what was delivered by the Inspired writers' would interpret it. He too had found the glosses

---

[53] In 1697 Bold appended 'Some Animadversions on Mr. Edwards Reflections on the Reasonableness of Christianity, and on his book, Entitled, Socinianism Unmasked' to his *A Short Discourse on the True Knowledge of Christ Jesus* (London: A. and J. Churchill, 1697). He later wrote *Some Considerations on the Principal Objections and Arguments against Mr. Locke's Essay* (London: A. Churchill, 1699) and, after Locke's death, *A Discourse Concerning the Resurrection of the Same Body* (London: S. Holt, 1705). The last two works came to the defence of Locke's suggestion in the *Essay* (4. 3. 6) that God might annex the power of thought to matter. Their friendship remained firm until Locke's death. In 1703 Locke wrote 'Some Thoughts Concerning Reading and Study for a Gentleman' at the prompting of Bold. The manuscript copy of the work is in Bold's hand. See *Thoughts on Ed.* 397–401.

[54] Bold to Locke (26 Mar. 1697: vi, no. 2232).

[55] Bold, *Short Discourse*, 9, 29, 33.

of the learned over the ages to be a major source of confusion and division within the Protestant Churches of England, making knowledge of the moral law even more difficult for men to attain.[56] But the purpose of both men in their respective undertakings, as it had been for Limborch and Popple in theirs, was not to dismiss or to mitigate the seriousness of the Fall: rather, both sought to highlight the nature of mankind's individual responsibility for a condition brought on by Adam's transgression in Paradise—his loss of righteousness—and the impossibility of avoiding sin in the aftermath of that signal failing. Their mutual emphasis on the importance of the work of Christ, where the first movement towards salvation had to be initiated by God in his accounting faith for righteousness, emphatically and unambiguously rejected both the misconceptions of the Deists and the creedal excesses of the Calvinists. For Bold, as for Locke, as for their Broad-Church sympathizers, the final result could be salvation for all, but the starting-point, unlike that of the Deists, had to be a recognition of mankind's voluntary repudiation of God's sovereignty, which after all was the Christian definition of original sin. As the Latitudinarian Archbishop of Canterbury wrote with regard to the instruction of young children, 'they are to be made sensible of the great degeneracy and corruption of human nature . . . and our way of Recovery out of this miserable state by Jesus Christ; whom God hath sent in our Nature to purchase and accomplish the Redemption and Salvation of Mankind, from the captivity of Sin and Satan, and from the Damnation of Hell.' The words were those of John Tillotson, Locke's closest friend within the Anglican clerical establishment after the Glorious Revolution and a churchman long considered by historians to have been instrumental in helping usher in the Augustan age of prudential ethics and rational religion. Perhaps the claim is justified, but not on the basis of statements similar to the one above. Tillotson's death in 1694 left Locke 'scarcely anyone whom I can freely consult about theological uncertainties'. He undoubtedly could have used the Archbishop's support the following

---

[56] Bold to Locke (11 Apr. 1699: vi, no. 2567). Samuel Bold, *A Brief Account of the First Rise of the Name Protestant* (London: n.p., 1688), 32.

year, when he attempted to settle many of those uncertainties for himself with the publication of *The Reasonableness of Christianity*.[57]

Locke returned to the issues first raised in his book on religion five years later, after his retirement in 1700 from public life. He had spent a good part of those years in the public service as a political adviser to such Whig luminaries as John Somers and as a Commissioner on the influential Board of Trade. When not in London researching, holding meetings of the Board, and making recommendations on everything from the appointment of colonial governors to the best remedy for rising domestic pauperism, Locke retreated to his home at Oates, there to recoup his health and to combat the growing criticism of his religious ideas as set forth in both the *Reasonableness* and the *Essay*.[58] The sudden negative commentary which descended upon the latter work bothered him in particular, especially since so few objections to his way of ideas had been raised prior to 1695.[59] Turning his attention to a systematic study of St Paul's Epistles, Locke undertook for himself a further explication of right belief as he understood it. Once again he would be guided by the principle of free enquiry as set forth in his *Essay*, where 'The floating of other Mens Opinions in our brains makes us not one jot more knowing, though they happen to be true.' His method was exhaustive, tedious even, and reflected the sort of textual analysis carried out by his friend Isaac Newton, who as early as the winter of 1690–1 had visited Locke at Oates and begun to exchange ideas with him on Biblical interpretation— an undertaking which Newton considered as important as his scientific work in forwarding true worship and knowledge of

[57] Tillotson, 'Of the Education of Children' (*Works*, iii. 495); Locke to Limborch (11 Dec. 1694: v, no. 1826); Cragg, *Reason and Authority*, 20–1; L. G. Locke, *Tillotson*, 67, 164; I. Simon, ed., *Three Restoration Divines*, 125, 126. In 1703 Locke recommended Tillotson's books as models of 'clearness and propriety in the language that a man uses' (*Thoughts on Ed.* 399).

[58] On the Board of Trade and Locke's duties, see Andrews, *Colonial Period*, iv. 272–315; D. Ogg, *England in the Reigns of James II and William III* (Oxford: Clarendon Press, 1969), 305–6; S. S. Webb, *The Governors-General: The English Army and the Definition of the Empire* (Chapel Hill, NC: University of North Carolina Press, 1979), 98–9, 111–12, 264–5, 463. Locke's proposal to the Board for reform of the Poor Laws is printed in Fox Bourne, *Locke*, ii. 377–90.

[59] 'My book crept into the world about six or seven years ago, without any opposition' (Locke to Molyneux, 22 Feb. 1697: vi, no. 2202).

God.[60] Locke first copied out the full text of each Epistle, paraphrased the original words, and then added his own explanatory notes at the end. His commentaries on Romans, the Epistle which he considered essential for anyone 'that would have an enlarged view of true Christianity', and which contained that most troublesome of passages for the historic Pauline conception of original sin, Romans 5:12, are of greatest interest for our purposes.[61]

˙ In the notes, Locke reiterated his unorthodox interpretation of Paul's words. The text 'Wherefore, as by one man sin entered into the world, and death by sin; and so death passed upon all men for that all have sinned' he took in what was an unquestionably Pelagian sense. The final three words, Locke explained, indicated only that all of Adam's offspring had become mortal as a result of the Fall. He identified the parallel to the entire clause in 1 Corinthians 15:22 ('For as in Adam all die, even so in Christ shall all be made alive') and refused to view the state of mortality as in any sense a punishment inflicted upon the descendants of the first man. The gift of eternal life had been first restored through the promulgation of Mosaic law; then, failing our obedience to that, through the atoning sacrifice and the new covenant. Christ had redeemed men from · their bondage to a life of sin, said Locke, but a self-imposed bondage remained where the carnal appetites overruled the promptings of reason. For the first time he directly equated the natural inclinations of man, the attractions of sense and present pleasure, with sin against God, and he did so in conjunction with

---

[60] *Essay*, 1. 4. 23. This theme was actually one of long standing for Locke: see *Two Tracts*, 174, and Locke's advice regarding study written in 1677 (MS Locke f. 2, fols. 90–2, printed in *Thoughts on Ed.* 408–9). Newton to Locke (7 Feb. 1691: iv, no. 1357; 30 June 1691: iv, no. 1405). Locke sent Newton a manuscript copy of the *Third Letter for Toleration* for criticism and advice: Locke to Newton (26 July 1692: iv, no. 1517). Frank Manuel (*A Portrait of Isaac Newton* (Cambridge, Mass.: Belknap Press, 1968), 184) writes that 'Later eighteenth century anticlerical rationalists for whom these two men were ideal heroes of pure reason would have been incapable of comprehending a relationship in which such dark superstitions as alchemy or interpretation of prophecy and other Biblical texts played the central role.' Locke's influence on Newton, especially on his rejection of innate ideas, is discussed by G. A. J. Rogers, 'Locke, Newton and the Cambridge Platonists', *Journal of the History of Ideas*, 15 (1979), 195–205.

[61] Locke, *Paraphrase and Notes*, 486. This particular paraphrase was first published by the Churchills in 1707. Newton received a copy of the manuscript for comment in 1703 (Newton to Locke, 15 May 1703, printed in King, *Life of Locke*, 225–6).

a discussion of what was probably the second most controversial passage in Romans. We recall that Limborch had spoken of mankind's 'natural Inclination of attaining that which is grateful to the Flesh' as being only a 'propensity to sin' and 'Not sin properly so called'; now in commenting on Romans 6:6, where 'our old man is crucified with him, that the body of sin might be destroyed, that henceforth we should not serve sin', Locke expressed the opinion that Paul meant to imply by the last two words 'the gieving our selves up to the conduct of our *sinful,* [emphasis mine] carnal appetites'.[62] It was a telling statement, this equating sin with the immediate attractions of the flesh; but in making it Locke appeared to be drifting in the direction of the type of dualism suggested in Romans 7:22–4 but ultimately rejected by Paul. The 'old man', Locke believed, was for Paul 'our wicked and corrupt fleshy self' or 'our carnal sinful propensities'.[63] Too much movement here and the philosopher would have become entrapped by the always suspect Platonic definition of sin—where the divine element in man, the faculty of reason, struggles first to bridle and then to transcend the sinful demands of the flesh, where there was believed to be no essential defect at the centre of human personality.

But Locke was plainly unwilling to go this far. His previous observations in the *Essay* concerning the complicity of reason where individuals eschew the greater good whenever it is not seen to be within their immediate interests, and on the power of the mind to withhold judgement until one's true self-interest is discerned, effectively precluded his ever falling prey to the dualistic error. Sin remained at bottom for Locke a matter of choice, of Pelagian deliberation. But sin was also very un-Pelagian in its universality, in the sorry fact that each and every individual had opted for the way of sin at some point in his life, thus making necessary Christ's sacrifice. No longer could men save themselves. He had said so in the *Reasonableness*, and now, in his notes on Paul's Epistle to the Ephesians, he reconfirmed it as if to make even more obvious to those who might suspect his larger motives his objection to the Pelagian notion of unaided perfection: salvation was by faith alone and with faith came the

---

[62] Locke, *Paraphrase*, 523, 533.
[63] Ibid. 533.

assisting grace of God to help men live lives of greater rectitude; but 'for the attaining this Gift of Faith, Men do, or can do, nothing: Grace hitherto does all, and Works are wholly excluded'.[64] One would be hard put to find a more Calvinistic definition of prevenient divine favour in all the literature of the seventeenth century.

· 'A Christian I am sure I am,' Locke had asserted defensively in 1697, 'because I believe Jesus to be the Messiah, the King and Saviour promised, and sent by God'. The charges of Socinianism he had perhaps half expected, knowing the prevailing climate of religious opinion in the 1690s, so all-encompassing was that ill-defined term of opprobrium.[65] But that he was troubled enough by them to begin anew an exhaustive re-evaluation of the foundations of his belief so late in life attests his deep religiosity. And that the vision of sinful humanity remained with him until those last autumn days in 1704 when Damaris Masham read Scripture by his bedside as life slowly deserted him is indicative of something about the man that was very different from the myth of Locke as the inaugurator of the Age of Reason.

There is no denying the fact that Locke had travelled some distance away from the declaration of the Elizabethan bishops on the matter of original sin. Back in 1692, replying to criticisms made by the Reverend Jonas Proust to his *Letter on Toleration*, he had asked whether 'one who is in the communion of the church of England, sincerely seeking the truth, may not raise to himself such difficulties concerning the doctrine of original sin as may puzzle him, though he be a man of study; and whether he may not push his inquiries so far, as to be staggered in his opinion?' Locke believed it necessary for all thinking Christians to untangle the interpretative quagmire for themselves, and so he took the strongest exception to anyone who would impose upon others their special understanding of Articles 9–13.[66] He was

---

[64] Locke, *Paraphrase*, 629. Locke is here commenting on Eph. 2:8 'For by grace are ye saved, through faith; and that not of yourselves; it is the gift of God.' Recall the discussion in ch. 1 above.

[65] McLachlan, *Socinianism*, 3. Charges of atheism also covered a broad spectrum of unorthodoxy and did not always indicate disbelief in God: see S. G. Hefelbower, *The Relation of John Locke to English Deism* (Chicago: University Press, 1918), 84; Mintz, *Hunting of Leviathan*, 39. Locke, *Second Vindication* (*Works*, vii. 359).

[66] Locke, *A Third Letter for Toleration* (*Works*, vi. 411). On Proust see Wood, *Life and Times*, iii. 263.

convinced that no one deserved God's 'wrath and damnation' for the sins of another man, nor were the sons of Adam utterly incapable of participating in the work of salvation by faith with their voluntary works of repentance. He had early on in his life come to associate the Calvinist-Augustinian tincture of the Thirty-Nine Articles with a Christianity devoid of moral urgency and singularity of purpose; he had stepped into the shadow of his fifth-century predecessor, and revived the controversies of Pelagius' Rome in Restoration London. But he refused to countenance the extreme environmentalism of the Pelagian intellectual world, refused to accept the assertion that 'Everything good, and everything evil . . . is not born with us but done by us.' Perhaps, under the best of circumstances, most things good and most things evil might be predicated on one's education in the larger sense—Locke might have been willing to entertain this notion in his more hopeful moments. After all, he had devoted a good part of his adult life to trying to alert his fellows to the need for and the possibility of moral reform. The chances for success may have been sharply diminished as a result of the Fall, but they had never been annulled by it. Still, that they had been, in Locke's view, unquestionably straitened is certainly one significant measure of the difference between Locke's Christianity and that of the fifth-century monk with whom he is so often compared.

6

Finding Common Ground

IN the spring of 1695 an obscure Staffordshire attorney by the name of Henry Hatrell wrote to Locke of the 'pleasure and profit' which he had received from reading the *Essay* and wondered whether the author might share with a man 'of the meanest Rank' his thoughts on baptism and faith. Unfortunately, the reply is no longer extant, but it seems more than likely that Locke's letter touched upon these matters; for in June the attorney was writing again, this time to announce that the *Essay* had greatly aided him in rethinking 'severall Doctrines that I had taken upon trust'. Enclosed with the letter was a short fragment entitled 'An Enquiry touching originall sin', Hatrell's attempt to clarify for himself the meaning of the Fall in light of the new insights contained in *An Essay concerning Human Understanding*. It is a revealing document, an apposite statement of just how dexterously the Lockean polemic against innate ideas might be enlisted on the side of straightforward Pelagianism in the late seventeenth century. And given the more general rise of Deism in the 1690s, Hatrell's unambiguous logic could easily have contributed additional tension to a spiritual atmosphere in which Locke's pleas on behalf of his own religious orthodoxy seemed, at least to his numerous critics, wholly disingenuous. That it did not, that the logic was ignored by most, is of more than minor significance in our attempt to gauge the religious sensibilities of the age.

It was impossible, thought Hatrell, for the children of Adam to be infected with original sin, for if in fact all ideas were the product of sensation and reflection, and if, as Locke had argued, no law was binding until it was known, 'and if Sin be a transgression of a knowne Law either in thought word or deed, and if Children before growne up to some maturity cannot understand the Law, I infer that all the thoughts and actions of Children whilst uncapable of knowing the Law are not sins'. The unruliness of excessive appetite in opposition to a known law was indeed sin, he maintained, but mere 'irregularity in his affections', the product of Adam's fall from grace and the normal state of his posterity, did not constitute original sin as most divines had interpreted it since the time of St Paul. For Hatrell, the epistemology of the *Essay* made the notion that all men enter into the world defiled by sin 'altogether unintelligible': Augustinianism had become as dubious as innateness.[1]

The *Reasonableness of Christianity* had yet to appear in print when Hatrell forwarded his second letter, but it would not be long before a wave of negative commentary descended upon the *Essay*, criticism provoked by what appeared to be a general concern that Locke's doctrines undermined orthodox religion, promoted epistemological scepticism, and forwarded the cause of Deism. Locke did not respond to most of these hostile observations (the bulk of which he believed to be the product of a deliberate plot to discredit him), telling his friend Molyneux in June 1694 that there was 'so little material, in the objections against me, that I have passed them all by, but one Gentleman's'. When he did respond to selected individuals, it was with barely concealed impatience for what he perceived to be his opponent's obtuseness or deliberate obstinance in the face of clear and credible evidence; and he refused to waste his time 'at the pleasure of every one, who may have a mind to pick holes in my book, and shew his skill in the art of confutation'.[2] The fear of some cabal working against him was unwarranted, but his more general apprehension was not totally without foundation. For despite more than one voice raised in dissent after the initial publication of the book in 1689, Locke had fared none too badly at the hands of his reading public before the middle years of the decade. His college friend Tyrrell reported from Oxford in early 1690 'that your booke is received here with much greater applause: [*sic*] then I find it is at London; the persons here being most addicted to contemplation, as there to action'. One Oxford

---

[1] Hatrell to Locke (25 Mar. 1695: v, no. 1866; 3 June 1695: v, no. 1914); cf. *Two Treatises*, 2. 6. 57. Hatrell was a Dissenter active in Newcastle politics and administrator of a grammar-school trust created for the instruction of the poor of the city: *Victoria County History: Staffordshire*, ed. R. B. Pugh (London: Oxford University Press, 1963), viii. 56, 65.

[2] Locke to Molyneux (28 June 1694: v, no. 1753); id., 'Answer to Remarks upon an *Essay concerning Human Understanding*', in *Works*, iv. 189. Locke was responding here to Thomas Burnet's *Remarks* (1697).

don, Dr John Wynne of Jesus College, requested permission to print an abridgement for use by undergraduates, while fellow-physician and philosopher Richard Burthogge found the epistemology of the *Essay* so similar to that contained in his own earlier *Organum Vetus et Novum* (1678) that he dedicated his new *Essay on Reason* to Locke in 1694. The influence and popularity of the text was such by 1692 that Molyneux's friend George Ashe, Provost of Trinity College, Dublin, made it required reading for every undergraduate; and by September of that year the first edition had been sold out in London.[3]

Nevertheless, by 1697 the *Essay* and its author were under what seemed like constant assault, especially from the religious community. Something in the book, he told Molyneux in February, 'I know not what, is at last spyed out in it, that is like to be troublesome, and therefore, it must be an ill book, and be treated accordingly'.[4] Locke was deeply disturbed by the criticism, convinced as he was of his firm commitment to the spirit and letter of the Christian faith as revealed to him in the Scriptures. He believed himself to be as devout a Christian as the most vociferous of his detractors, and, as we shall see, examination of the religious sensibilities of those principal detractors will bear him out. Locke's assailants have already been treated in conjunction with the dispute over the epistemological doctrines of the *Essay*;[5] in some respects, these men simply followed Hatrell in drawing their own special conclusions concerning the intentions of the author. The clash between Locke and his critics proved to be of such magnitude that their shared Protestant position was again obscured by the smoke of battle over what were really quite peripheral issues. For the contemporary critics, and this includes the irascible Edwards, never fastened on to the issue of original sin in the manner that

---

[3] The *Essay's* reception is thoroughly treated by Yolton, *Locke and Way of Ideas*. Tyrrell to Locke (18 Feb. 1690: iv, no. 1248); Locke to John Freke (11 Mar. 1695: v, no. 1859; 2 Apr. 1695: v, no. 1872); Molyneux to Locke (22 Dec. 1692: iv, no. 1579); Locke to Molyneux (20 Sept. 1692: iv, no. 1538); John Wynne to Locke (21 Jan. 1695: v, no. 1843). Burthogge is uncharitably discussed by Wood, *Athenae*, iv. 560: Margaret W. Landes (ed., *The Philosophical Writings of Richard Burthogge* (Chicago: Open Court, 1921), introd.) offers a more balanced assessment.

[4] Locke to Molyneux (22 Feb. 1697: vi, no. 2002).

[5] By John Yolton in *Locke and Way of Ideas*.

Hatrell and, later on, eighteenth-century commentators did.[6] The matter simply did not greatly trouble the individuals who opposed the *Essay*, and for that reason it might be worth taking another look at some of them to try to understand how, at one level, men could seem to each other unalterably at odds over issues of no small import to religion, while at another they had so much in common, their ideas converging on the shared ground of Protestant anthropology and the defence of Augustine's *City of God*.

The first critic to appear in print against the *Essay* was John Norris, a churchman from the parish of Newton St Loe outside Bristol. He was the son of a Nonconformist divine from Wiltshire who had been ejected from his living at the time of the Restoration. Educated first at Winchester and then at Exeter College, Oxford, Norris had early in his undergraduate career become enamoured of Platonic and Cartesian philosophy, with a special interest in Descartes's metaphysical dualism. After receiving his BA in 1680, he was elected Fellow of All Souls College in the summer of that year, was ordained in 1684, and continued in residence at Oxford until 1689—at which time he left academia, married, and became Rector of Newton St Loe.[7] In 1690 he appended to his *Christian Blessedness* some thoughts on the *Essay* from the perspective of one who had just recently been converted to the epistemological and metaphysical theory of Occasionalism, as formulated by the French thinker Nicolas Malebranche. There Norris expressed serious reservations about the *Essay* because of what he thought to be its single-minded concern with naturalistic explanations to the problem of knowledge, and because of its alleged assumption that an intimate connection existed between the world of nature and Norris's Neoplatonic world of pure ideas.

In the *Essay*, ideas had been vaguely defined alternatively as 'whatsoever is the Object of the Understanding when a man

---

[6] Edwards (*Some Thoughts Concerning Atheism*, 110) noted Locke's unorthodoxy here, but he did not press the matter. John Milner (*An Account of Mr Locke's Religion* (London: T. Nutt, 1700), 186) thought that Locke had denied original sin.

[7] R. Acworth, *The Philosophy of John Norris of Bemerton, 1657–1712* (New York: Hildesheim, 1979), 1–8; F. Powicke, *A Dissertation on John Norris of Bemerton* (London: George Philip and Son, 1894), 1–7; F. I. Mackinnon, *The Philosophy of John Norris of Bemerton* (Baltimore, Md.: Review Publishing Co., 1910), 4–10; Kippis, *Biographia Britannica*, v. 3246–8.

thinks', and 'Whatsoever the Mind perceives in it self, or is the immediate object of Perception, Thought or Understanding'. At the very outset of the work, Locke had dismissed any possible effort on his part to 'meddle with the Physical Consideration of the Mind . . . wherein its Essence consists, or by what Motions of our Spirits, or Alterations of our Bodies, we come to have any Sensation by our Organs, or any Ideas in our Understandings', as being beyond the scope of his immediate investigation. Norris, however, while agreeing with Locke in his rejection of innate ideas, thought that the author should first have explored the nature of the thing that he was discussing before attempting to discover its origins. 'For how can any Propositions be form'd with any certainty concerning an Idea,' he asked, 'that it is or is not Innate, that it does or does not come in at the Senses, before the meaning of the Word Idea be stated, and the nature of the thing, at least in general, be understood?'[8] Following Descartes, Norris thought it impossible for bodies existing outside us to have any connection with mind or spirit; thus they were, according to him, incapable of producing ideas of themselves within the mind. Locke's view that external objects, while not united to our minds, have the power to produce ideas in them 'by Impulse' had for Norris the appearance of dangerous materialism. If bodies be the cause of all sensation, he later wrote, 'then it would be in the power of Bodies to make us happy or miserable, to reward or punish us, to perfect or deteriorate our Condition', and to become the final end of our esteem and devotion. The Occasionalist theory of Malebranche, where God acted to communicate ideas to us directly at specific moments when bodies affect one another, seemed to Norris the only plausible solution to the dilemma: 'What else need, and what else can be the immediate Object of our Understanding but the Divine Ideas, the Omniform Essence of God?' Finite men thus have their ideas directly from the infinite Creator, who is the embodiment of every perfect idea in the universe: the appearance of bodies acting on our senses was simply the occasion for God to place certain ideas in our minds; these ideas had no

---

[8] *Essay*, 1. 1. 8; 2. 8. 8; John Norris, 'Reflections Upon a Late Essay Concerning Human Understanding', in *Christian Blessedness: or Discourses Upon the Beatitudes* (London: S. Manship, 1690), 3.

natural connection whatsoever with those bodies and their motions.[9]

Despite this criticism, Norris thought very highly of the *Essay* on many points, and even recommended it to a friend as amongst the more worthwhile books in any programme of reading and education. He openly acknowledged 'that the Author is just such a kind of Writer as I like, one that has thought much, and well, and who freely writes what he thinks'; and trusting Locke to be a man of 'Ingenuity and Candor', he assumed that his criticisms would be received in the best spirit of free intellectual enquiry.[10] For his part Locke refrained from taking up this early challenge to his epistemological views—and even went so far as to assist the young clergyman in forwarding his career in the Church. It appears that Norris had befriended Lady Masham in the 1680s, probably before Locke began exchanging letters with her in 1682. The fondness was deep on Norris's side; he addressed two of his Neoplatonic essays to her and assumed, incorrectly as it turned out, that the daughter of Cudworth shared his belief in the revised Cartesianism of Malebranche.[11] By 1691, Norris's situation at Newton St Loe had become less than satisfactory. His penetrating sermons, laced as they undoubtedly were with a strong dose of Platonic idealism, were not being very well received by the provincial

---

[9] *Essay*, 2. 8. 11, 12. In his *Conduct of the Understanding* (ed. T. Fowler (New York: Burt Franklin, 1970), 28) Locke stated that 'Outward corporeal objects ... constantly importune our senses, and captivate our appetites'. Norris, 'A Discourse Concerning the Measure of Divine Love', in *Practical Discourses Upon Several Subjects*, 3 vols. (London: S. Manship, 1693), iii. 36; id., 'Cursory Reflections', 31. On Norris's borrowings, see J. H. Muirhead, *The Platonic Tradition in Anglo-Saxon Philosophy* (London: Allen and Unwin, 1931), 72–105; M. H. Carre, *Phases of Thought in England* (Oxford: Clarendon Press, 1949), 271–2; K. Fisher, *History of Modern Philosophy: Descartes and His School*, trans. J. P. Gordy (New York: Scribner's Sons, 1887), 554–60; Martineau, *Types of Ethical Theory*, i. 159–66.

[10] Norris, 'Reflections Upon a Late Essay', in *Christian Blessedness*, 41–2; 'Letter from Mr Norris to Corinna for the Direction of Her Studies', in *Pylades and Corinna*, ed. Richard Gwinnett (London: n.p., 1732), 204.

[11] While Neoplatonism did not take hold at Oxford, Norris corresponded with Henry More from 1683 and may have met Lady Masham, at that date Damaris Cudworth, through More. The correspondence is appended to Norris's *The Theory and Regulation of Love* (Oxford: Henry Clements, 1688). Gilbert D. McEven, in his introduction to the Augustan Reprint Society's edition of Norris's 'Reflections', (Los Angeles: 1961), p. 2, thinks that Masham admired Norris solely 'as one who followed in her father's footsteps'. Her own early Platonism is evident from the correspondence with Locke: see, for example, Damaris Cudworth to Locke (16 Feb. 1682: ii, no. 682) where she discusses John Smith's *Select Discourses* with Locke.

parishioners, most of whom were more concerned with scratch-
ing a meagre living from the Somerset soil than with their
rector's weekly flights into the insubstantial realm of ideas. At
any rate, by the spring of 1691 Norris was actively seeking a new
(and preferably more hospitable) parish. With the help of Lady
Masham, and the timely intervention of Locke, the clergyman
was presented by Locke's good friend Thomas Herbert, earl of
Pembroke, to a more lucrative living at Bemerton near
Salisbury. 'Sir I have a very gratefull sense', Norris wrote to
Locke after learning of the philosopher's role on his behalf, 'of
your great generosity towards me, which indeed is of so rare and
singular a nature that it surprises me no lesse than it obliges me,
and raises my wonder to as high a pitch as it does my gratitude.'
Locke answered that there was no need for Norris to feel in any
way obliged to him, for he acted entirely to advance the interests
of 'a person [whose] learning and parts I very much estemd and
with a Lady I thought deserved a better station in the world'. In
fact, he enjoyed being of some small service to 'a worthy man' of
'reason and thought'. To all appearances relations seemed good
between the philosopher and his critic in that summer of 1692.[12]

Unhappily for Norris, however, he remained in Locke's eyes
'a worthy man' for less than six months. The rather mundane
occasion for Locke's displeasure had to do with a letter which
Lady Masham had entrusted to Norris for delivery to Locke at
his lodgings in London. When the letter finally reached its
intended recipient through another intermediary, the seal had
been broken and, rightly or wrongly, Norris was blamed.
Protesting his innocence, he appeared nonplussed by Locke's
'hast to expres a Resentment upon so doubtful an Occasion'.
Others, meanwhile, came to Norris's defence, but the regrettable incident signalled the abrupt end of their friendship and
also apparently provoked Locke into writing three separate
rejoinders to Norris's Neoplatonic alternative to the epistemology of the *Essay*. As John Yolton has observed, Locke never took
criticism very well anyway. His growing contempt for the
follower of Malebranche was made plain in a fragment written
late in the year, where he defended his own refusal to discuss the

---

[12] Norris to Locke (14 Apr. 1692: iv, no. 1492); Locke to Norris (6 June 1692: iv,
no. 1505). Norris hinted at his problems in the parish of Newton St Loe in his preface to
Christian Blessedness. See also Powicke, *Norris*, 17; R. Acworth, *Philosophy of Norris*, 9.

nature of ideas while labelling Norris one of those 'happy Genius's who thinke they either are not or ought not to be ignorant of anything'.[13] He followed this with a more extensive 'Examination of Malebranche', composed in 1693, but only published in 1706, and with 'Remarks upon Some of Mr. Norris's Books', written soon after the 'Examination' and first appearing in 1720. In the latter piece Locke ridiculed the notion that men know the nature of their ideas any better when they consider them to be somehow part of the divine essence. Malebranche and his English disciple, Locke was convinced, had done nothing to explain the manner in which ideas were produced in the mind, 'in what alteration of the mind the perception consists'. In point of fact, the doctrine of 'seeing all things in God', by making the mind of man a passive instrument in the knowing process, actually pointed (or so Locke believed) in the direction of determinism, 'to the religion of Hobbes and Spinosa, by resolving all, even the thoughts and will of men, into an irresistible fatal necessity'.[14]

The unfortunate incident of the letter quite finished whatever hopes Norris might have entertained about Locke's interest in the friendly give-and-take of honest intellectual exchange; but in spite of the break in relations, Norris remained open-minded enough to extend to his erstwhile friend the benefit of the doubt regarding Locke's meaning when discussing ideas in the *Essay*. Referring to that work in his own major statement on the Occasionalist way of ideas, Norris conceded that Locke might not have meant to imply 'that sensible Objects do send or convey Ideas from themselves to our Minds by the mediation of the Senses' (which would have validated his earlier suspicions),

---

[13] Yolton, *Locke and Way of Ideas*, 13. Locke's first reply is entitled 'J. L. to Mr. Norris' (MS Locke c. 28, fols. 108–13; printed in R. Acworth, 'Locke's First Reply to John Norris', *Locke Newsletter* 2 (1971), 7–11.

[14] The incident and Locke's critical response to Norris are discussed by C. Johnson, 'Locke's Examination of Malebranche and John Norris', *Journal of the History of Ideas*, 19 (1958), 551–8. Locke's friend Martha Lockhart, while suggesting that Norris did indeed break the seal, told Locke 'I believe what he did, was out of a very good designe, that he might take an occasion to advise you both' (Lockhart to Locke, 25 Oct. 1692: iv, no. 1550). Robert Pawling, who suspected Norris, wrote sarcastically 'they talk of Platonic love but it usually ends thus but his peeping is a crime unpardonable' (Pawling to Locke, 3 Nov. 1692: iv, no. 1560). Both the 'Examination of Malebranche' and the 'Remarks' are contained in Locke's *Works* (ix. 211–55; x. 247–59). Quotations are from 'Remarks', 248, 255–6.

but rather that they served only as the occasions for our having any ideas. Given that Locke, probably out of consideration for Lady Masham, did not publish any of his criticisms of Norris, it is fair to say that the churchman continued to try to read the *Essay* as sympathetically as he possibly could. Indeed, in retrospect it seems clear that Norris was seeking to promote in his own work the very same spirit of enquiry after moral knowledge that had been one of the principal objectives of the *Essay*. Both philosophers were writing in pursuance of the selfsame end; unfortunately the radically different means that each man employed, together with the rupture caused by the letter incident, hopelessly beclouded the fact.[15]

In 1693 Norris dedicated his third volume of *Practical Discourses* to his benefactor, the earl of Pembroke. And if Pembroke ever bothered even to peruse the volume, he would have discovered more than a few similarities between that collection of occasional pieces and another work recently dedicated to him, the *Essay concerning Human Understanding*. For in the *Discourses* Norris, following his Platonic vision, called men to turn from their delusive earthly preoccupations and to devote their admittedly limited resources to the business of morality and godly living. In language strikingly similar to Locke's, he invited each man 'to learn the true Bounds that divide Opinion from Knowledge, to study the Extent of his own capacity . . . and to sit down in a quiet Ignorance of those things to which his Understanding is not proportioned'. The only truths really necessary for mankind, he argued, were those which served to further moral conduct, the government of the passions, and the direction of life 'in such a way as may lead him to Eternal Happiness'. Other intellectual pursuits may in their own way 'be perfective of Human Understanding', but 'considering the present Station and Order of Man, he is to trouble himself about no other than what serves to the Regulation of his Life and Manners, that being the only Business he has to do in this World'.[16] Here was the central reason that Norris repeatedly

---

[15] John Norris, *An Essay Towards the Theory of the Ideal or Intelligible World*, 2 vols. (London: S. Manship, 1701, 1704), ii. 371–2. Locke did not respond to this, except in a letter to the Deist Anthony Collins (21 Mar. 1704: *Works*, x. 282–6). His earlier criticisms were directed against Norris's *Reason and Religion* (London: S. Manship, 1689), which was his first full exposition of Malebranche's ideas.

[16] John Norris, 'A Discourse Concerning the Natural, and the Moral Vanity in Man', in *Practical Discourses*, iii. 107, 108. See the near parallel passage in the *Essay*, 1. 1. 4.

took exception to the seventeenth century's increasing concern with the natural world, the world of sensible objects:

The Soul by her Body has contracted such an Alliance with the Material World, that we have a sort of Magnetick Inclination towards sensible things which in some Men is exalted to that degree, that instead of loving God with all their Hearts, Souls and Minds, they love the World at that rate, making that their God, their End, their Supream Good.[17]

God did not make men rational that they might puff themselves up with knowledge for its own sake, but in order that their knowledge might centre on and serve the interest of religion: the question, as Norris saw it, concerned 'whether we ought to be more Solicitous for that Intellectual Perfection which we cannot have here, and shall have hereafter, or for that Moral Perfection which we may have here, and cannot hereafter?'[18] The whole spirit of Norris's idealist philosophy, with its basic premisses that the real world consisted of divine ideas and that truth was to be acquired through an intense application of mind to the immediate realm of the divine essence, was admittedly opposed to the empirical, naturalistic temper of his own day; and his reputation has suffered accordingly. Norris's was a philosophy that eschewed action within the world as of little importance to the business of religion and morality; making God the immediate object of our minds seemed to him a good deal more pious and intellectually reassuring than having the mere sensible objects of divine creation as the only material for thought. There was a certain cosmic intimacy in the doctrine of Occasionalism, as indeed there was for Neoplatonism as a whole at this time; but the price to be paid for this entrance into the mind of the Deity seemed a bit too high, and the technique of attaining understanding too saturated with mysticism, for most of Norris's contemporaries, including the ever-sensible Locke.[19] For all of that Norris, like

---

[17] Norris, 'Measure of Divine Love' (op. cit. iii. 79).

[18] John Norris, *Reflections Upon the Conduct of Human Life* (London: S. Manship, 1690), 138. See also his *An Account of Reason and Faith* (London: S. Manship, 1697), 286; *A Practical Treatise Concerning Humility* (London: S. Manship, 1707), 46, 111; 'A Discourse Concerning Perseverence in Holiness' (1687), in *A Collection of Miscellanies* (London: S. Manship, 1717), 263.

[19] John Norris, *Letters Concerning the Love of God* (London: S. Manship, 1705), 1–3; id., *Reason and Religion*, 52, 176, 196. Powicke, (*Cambridge Platonists*, 22–3) and Cassirer

Locke, wanted to check the perceived breakdown of godly behaviour in English society. And in order to do that he had to concern himself with the fall of Adam; he had to come to terms with original sin.

Now this was always a difficult matter for men imbued with the spirit of Platonic idealism. One of Norris's intellectual mentors, Henry More, believed along with the other Cambridge Platonists that all depravity in man 'is repugnant to human Nature'. That depravity, of course, had its root opposite the rule of reason, in certain 'Brutal Additions' or bodily passions, and it was due to these troublesome passions that, according to More, 'The Life of this body is the Prison of the Soul, and Passion its very Crucifixion'.[20] But as we have seen in our previous discussion of Benjamin Whichcote, the Platonists were more often than not apt (when making their hopeful estimates of mankind's potential for good) to describe human nature as it had proceeded from the hands of God, leaving a veil over what it had since become. Norris likewise dwelt upon man's rational side more often than he treated its obverse; and on more than one occasion he even argued in favour of that most damnable affront to Pauline Christianity, the notion that sin was the product of human ignorance and lack of consideration on the part of those who would never knowingly transgress the obligations of the moral law.[21] Yet the Neoplatonic formulae were never entirely satisfying to Norris, and he freely acknowledged that man's 'deeply lapsed and degenerated' present condition 'is now too faulty and defective to be the first and original workmanship of God'. All things that share in the divine nature, he asserted, must be created in the image of that

---

(*Platonic Renaissance*) discuss the Neoplatonic setting. Standard treatments of the empirical temper of the Restoration era include G. N. Clark, *Science and Social Welfare in the Age of Newton* (Oxford: Clarendon Press, 1937); R. K. Merton, *Science, Technology and Society in Seventeenth Century England* (New York: Harper Torchbooks, 1970); and, more generally, A. R. Hall, *The Scientific Revolution, 1500–1800* (London: Longman, 1954), chs. 6, 7.

[20] Henry More, *A Collection of Aphorisms* (London: J. Downing, 1704), 1; id., *An Account of Virtue: or Dr More's Abridgement of Morals, put into English* (London: Benjamin Tooke, 1690), 6.

[21] John Norris, *Spiritual Counsel: or the Father's Advice to His Children* (1694), in *Treatises Upon Several Subjects* (London: S. Manship, 1697), 473; id., *Reason and Religion*, 252–3, 256; id., 'Considerations Upon the Nature of Sin', in *Miscellanies*, 386.

nature, 'because nothing can be but by partaking of the Perfection of God', and any contumacy and declension must be the entire responsibility of the individual moral agent. Therefore it was necessary to 'pre-suppose some real sin or other in Man as the cause of his great depravation and proneness to Irregular Love'. And the fact that man's propensity to sin appeared to be even stronger since Christ had reinforced the laws of nature with divine law 'we shall the less wonder at, if we consider the universal pravity and corruptness of Human Nature'.[22] For Norris, the effects of original sin were so overwhelmingly manifest in mankind's refusal even to consider the perfections of the ideal world, that something more than simple encouragement was needed to set them aright. Christ had sacrificed himself for sinners in order that man might be put into 'a Capacity or Possibility of Pardon and Reconciliation', he wrote; but the efficacy of that sacrifice was contingent upon true belief and repentance, 'does ordinarily depend upon the Disposition in which it finds us, in relation to sensible good'. Echoing the *Reasonableness of Christianity*, Norris insisted that Christianity 'both as to Faith and Practice does approve it self to be the most Rational thing in the world', and he refused to believe that God would require 'any thing from us but what is good and consistent with Reason'. Unfortunately, most men 'understand not the Dignity of Human Nature' as God had originally intended it.[23] In the final analysis Lockean educational principles were required if the situation were ever to be reversed.

Although we have no direct evidence that Norris read or even consulted *Some Thoughts concerning Education*, it is clear that he shared, along with so many other late seventeenth-century educational theorists, Locke's broader concern with shaping the individual child through proper habits inculcated early and often. Norris's own book on pedagogy, the *Spiritual Counsel*, was

---

[22] John Norris, 'A Discourse Concerning Heavenly-Mindedness', in *Practical Discourses Upon Several Divine Subjects* (London: S. Manship, 1691), 169; id., 'A Discourse Concerning Religious Singularity', ibid. 85; id., *Reason and Religion*, 259; id., *Christian Blessedness*, 23. See also his *Theory and Regulation of Love*, 66.

[23] Norris, *Reflections Upon Human Life*, 120; *Spiritual Counsel* (above, n. 21), 495; id., 'A Discourse Concerning Perseverance in Holiness', in *Miscellanies*, 253; id., 'The Christian Law Asserted and Vindicated', ibid., 225; id., 'An Idea of Happiness', ibid. 416.

written for the benefit of his three young children; but it is really
little more than an extended appeal on behalf of rational living
and idealist philosophy, an odd work where practical directives
are few and where pious pleading takes the place of system or
method. Nevertheless, scattered throughout his other books and
short discourses are commentaries on the plastic nature of
children, who, although naturally prone to the evils of passing
pleasure, can be brought into morality through careful and
considered design. Custom and habit, he said, must create a
second nature, for 'being born Infants, and passing so many
Judgments upon things as we do, before we have reason enough
to judge of any Thing as we ought, we take up abundance of
Prejudices which indispose us for the Knowledge of Truth'. All
children 'take their Impressions like Wax', and because of their
constant exposure to so many dangerous allurements, worldly
reward takes 'an early Possession of [their] Hearts' which, once
established, cannot easily be dislodged. 'To be vertuous at any
rate is work enough,' he cautioned, 'but to do Good while we
have Habits to Evil upon us, with the confederate disadvantage
of a corrupt Nature' is a work of imposing proportions where
'the very entrance into the School of Wisdom and a vertuous
course, is a state of Discipline, Difficulty and Hardship'. Norris
discussed the inevitable confusion of thought brought on by our
faulty and ambiguous use of words, again following Locke's
treatment of the same issue in Book Three of the *Essay*, and,
despite his idealist philosophy, posited a hedonistic ethic similar
to Locke's where 'Interest and Duty are immediately link'd
together in this life' in anticipation of the glories of the afterlife.[24]
Norris was also committed to a programme of early intervention
and remedy, because without it God's plan for mankind and
promise of salvation would be instinctively brushed aside by
fallen humanity. His aim, in his essays and larger treatises, was
to move men towards reform by appealing to their rational sense
of greater self-interest: 'For as Corrupt as our Nature is,' he
wrote in 1707, 'we have nothing Substantial in us but what is
Good, and a great deal that is Excellent, being made in the

---

[24] John Norris, *A Treatise Concerning Christian Prudence* (London: S. Manship, 1710),
26, 27, 28; id., 'Of the Advantages of Thinking', in *Miscellanies*, 147, 149; id., 'A
Discourse Concerning Perseverence in Holiness' ibid. 263–4; id., 'Of Courage', ibid.
165; id., *Account of Reason and Faith*, 23.

image and likeness of God, which still in great Measure shines forth in us.'[25] This abiding faith, shared to some degree by Locke, together with Norris's conviction that so much of sin was due to ignorance and error, steeled his hopes of doing some good for any one who would but consider his appeals. On this score, at least, the greater popularity of Locke's approach to education is easily comprehensible: Locke understood the futility of appeals to the rationality of mankind much better than his opponent. The Platonic means to the moral end, Locke believed, was based upon an unduly optimistic estimation of the human condition. One suspects Norris knew something of that, too, but he could never quite bring himself to fashion a workable alternative to edification and hortatory appeals to diminished reason; he staked the outcome of his own struggle with the forces of sin on the greatly attenuated illumination of the 'Candle of the Lord', and the obscurity into which he has fallen is perhaps the best indicator of the insufficiency of that light against those forces.

Although Norris plainly irritated him, Locke did not think that the doctrine of Occasionalism would ever gain a solid foothold in educated circles.[26] His real concern was not so much with that ineffectual challenge, as with those churchmen and lay authors who took exception to his abandonment of innate ideas and to other of his novel suggestions in the *Essay*. We have already mentioned Thomas Burnet's strictures in this regard and have briefly discussed the position of those who defended innate ideas as essential to the stability of universal morality. The critics of the polemic in Book One of the *Essay* almost to a man questioned, either implicitly or expressly, the sincerity of Locke's faith because of his attack on innateness. They consciously set themselves up as the standard-bearers, the guardians of religious orthodoxy; and whether they styled themselves liberal churchmen or Calvinists, none of them ever expressed the slightest sympathy with Locke's attempt to solidify common morality by grounding it in natural law. Most agreed with William Sherlock, Dean of St Paul's from 1690, who found in the *tabula-rasa* theory 'the Old Atheistick

---

[25] Norris, *Practical Treatise Concerning Humility*, 25.

[26] Locke to Peter King (25 Oct. 1704: printed in Cranston, *Locke*, 478). He recommended to King that his 'Examination of Malebranche' should not be published after his death, but he did not specifically forbid it.

Hypothesis, which banishes Original Mind and Wisdom out of the World, makes Mind younger than Matter, later than the making of the World and therefore not the Maker of it'.[27] To exonerate himself in the eyes of these critics, Locke would have to reinstate natural conscience, recant his suggestions that God might annex to matter the power of thought, and prove his belief in the immateriality and immortality of the soul by acknowledging that there was no intermission in its operation as a thinking substance. These things he would not do, concerned as he was more with vindicating the power of God and with coupling the moral law to the rule of reason than with making dogmatic statements about questions beyond the pale of human understanding. As he wrote snappishly to Burnet:

The world now has my book, such as it is; if anyone finds, that there be many questions that my principles will not resolve, he will do the world more service to lay down such principles as will resolve them, than to quarrel with my ignorance (which I readily acknowledge) and possibly for that which cannot be done.

If Burnet and others remained unsatisfied with his treatment of the soul's immortality, certainly no small issue to Christians everywhere, Locke advised their careful consideration of another of his firmest canons: 'and that is, the revelation of life and immortality of Jesus Christ, through the Gospel'.[28]

The men who challenged Locke over the issue of innate ideas were in the end, we know, working to protect Reformed Christianity from the advance guard of religious free-thinking, spearheaded by the abhorrent Deists. The friendship which emerged between Locke and the youthful Deist Anthony Collins

[27] William Sherlock, 'A Digression Concerning Connate Ideas', in *Discourse Concerning the Happiness of Good Men* (London: W. Rogers, 1704), 124. The contents of the 'Digression' were first aired in a sermon of 1697: see Locke to Molyneux (22 Feb. 1697: vi, no. 2202). Throughout the 1690s Sherlock was embroiled in the Trinitarian Controversy: see Wallace, *Antitrinitarian Biography*, i. 236–8, 267–73, 347–51, 354–8; Kippis, *Biographia Britannica*, vi. 3676–8. T. B. Macaulay offers an interesting account of his reputation around the time of the Glorious Revolution: *History of England*, 2 vols. (London: Longman, 1873), ii. 260–2.

[28] Locke, 'An Answer to Remarks Upon an Essay Concerning Human Understanding' (1697), in *Works*, iv. 188. Locke had suggested that the soul may not always think in the *Essay* (2. 1. 10). He discussed the possibility of thinking matter in 4. 3. 6, saying that to deny the possibility is to question God's omnipotence and make man's puny reason the measure of all; for Locke the attempt to set limits on God's power was supreme arrogance, and another sign of human depravity.

in 1703 only served to intensify the distrust surrounding the philosopher and his ideas.[29] So it is not surprising that the failure of these critics to apprehend and appreciate Locke's larger purpose in doing away with innate ideas was matched by their lack of insight into his view of fallen humanity, a view very much similar to their own. James Lowde, who was only one of many authors to err in their reading of the *Essay* and mistakenly to charge Locke with reducing morality to custom and habit, did not quarrel with the original motivation behind the work: 'The Knowledge of our selves, and of Human Nature', he conceded, 'was always counted a good Foundation of both Piety towards God, and of Justice and Charity towards Men.' Nor did he doubt that most errors in religion, as Locke had concluded, 'have been occasion'd by the want either of true knowledge, or due consideration of our Natures, as rational, and of the Duties and Obligations that lye upon us therefrom'. In fact, if it were not for his confusion over Locke's distinction between the divine law and the law of opinion, there would have been little substantive disagreement between the two men. Lowde's hedonistic ethics were based, like Locke's, on the individual's recognition of true self-interest, helped along by eternal punishments and rewards; 'yet such is the disorder and confusion which Sin has introduc'd into human Nature, such is the general depravation of Mankind', that even with the aid of other-worldly sanctions men will still mistake the moral good. The ancients had some understanding of original sin, he observed in a sermon published in 1684, but no real apprehension of its cause and thus no plan for its remedy. Only Christianity, which shows men the origin of sin in Adam, provides 'a sufficient means for the removal of it, viz. the blood of Christ, and the Grace of the Gospel'. For Lowde, moral virtue might have been based on ideas 'connatural to the Soul', but its true realization consisted in a Lockean 'Habit of Mind, founded indeed in Nature, but perfected by frequent use and exercise'. And while he directly associated the current depravity of all men with Adam's fall in Paradise, the consequences, as he interpreted them, did not go beyond 'ignorance of the Understanding, and impotence and irregularity of the Will'—the very same

---

[29] Cranston (*Locke*, 460) thinks Locke was rather taken in by the young man's uncritical praise for all his work.

conclusion which Locke would draw in the *Reasonableness of Christianity*.[30]

There were others who fit a similar pattern of public disdain for Locke's way of ideas, and unacknowledged agreement with his assumptions about man which, perhaps as much as anything else, had prompted his initial investigation into the origins of human knowledge back in 1671. The Revd John Hartcliffe, former head of Merchant Taylors School and nephew of Locke's old Christ Church Dean John Owen, while confident that there had always existed 'a secret impression upon the Minds of Men, whereby they are naturally directed to approve some things as good, and avoid others as evil', nevertheless worried that human nature, although 'framed for great and noble ends', was at present 'in a state of Weakness' and 'much below its own Perfection, as Infancy is short of Manhood'. He as much as admitted the cogency of Locke's position when he observed that all have a 'propension to evil, and Men are generally vicious; which seems to contradict that natural Instinct, which shews us, as we say, what is Virtue, and what is Vice'. Hartcliffe's theological training and his pedagogical experience had awakened him to the hard fact that 'Man is first born into the World little higher than the Beasts that perish' and impressed upon him the urgent need for systematic education. Whereas in Adam 'the Understanding was a Noble and pure Faculty, could lead and controul the Passions', since the Fall 'Vertue is Gotten by Care and Study. Now it was never known, that any Man was born virtuous, but attain'd unto it by long Practice. Virtue therefore must be reckon'd amongst Habits; for they only are contracted by Labor and Industry.'

That most men would freely prefer to 'doze away their days', 'unravel their natures', he took for granted, comforted by the fact that education might at least serve as a needed counterweight in a handful of cases.[31] Matters were much the same for

---

[30] Lowde, *A Discourse Concerning the Nature of Man*, 4, 36–7, 203; id., *The Reasonableness of the Christian Religion* (London: Walter Kettilby, 1684), 20. Locke received a copy of the *Discourse* on 23 June 1694: MS Locke f. 10, fol. 217. He responded to Lowde's criticism in the Epistle to the Reader in the second edition of the *Essay*.

[31] John Hartcliffe, *A Treatise of Moral and Intellectual Virtues* (London: C. Harper, 1691), preface and pp. 17, 352, 357. For additional observations on the Fall, see his *A Discourse Against Purgatory* (London: Brabazon Almer, 1685), 19, and *Sermon Preached at the Oxfordshire Feast* (London: Ralph Holt, 1684), 17–18, where Hartcliffe refers the reader to Hobbes for confirmation of his view of man outside civil society.

the first Boyle Lecturer, Richard Bentley, who also spoke in support of innate ideas, 'characters that can never be defaced', as the strongest weapon against irreligion; and who insisted, much as Locke would do in the *Reasonableness*, that men were fully competent to fulfil the most difficult requirements of the eternal law by virtue of their having been created rational beings. But even Bentley, whose buoyant arguments from design later gave much credence to the notion that divine wisdom had planned and executed the best of all possible words, even he dared not disown 'the vicious ferment' of original sin, the leaven of evil 'perpetually diffusing and propagating itself through all generations'. Again like Locke, Bentley identified evil example, imitation, and the ignorance, prejudice, fervour, and temerity of childhood, along with 'the force and frequency of temptation' as the objective characteristics of our depraved station. His law of nature presupposed man in a prelapsarian state; but seventeenth-century Englishmen, he believed (innate ideas of God, good, and evil notwithstanding), were criminals all in the eyes of their Maker, languishing between hope and despair, and must call upon Christ 'to retrieve a perishing world'.[32]

The most formidable and respected of Locke's opponents during the final years of the seventeenth century was King William's choice as Bishop of Worcester, Edward Stillingfleet. Universally respected for his vast learning and unflinching commitment to the Reformed Church of England, Stillingfleet directed an assault at Locke's work that was neither impulsive nor ill-considered; and Locke, recognizing the great weight of authority that any observations from the pen of Stillingfleet would carry, responded in what was an uncharacteristically civil and thorough fashion, determined not to let this one-time exponent of Latitudinarian principles undermine his reputation in the eyes of liberal churchmen.[33] The evolution of Still-

[32] Richard Bentley, 'The Folly of Atheism,' in *Works*, 3 vols. (London: Francis MacPherson, 1838), iii. 3; id., 'Of Revelation and the Messiahs', ibid. 226–30. Locke knew Bentley while the latter was living in London between 1691 and 1700: R. J. White, *Dr Bentley* (London: Eyre and Spottiswoode, 1965), 66. His success as the first Boyle Lecturer is attested to by John Evelyn, *Diary*, ed. W. Bray, 2 vols. (London: Walter Dunne, 1901), ii. 315.

[33] Stillingfleet's considerable reputation was attested to by Burnet (*History of Own Time*, i. 264, H. C. Foxcroft, ed., *A Supplement to Burnet's History* (Oxford: Clarendon Press, 1902), 102, and by Pepys, *Diary*, vi. 87. For Locke's concern that Stillingfleet's name alone would legitimize what in his mind was groundless criticism of the *Essay*, see Molyneux to Locke (3 Feb. 1697: v, no. 2189); Locke to Molyneux (22 Feb. 1697: vi, no. 2202).

ingfleet's own views (he was three years younger than Locke) constituted, at least as regards the respective roles of Church and State in the life of the community, the inverse of Locke's. His youthful *Irenicum: A Weapon-Salve for the Churches Wounds*, appearing when he was only twenty-four and when, one year after the death of the Lord Protector, religious uncertainty was at its height, was written in the best tradition of Great Tew liberalism and comprehension, an animated yet reasoned plea on behalf of mutual forbearance and peaceful reconciliation. In it, Stillingfleet declared that there was nothing divinely ordained regarding episcopacy, the proper church order or ceremony, and concluded that 'as long as mens faces differ, their judgments will'. The only responsible solution to decades of religious bickering, where every element of faith was being questioned by 'Weaker Heads' who were 'apt to suspect that the Foundation it self is not firm enough', was, in Stillingfleet's mind, the construction of a new church order, on the form of which he declined to speculate, where the needs of both doubters and dissenters might be equally accommodated.[34] Locke, we recall, was at this same time moving swiftly in the direction of greater absolutism and religious conformity, towards accept-ance of a Church where matters indifferent were to be adjudicated not through compromise and accommodation, but *ex cathedra* by the soon-to-be restored monarch.

All this had changed by the time of the Popish Plot. Appointed Dean of St Paul's in 1678, Stillingfleet had by that date come to view toleration as a grave threat to the stability of religion and the peace of society. Universal forbearance seemed now to breed nothing but contention; while sectarian rivalry and the failure of the different Churches to agree upon the essential tenets of the Christian faith would ultimately, he thought, drive men back into the authoritarian embrace of the Catholic fold, there to find the organizational cohesion and unsullied doctrinal uniformity missing in the Protestant world. Locke, on the other hand, by now many years a convert to the

---

[34] Edward Stillingfleet, *Irenicum: A Weapon-Salve for the Churches Wounds* (1659), in *Works*, 6 vols. (London: n.p., 1707–10), ii. 148–9, 156, 417. See also Tulloch, *Rational Theology*, i. 411–63; J. H. Overton, *Life in the English Church* (London: Longman, 1885), 74–6; G. Every, *The High Church Party, 1688–1718* (London: SPCK, 1956), 10–11; J. J. Taylor, *A Retrospect of the Religious Life of England* (London: Trubner, 1876), 72.

doctrine of toleration, was one of a number of individuals who took up the defence of Nonconformity against Stillingfleet. James Tyrrell assisted him in one undertaking during the summer of 1680, and although the resulting pamphlet was never published, the argument put forward there would eventually find public expression in the *Epistola de Tolerantia* of 1689.[35]

Stillingfleet's quarrel with Locke after 1696 was not directed against the philosopher's religious convictions, for the Bishop was thoroughly familiar with the nature of Latitudinarian belief; but, rather, against the use to which Locke's way of ideas had been put by Deists like Toland. It was in his *Discourse in Vindication of the Trinity* (1696)—written ostensibly to refute Toland's *Christianity Not Mysterious*, but containing trenchant observations on the *Essay*—that Stillingfleet first confronted Locke's radical epistemology. More specifically, Stillingfleet found the polemic against innate ideas hostile to the concept of substance and ultimately to such Christian doctrines as the Trinity and Incarnation. The idea of substance, Locke had indicated in the *Essay*, 'we accustom our selves' to suppose, 'So that if any one will examine himself concerning his Notion of pure Substance in general, he will find he has no other Idea of it at all, but only a Supposition of he knows not what support of such Qualities, which are capable of producing simple Ideas in us; which qualities are commonly called Accidents.'[36] Stillingfleet complained that by making knowledge contingent upon our having clear and distinct ideas derived solely from the twin sources of sensation and reflection, all possibility of proving the existence of substance would be eliminated. In response to Locke's protest that he had never once doubted the existence of substance, Stillingfleet responded that the issue in question was not Locke's sincerity, but rather the sceptical implications inherent in his simply supposing that substance supports the sensible qualities which we perceive to be outside us: 'I do not

---

[35] Stillingfleet, *The Mischief of Separation* (1680), in *Works*, i. 279–300; MS Locke c. 34. Others who wrote against Stillingfleet included John Owen and Richard Baxter: see R. T. Carroll, *The Common-Sense Philosophy of Bishop Edward Stillingfleet* (The Hague: Nijhoff, 1975), 26. Stillingfleet's unpopularity at the time of the Popish Plot is discussed by J. Nankivell, *Edward Stillingfleet, Bishop of Worcester* (Worcester: Ebenezer Bayliss and Son, 1946), 6–7.

[36] *Essay*, 2. 23. 2. For a discussion, see Aaron, *Locke*, 174–9; J. Bennett, *Locke, Berkeley, Hume: Central Themes* (Oxford: Clarendon Press, 1977), 59–63.

charge them [the Lockeans] with disgarding the Notion of Substance, because they have but an imperfect Idea of it; but because upon those Principles there can be no certain Idea at all of it.' Men, Stillingfleet thought, would never have the sort of clear and distinct ideas of substance, the triune nature of the Godhead, and the many other legitimate mysteries of the Christian religion necessary to qualify as knowledge according to Locke's definition. Should they then, he asked, abandon all hopes of knowledge in those areas? Was Locke suggesting complete fideism here? Were Protestants no better situated to know these essential truths than their Roman Catholic adversaries? Worst of all, how did Locke propose to escape Hobbesian materialism when his supposition of substance was based upon little more than the simple ideas of 'accidents', sensible objects existing outside us which could never have any connection with non-material substance? For Stillingfleet this was where the dangerous principles of the *Essay* were bound to lead their purblind exponents.[37]

Toland had already taken the first steps towards religious scepticism by holding the veracity of Scripture to the inappropriate standard of clear and distinct ideas; and Locke's conclusion in Book Four of the *Essay*, where he linked all improvement in knowledge with clear ideas, seemed to presage nothing but ill for man's understanding of God's creation and of himself, because so many of our ideas have been and will remain for ever imperfect and confused. The prophylactic endorsed by the Bishop was a flat rejection of Locke's empiricism. 'The Relative Idea of Substance', he said, 'arising from the necessary Support of Accidents is a mere effect of Reason and Judgment, and no effect of any simple Ideas . . . it comes only from the Mind it self.' He admitted that his innate conception of substance was no clearer than Locke's, but felt confident that his proof of its existence on the basis of ratiocination went—with important epistemological implications—far beyond mere Lockean supposition.[38]

What Stillingfleet was attempting to do here should have

---

[37] Locke, *A Letter to the Right Reverend Edward, Lord Bishop of Worcester* (*Works*, iv. 5–11); Stillingfleet, *An Answer to Mr. Locke's Letter* (*Works*, iii. 524, 526); W. C. DePauley, *The Candle of the Lord* (London: SPCK, 1937), 214–21.

[38] *Essay*, 4. 12. 3; Stillingfleet, op. cit. 527.

been familiar to Locke. The churchman was reaching back into his Latitudinarian past to revive the notion of probable knowledge, arguing, as the members of the Great Tew Circle had done before him, that different sorts of knowledge demanded different degrees and types of evidence. He was well equipped for the undertaking, having been engaged in the rule-of-faith controversy against Catholic opponents earlier in his career, and having at one point even joined with Locke's friend Tillotson in refuting the fideistic claims of the Jesuit controversialist John Sergeant.[39] Stillingfleet's position was perhaps best stated in a short tract against Deism, where he acknowledged that while the same evidence could not be marshalled for the truths of religion as for the truths of sense, it remained 'a great part of Judgment and Understanding, to know the proportion and fitness of evidence to the Nature of the thing to be proved. They would not have the Eye to judge of Tastes, nor the Nose of Metaphysicks; and yet these would be as proper, as to have the Senses judge of Immaterial Beings.'[40] The principles of religion, he thus concluded, were to be proved on the basis of the preponderance of reasonable evidence assembled to test them. In his own first effort in this area, the lengthy and erudite *Origines Sacræ*, he attempted to defend the historical accuracy and reasonable nature of the Christian faith against those who might question them. The weight of the evidence he of course found to be in favour of Christian revelation, just as the evidence of reason had proved to him the existence of substance and the validity of other truths above reason, such as the Trinity.[41] What Stillingfleet found so disturbing about Locke's epistemology was that in the final account, if the philosopher were to remain true to his principles, he would have to separate the realms of reason and faith, would have to accept fideist scepticism—and this he appeared to do in the *Essay*. Faith was distinguished from reason in Locke's book as something 'not thus made out by the

---

[39] Stillingfleet's entrance into the debate began in 1664 with his *Rational Account of the Grounds of the Protestant Religion* (*Works*, iv. 626–58). He next replied to Sergeant's *Sure Footing in Christianity* (1665) in an appendix to Tillotson's *The Rule of Faith* (London: n.p., 1666). See R. Popkin, 'The Philosophy of Edward Stillingfleet', *Journal of the History of Philosophy*, 9 (1971), 303–19.

[40] Stillingfleet, *A Letter to a Deist* (1677), in *Works*, ii. 118.

[41] Stillingfleet, *Origines Sacræ* (*Works*, ii. 68–9); *A Rational Account of the Grounds of the Protestant Religion* (ibid. iv. 138).

Deductions of Reason; but upon the Credit of the Proposer, as coming from GOD, in some extraordinary way of Communication'.[42] Stillingfleet's common-sense approach to revelation denied this important distinction, and in making this the fundamental issue separating him from Locke, he could portray himself as the true defender of the reasonableness of Christianity, while Locke appeared, with his way of ideas in the *Essay* anyway, to be one of traditional Christianity's more articulate, and for that reason more dangerous, enemies.

Molyneux's friends in Ireland seemed convinced that Locke had effectively thwarted the Bishop's attempts to link his ideas with the rise of Deism and scepticism, but Locke himself was less confident.[43] At any rate the battle continued until Stillingfleet's death in 1699, with Locke's three responses (the last of which reached some three hundred wearisome pages) alone filling one large volume. In the end, Stillingfleet's performance convinced others that their own assaults on the *Essay* were justified and in the best interests of orthodox Christianity. One individual thus convinced was Daniel Whitby of Salisbury. This churchman attacked Locke on another issue raised by Stillingfleet, namely Locke's suggestion in the *Essay* that the resurrection of the same body could neither be found discussed in Scripture nor be proven by man. In a polite letter to the philosopher, Whitby forwarded his objections to Locke's argument, objections which Locke found as untenable as the Bishop's. Yet despite this difference of opinion, Whitby's own major statement on Scripture published in 1700, *A Paraphrase and Commentary Upon All the Epistles*, pictured man and the nature of original sin in a manner that was virtually indistinguishable from the interpretation offered by Locke in 1695. Whitby's notes on Romans 5:12 in particular recalled Locke's words in the *Reasonableness*, and anticipated Locke's further statements in the posthumously published notes on St Paul's Epistles. When later challenged for his denial that the sin of Adam was directly imputed to his posterity, Whitby responded by claiming the support of Jeremy Taylor for his views. 'I deny not that Man is

---

[42] *Essay*, 4. 18. 2. David Snyder ('Faith and Reason in Locke's Essay'. *Journal of the History of Ideas*, 47 (1986), 197–213) discusses Locke's exclusion of faith from the purview of knowledge.

[43] Molyneux to Locke (15 May 1697: vi, no. 2262).

very far gone from Original Righteousness,' he wrote, 'and is of his own Nature enclined to Evil, so that the Flesh (as soon as it can do it) lusteth always contrary to the Spirit'; but he added that actual guilt and just punishment can only follow free choice, that 'Men sin, not because they cannot, but because they will not observe the law which forbids it.' The gift of free choice magnified, for Whitby, the seriousness of all offences in a manner that he believed was impossible under the Calvinist reading of Romans (which appeared to make God the author of man's hardness of heart); but 'This liberty is indeed no Perfection of Human Nature, for it supposes us imperfect, as being subject to fall by Temptation.' Whitby's criticism of Locke over the resurrection was, then, in no sense symptomatic of a deeper rift in their Broad-Church vision of man, and this was to be the case with Stillingfleet's criticisms as well.[44]

The fact that the Bishop of Worcester, despite his efforts to induce Locke into making some positive statement concerning the mystery of the Trinity, never really doubted his religiosity, seemed to escape others who took the offensive against the way of ideas. Not only did Stillingfleet trust Locke's commitment to Latitudinarian principles, but he never once suggested, as Henry Hatrell had done, that the *Essay* undermined the concept of original sin as interpreted by the Church of which Stillingfleet was such an influential member. One would expect the Bishop to have been as deeply concerned with the corrosive force of Locke's purported scepticism in this crucial area as in any other. Having doggedly scrutinized the atheistical tendencies of the *Essay* for three years, it is a bit surprising—and, ultimately, revealing—that a similar scrutiny of the work for Pelagian leanings produced no significant challenge to Locke from Stillingfleet.

The fact is, that even if he had wanted to broaden his attack against Locke to include the question of original sin, Stillingfleet would have been hard-pressed to find much in Locke's view of

<hr />

[44] *DNB* xxi. 28–9; Locke, *Mr Locke's Second Reply to the Bishop of Worcester*, in *Works*, iv. 303–44; Whitby to Locke (11 Jan. 1699: vi, no. 2533); Locke to Whitby (17 Jan. 1699: vi, no. 2536); Samuel Bold to Locke (9 Sept. 1700: vii, no. 2771); MS Locke e. 11; Daniel Whitby, *A Paraphrase and Commentary Upon All the Epistles of the New Testament* (London: W. Bowyer, 1700), 26, 28–9; id., *A Full Answer to the Arguments of the Reverend Dr Jonathan Edwards* (London: John Wyat, 1712), p. xxiii. See also Whitby's *A Discourse Concerning the True Import of the Words Election and Reprobation* (London: John Wyat, 1710), 307, 310.

Adam's fall that differed from his own. In this respect more than any other, perhaps, the Bishop remained faithful to the ideals of his Latitudinarian youth. Indeed, it might not be inaccurate to suggest that Stillingfleet's conception of the Fall carried within it a view of man's nature much closer to the classical outlook than any interpretation that Locke was ever willing to countenance. For Stillingfleet often associated mankind's corruption and degeneracy directly with our inability to control the passions, the 'folly' of imagination, and 'the distempers of our wills'. There was little discussion of deliberate transgression in the Augustinian sense to be found either in his sermons or in his more formal treatises.[45] He seemed less concerned with detailing the specific moral infirmities of man in their relation to the first sin than he was with devising an effective strategy by which those infirmities might be excused. The work of combating the depravity of men, he told the clergy of his diocese in 1690, required great pains on their part, 'for few love to hear of their Faults, and fewer to amend them'. Locke had made much the same statement in the *Essay*, when he observed that 'it carries too great an imputation of ignorance, lightness, or folly, for Men to quit and renounce their former Tenets', and for both men the only feasible solution to this regrettable situation lay with the enlightened pedagogue. There was little probability 'of prevailing on those who have accustomed themselves to vicious habits, and are hardened in their Wickedness', thought Stillingfleet; but much could be done 'to soften the Fierceness, to direct the Weakness, to govern the Inclinations of Mankind' in its youth. Stillingfleet's own personal experience as a private tutor in the 1650s may have helped bolster his confidence in the ameliorative power of education, but the more general Latitudinarian emphasis upon each individual's personal responsibility and ability to prove the sincerity of his faith through works really made this attitude imperative if that special theological perspective were to survive.[46]

Of greater significance to Stillingfleet's overall view of human nature was his understanding of the state of nature and of the

[45] Stillingfleet, *Origines Sacræ* (*Works*, ii. 380); id., 'Of the True Happiness of Mankind and the Immortality of the Soul' (ibid. i. 632, 633); id., 'Fools Make a Mock at Sin' (i. 23).

[46] Stillingfleet, 'The Bishop of Worcester's Charge to the Clergy of His Diocese' (1690), in *Works*, iii. 621, 627–8; Locke, *Essay*, 4. 16. 4; Nankivell, *Stillingfleet*, 2.

role of government in ensuring that God's laws were maintained. In fact, his analysis of man's hypothetical flight from the state of nature into civil society was markedly similar to the one presented by Locke in his *Two Treatises of Government*. Now there has been much dispute in recent years about Locke's intentions in chapter 2 of the Second Treatise, and the issue of Hobbesian influence is still unresolved.[47] What is of interest to us, however, is the fact that neither Locke nor Stillingfleet believed that men as they were presently constituted could achieve lasting happiness outside civil society. Both were in essential agreement that, in the state of nature, the law of nature (or God's eternal law) was the standard by which men were obliged to regulate their lives.[48] In order, then, for individuals to realize their full potential without civil society they were required to abide by that law of reason; and 'every man upon this score', to use Locke's words, had then a personal right to punish any who would violate the law, who would 'trespass against the whole Species, and the Peace and Safety of it, provided for it by the Law of Nature'. Locke was, however, wary enough to admit that in this situation, the self-love of men would render all hopes of peaceful coexistence impossible, 'Ill Nature, Passion and Revenge' carrying individuals beyond the bounds of just and equitable punishment.[49] So for him the establishment of civil

[47] Leo Strauss (*Natural Right and History* (Chicago: University Press, 1953), 202, 224, 232), Richard Cox (*Locke on War and Peace* (Oxford: Clarendon Press, 1960), 1–7, 21, 142), C. B. MacPherson, (*Political Theory of Posessive Individualism*, 238–47) and J. D. Mabbott (*Locke*, 143–6) all see some parallels between Locke's state of nature and Hobbes's: John Yolton ('Locke on the Law of Nature', 477–98), J. Anglim ('On Locke's State of Nature', *Political Studies*, 26 (1978), 78–90), W. Von Leyden (*Hobbes and Locke: The Politics of Freedom and Obligation* (New York: St Martin's Press, 1982), 110), and Peter Laslett (*Two Treatises*, 111–14), deny that Locke's vision was in any important sense comparable. More récently John Dunn has written that Locke 'does not differ widely from Hobbes (or indeed from Filmer) in his judgment of what men are like and how they can be expected to behave' (*Locke*, 46).

[48] Stillingfleet wrote much of man's inherent rationality, declaring like Locke that those who repudiate reason repudiate God: see *Irenicum* (*Works*, ii. 172); 'Sermon Preached at St Margaret's: Being a fast-sermon for the fire of London' (1666), ibid. i. 23); 'Of the Differences of Good and Evil' (i. 575); 'Of Tranquility and Peace of Mind' (i. 589).

[49] Locke, *Two Treatises*, 2. 2. 8, 13. Elsewhere he observed that 'the greater part are no strict observers of equity and justice' and that the natural state 'is full of fears and continual dangers' (ibid. 2. 2. 123). Even stronger sentiments were expressed in an undated manuscript fragment: 'If all things be left in common, want, rapine and force will unavoidably follow, in which state, as is evident, happinesse cannot be had, which cannot consist without plenty and security' (MS Locke c. 28, fols. 139–40: quoted in Cox, *Locke on War and Peace*, 6).

government was 'the proper Remedy for the Inconveniencies of the State of Nature', and in this Stillingfleet fully concurred. Most men, the Bishop believed, simply would not obey the law of their nature outside civil society; 'we must suppose nothing but Disorder and Confusion', and a condition 'having all imaginable Uneasiness attending it'. The 'great Inconveniencies' that Stillingfleet saw in the state of nature were precisely those outlined by Locke in the Second Treatise.[50] Neither man could conceive of a world in which mortal men acted on the basis of their true interests. And while both believed that a legitimate government could only be the product of an equitable social compact, where free men gave up some of their natural rights in order better to secure others, both were also convinced that man's fallen nature made necessary a strong civil order—and a legal system—whose purpose was to enforce the very law of right reason that so few would obey of their own volition. Theirs, surely, was a picture of human nature in its natural state far different from the brutal, fratricidal world summoned up by Thomas Hobbes. But it was not an especially pleasant place either. Their state of nature mirrored their larger view of man: an always-shifting amalgam of good and bad, where man's vulnerability to the lure of present interest made the task of the educator something less than attractive. As Stillingfleet remarked, it was problematical enough to bring the sinner to a recognition of his evil ways, 'but it is far more difficult to change the inward Disposition of the Mind, and to alter all the great Designs and Pleasures of Life'.[51] That men at least had the presence of mind to depart from their natural state bespoke their inherent rationality, their ability to understand and to remedy a very distressing situation; but that they were in the first place compelled to retreat to a state (civil society) admittedly less flattering said something else about the children of the only two beings who had ever really lived in a historical state of nature. And the lamentable story of their behaviour in that earthly paradise was common knowledge to all.

[50] Locke, *Two Treatises*, 2. 2. 13; Stillingfleet uses the term 'great Inconveniencies' when describing the state of nature in 'Sermon preached before the Queen at Whitehall, 1 March 1691', in *Works*, i. 469. See also his 'Of the Nature of the Trust Committed to the Parochial Clergy', (iii. 649); *Irenicum* (i. 237–8).

[51] Stillingfleet, 'Of the True Happiness of Mankind' (*Works*, i. 380).

It was because of this state of affairs that Stillingfleet adopted the same attitude towards the role of God's grace in the drama of salvation that Locke was to argue for in the *Reasonableness of Christianity*. The Mosaic law was clear and full, Stillingfleet said, and men were theoretically able to fulfil all its requirements and thus merit eternal salvation. But preferring to follow their passionate and sinful inclinations, the 'Reasons of Good and Evil are not so easily understood in this degenerate State'.[52] The new covenant of faith excused sinful men from the requirements of the law, but their apostasy was a fault entirely of their own making. In essence, Stillingfleet remained faithful to the Latitudinarian prescription for eternal salvation, and in that respect could find little fault with Locke's Christianity and the picture of man which it entailed. His celebrated controversy with the philosopher over the sceptical implications of the *Essay*, while certainly important in its own right, diverted attention from their agreement on the meaning of depravity in late seventeenth-century England.

That the kind of polemic against innate ideas undertaken by Locke did not involve as complete a rejection of original sin as Henry Hatrell had so confidently assumed, is perhaps best indicated by the fact that Richard Burthogge, himself an opponent of innateness and possibly the most important English thinker to anticipate Locke's way of ideas, conceived of the traditional Adam story in a manner which can only be described as strongly Calvinistic. He found no difficulty in denying innate ideas on the one hand and championing Pauline-Augustinian Christianity on the other. Like the Puritans, he thought it fully reasonable 'imputing unto all men the sin of One, when you consider that One was All; and that All are one'. Adam was once the whole of humanity, and his descendants 'proceeding out of him, were at first in him' and thus subject to death and damnation in similar fashion. Despite these views, however, Burthogge was able to win both the attention and the respect of Locke—and not on the basis of his epistemology alone. For Locke seems to have been equally impressed by Burthogge's religious ideas, especially his understanding of justification by

---

[52] Stillingfleet, 'Of the Differences of Good and Evil' (*Works*, i. 578).

faith, free will and its implications for morality, and the role of God's helping grace in the work of salvation.[53]

Burthogge's *Organum Vetus et Novum* anticipated Locke's *Essay* not only in discovering the origins of knowledge outside man in the world of sense experience—although he is best remembered in that context—but also in its plea for greater humility in opposition to what both men saw as the intellectual arrogance of the scholastic tradition. 'The most the Wisest know,' he insisted, 'is that their Own and other's Ignorance is the surest Object of Knowledge.' For Burthogge, all men might be created in the image of Adam, but they were also in possession of a free will which, if properly directed in accord with reason, would enable them to receive the assisting grace necessary for the forgiveness of those sins, including original sin, which none could avoid. The Creator of man, he asserted, would forgive the stain of original sin (which he described both as an affront to God's perfect nature and as a capitulation to the attractions of the flesh) along Latitudinarian lines.[54] Grace was universal on condition that each fulfilled the obligations of obedience to the best of his abilities, but perfection was impossible without this grace, and mankind's *tabula-rasa* status at birth provided no grounds for hope that someone somewhere might avoid the stigma and the consequences of Adam's apostasy.

Locke obviously would not accept Burthogge's Augustinian understanding of the Genesis story, but he was on common ground with him over the objective reality of man's sinful nature; and the means they envisioned by which men might be forgiven the inevitable transgressions associated with the Adamic human condition were all of a piece. The mistake that Hatrell had made, and that many after him in the eighteenth

---

[53] Richard Burthogge, *Divine Goodness Explicated and Asserted from the Exceptions of the Atheist* (London: S. and B. Griffen, 1672), 68; Burthogge to Locke (20 Nov. 1702: vii, no. 3214). Locke was interested in Burthogge's interpretation of various troublesome passages in Scripture: see above letter and Burthogge to Locke (4 May 1703: vii, no. 3278). For his part, Burthogge praised Locke as 'one of the greatest Masters of Reason' (Burthogge to Locke, 15 May 1694: v, no. 1737). In Feb. 1695 he sent Locke copies of his *Causa Dei* (1675) and *The Nature of Church Government* (1691): see MS Locke f. 10, fol. 265.

[54] Burthogge, *Organum Vetus et Novum* (London: Sam Crouch, 1678), 3–4; id., *Christianity a Revealed Mystery* (London: Lockyer Davis, 1755), pp. vi–vii; id., *Causa Dei: or an Apology for God* (London: Lewis Punchard, 1675), 42, 159.

century would continue to make, was in assuming that Locke's
theory of knowledge was in some primary respect determinative
of his theory of man, that his epistemology dictated his
anthropology. The former theory was, admittedly, stated
forcefully and unambiguously; the latter, unfortunately, was
less explicit. Still, that they were dissimilar is undeniable.
Locke's contemporary detractors seemed to recognize as much,
or at least they found no great threat to the idea of original sin in
his polemic against innateness. Many critics of the *Essay* could
agree with Locke on the practical consequences of the Fall and
the indispensability of saving grace in the Christian scheme of
things. Most would probably have agreed with him that 'were it
not for the corruption, and vitiousness of Degenerate Men' there
would have been no real need for them to have alienated certain
of their natural rights and entered into civil society.[55] But
searching out points of agreement was not, understandably, the
first thing on the minds of men who were consumed by the fear
that the religion taught by Christ might one day be ignored.
And that an intelligent man of affairs, a moulder of opinion like
Locke, whatever his intentions, might with his novel way of
ideas facilitate the downfall of that religion—thereby engaging
in the most reprehensible of all scholarly undertakings—seemed
altogether unpardonable.

[55] Locke, *Two Treatises*, 2. 9. 128.

7

Shaftesbury, Locke, and the Problem of the Moral Sense

IF in the search for common ground between Locke and his opponents, some of the underlying assumptions about human nature and human potential shared by liberal, rationalizing Christians of the late seventeenth century have been brought into sharper focus, we can now profitably turn our attention to the one relationship which in many respects clarifies that special vision even further, and in its own unique way underscores the important distinction to be made between Locke's view of man and that which was so often attributed to him by later generations. The relationship, it should be said, has been treated many times before, and to good purpose; but always with an emphasis on the issues that separated the principals, and only rarely with an eye towards those that brought them together. For an understanding of the problem of depravity in its seventeenth-century context, how the issue itself was becoming less a matter of Christian dogmatics and more a question of classical dualism restored, there is no better illustration than the story of Locke's friendship with the grandson of his former London patron.

Shaftesbury's celebrated disagreement with Locke over the question of the origin of moral ideas is fairly familiar to all Locke scholars. The third earl is perhaps best remembered as the principal founder of the so-called 'moral sense' school of English ethical theory, the forerunner of Joseph Butler, Francis Hutcheson, Adam Smith, and David Hume. The touchstone of this moral-sense doctrine, suggestions of which we have already seen in Cudworth, lay in the belief that true morality ultimately comes from within the individual who pursues the good for its own sake, rather than from the external, arbitrary decrees of a sometimes vengeful God. By inspiring a greater sense of confidence in human nature, Shaftesbury hoped to overturn one of the central assumptions of Pauline theology in general and of

Reformed Christianity in particular: the inability of men to live in accordance with the dictates of morality and right reason, to follow God's law without the intervention of Christ's prevenient saving grace and the promise of eternal reward. Shaftesbury posited a universe where everything had been designed for the best by a benevolent Creator, where men need not worry themselves overmuch about the apparent proximate cruelty of the world around them. To argue in favour of the independent existence of evil was, he maintained, to question either the omnipotence of that Creator or the essential goodness of his nature. Man's special duty in this wider system of the universe was to bring his own conduct, the product of myriad affections and passions, into accord with the greater harmony around him. The native ability to do this was there in everyone; all that was required in addition was the will and the determination to follow one's natural lights.[1]

Most discussions of Shaftesbury's philosophy leave off at this point. Indeed the overwhelming thrust of his collected works, *Characteristics of Men, Manners, Times* (1711), seems to confirm his endorsement of common deistic notions concerning the superfluity of Scripture and forgiveness. There is no mention made by Shaftesbury of the propitiatory sacrifice of Christ, the indelible stain of original sin, or the role of grace in any of his published writings. Nor is there any doubt that man can conduct himself, unaided, in a benevolent, public-spirited manner when guided by the moral sense.[2] But while this emphasis in the works of Shaftesbury upon man's inherent capacity for good is important in distinguishing him from the mainstream of seventeenth-century Protestant thinkers, it inevitably tends to direct our attention away from the extent to which the moral struggle, so

---

[1] R. L. Brett, *The Third Earl of Shaftesbury: A Study in Eighteenth Century Literary Theory* (London: Hutchison's University Library, 1951), 59–85; T. Fowler, *Shaftesbury and Hutcheson* (London: Sampson Low, 1882), 63–102; B. Willey, *The English Moralists* (London: Chatto and Windus, 1964), 216–32; L. Stephen, 'Shaftesbury's Characteristics', in *Essays in Freethinking and Plainspeaking* (New York: Putnam's Sons, 1905), 257–9; W. C. Swabey, *Ethical Theory*, 67–79; R. Toole, 'The Concepts of Freedom and Necessity in Shaftesbury's Philosophy', *Studia Leibnitiana*, 9 (1977), 190–6; J. Aronson, 'Shaftesbury on Locke', *American Political Science Review*, 53 (1959), 1101–4.

[2] J. A. Bernstein, 'Shaftesbury's Reformation of the Reformation: Reflections on the Relation between Deism and Pauline Christianity', *Journal of Religion and Ethics*, 6 (1978), 257–78; D. P. Walker, *Decline of Hell*, 168.

critical to the psychological foundations of original sin, was part and parcel of his overall philosophical position. Nowhere are the results of this latter aspect of Shaftesbury's thought more apparent than in his relationship with John Locke. Supposedly, Shaftesbury's formulation of the moral-sense doctrine put him irreversibly at odds with Locke over the latter's denial of innate moral ideas. In two much-quoted letters, both written five years after Locke's death, Shaftesbury accused the philosopher of undermining morality by substituting 'fashion and opinion' for universal 'virtue and honesty' with his denial of innateness. ''Twas Mr. Locke', he wrote to one correspondent, 'that struck at all fundamentals, threw all order and virtue out of the world, and made the very ideas of these (which are the same as those of God) unnatural, and without foundation in our minds.'[3] The philosophical gulf which developed between the two men was apparently unbridgeable because of this fundamental disagreement; in Shaftesbury's *Characteristics* we seem to witness a wholesale repudiation of one view of human nature which denied that man at birth possessed any specific nature, for a more sanguine estimate where his connatural disposition to good and intrinsic sense of right and wrong conducted him along the road to virtue and happiness.

The difficulty with this interpretation is that it fails to explain the genuine affection and mutual respect that both men continued to have for each other throughout their lives. Their experiences, their mutual friendships, their correspondence, and their formal published writings all bespeak a similarity of views on matters of vital import to their respective generations—similarities that go beyond the problem of the moral sense, and which ultimately place that special sense in its proper perspective. What needs to be examined here is the possibility that Shaftesbury's 'cosmic optimism' was always tempered by a

---

[3] Cooper to General James Stanhope (7 Nov. 1709; printed in Anthony Ashley Cooper, *The Life, Unpublished Letters, and Philosophical Regimen of Anthony Lord Shaftesbury*, ed. B. Rand (New York: Macmillan, 1900), 416); Cooper to Michael Ainsworth (3 June 1709: printed in id., *Several Letters Written by a Noble Lord to a Young Man at the University* (London: J. Roberts, 1716), no. 8); L. Stephen (*History of English Thought*, ii. 24) was probably the first scholar to mention Shaftesbury's 'unequivocal condemnation of Locke'.

strong dose of Lockean realism—and Lockean pessimism.[4] After all, if this were in fact the best of all possible worlds, one would expect Shaftesbury to have eschewed moral exhortation and resisted the reformist impulse. That he did not—that his life-long effort was to infuse others with a consciousness of the need for moral struggle and of the foibles of human nature—reflects, I think, an unwillingness to trust mankind with the unaided operation of the moral sense. Something else, it seems, was necessary if the moral sense were to be rendered fully operative in Shaftesbury's system.[5] And to the extent that Locke may have aided him in his search for that something else, the history of their friendship and its practical outcome is worth recalling.

It was, we know, through a chance meeting at Oxford in the summer of 1666 that Locke first made the acquaintance of Shaftesbury's grandfather Anthony Ashley Cooper, later first earl of Shaftesbury. The politician took an immediate liking to the young don, and subsequently attempted to assist him in his efforts to obtain the MD from the university.[6] During the spring of the following year Shaftesbury extended an invitation to Locke to come to London and join his household at Exeter House, located on the north side of the Strand. Locke's acceptance signalled the end of his career as a college tutor, and the beginning of a close friendship that would continue until the death of the older man in 1683. The relationship was significantly strengthened in 1668 when, in his capacity as family physician, Locke supervised an operation (to cauterize a liver abscess) that saved his friend's life.[7] Shaftesbury and his

---

[4] More recent studies of Shaftesbury correct the tendency to view his ethical teaching in an over-optimistic light, but Locke's contribution to Shaftesbury's thought in this area has been neglected. See R. Voitle, *The Third Earl of Shaftesbury* (Baton Rouge, La.: Louisiana State University Press, 1984), 131–2; S. Grean, *Shaftesbury's Philosophy of Religion and Ethics* (New York: Ohio University Press, 1967), 85–6, 224.

[5] 'The master motive of Shaftesbury', writes Ernest Tuveson, 'was reform—not through conversion, but by regeneration—the restoration of the human being to his true self' ('Shaftesbury on the Not So Simple Plan of Human Nature', *Studies in English Literature*, 5 (1965), 423).

[6] Cranston, *Locke*, 74, 93–5; Haley, *First Earl of Shaftesbury*, 203; Dewhurst, *Locke*, 23–4.

[7] On Locke and the first earl, see Pierre Coste, 'The Character of Mr. Locke', in Locke, *Works*, x. 167–8; Lady Masham to Jean Le Clerc (12 Jan. 1705: printed in Haley, op. cit. 217–18). On life and activities at Exeter House, see ibid. 215–19. Locke's residence there brought him 'much nearer to the places where decisions were actually made than Hobbes or Filmer had ever been' (ibid. 216; Cranston, op. cit. 116–21). On Shaftesbury's operation, see Dewhurst, op. cit. 37.

family were permanently grateful to Locke for the success of this dangerous procedure. Their confidence in his skill and judgement soon carried over into other areas of family concern, as in addition to his professional medical duties, Locke was placed in charge of the education and general welfare of Ashley's only son, and, subsequently, his grandson. Years later (again after the philosopher's death), the third earl recalled that he and six other siblings were educated according to the principles published by Locke in *Some Thoughts concerning Education*: 'I was his more peculiar charge, being as eldest son taken by my grandfather and bred under his immediate care, Mr. Locke having the absolute direction of my education'. Although doubtless expressive of Shaftesbury's fondness for his deceased friend, the claim was somewhat misleading in that Locke never actually tutored the youth; but his educational precepts were dutifully followed by the woman who was in charge of the day-to-day instruction.[8]

Within a year of the first earl's death in 1683, Locke had followed his former patron into exile in Holland. Young Ashley (the future third earl) was at this point sent off by his father to Winchester. He remained there for the next two years but was exceedingly unhappy at the treatment that he received on account of his grandfather's role during the Exclusion Crisis.[9] It was only after constant pleading with his father that he was excused from continuing with this ordeal and again placed under the supervision of a private tutor. Whether or not Locke endorsed this sojourn at a public school is unknown. But given the fact that he was at this time engaged in the correspondence which would eventually be published as *Some Thoughts concerning Education*, it is unlikely that he would have approved of the second earl's decision in the matter. In that work Locke advised against public-school education, declaring that the bad habits and vices endemic there would only undermine whatever virtue

---

[8] Third earl of Shaftesbury to Jean Le Clerc (8 Feb. 1705: in Cooper, *Life*, 332). The instruction was carried out by Elizabeth Birch, the daughter of a local schoolmaster. This woman remained in the Shaftesbury household as a tutor while Locke was away in France (1675–9) and was still in the family employ after his return: see Voitle, *Third Earl*, 7–12; J. G. Mason, 'Critical Interpretation', 113–15; *Thoughts on Ed.* 281–9.

[9] Anthony Ashley Cooper, fourth earl of Shaftesbury, 'A Sketch of the Life of the third earl of Shaftesbury', in Cooper, op. cit. p. xix.

the child had learned at home. Unless one could find a school, he cautioned his readers,

wherein it is possible for the Master to look after the Manners of his Scholars, and can shew as great Effects of his Care of forming their Minds to Virtue, and their Carriage to good Breeding, as of forming their Tongues to the learned Languages; you must confess, that you have a Strange value for words, when preferring the Languages of the Ancient Greeks and Romans, to that which made them such brave Men, you think it worth while, to hazard your Son's Innocence and Virtue, for a little Greek and Latin.[10]

What we do know is that by 1687 Locke was troubled by the paucity of letters from his former charge. He wrote to his kinsman Edward Clarke about the boy in April and was told that Ashley was planning to contact Locke during his forthcoming continental tour.[11] Shortly thereafter, Ashley and his new tutor Daniel Denoune visited Locke at the home of the expatriate Quaker Benjamin Furly and left some books with Locke in Rotterdam that November. Locke's considerable experience as a tutor in France during the 1670s (he had supervised the son of Sir John Banks at the first Lord Shaftesbury's request from 1676 to 1678), coupled with the wide-ranging ruminations on education in which he had been engaged between 1684 and 1687 (as attested by voluminous letters of advice to Clarke), ably fitted him to resume his role as adviser to the young man in this new setting. Ashley clearly valued the counsel, telling Locke in December that 'To thank you for the Advice I have Received in your Letters as well as from your mouth; would be a subject too bigg for this Paper, or indeed for my Toung, and is what I shall never attempt, or att least never Pretend to speak of as it deserves.'[12]

The separate return to England of Locke and Ashley in early 1689 marked the conclusion of what had been, in essence, a successful teacher-student relationship. After this time, we witness the emergence of a mature friendship—one which, despite their later philosophical differences, would remain firm for the rest of their lives. Instead of a dutiful Ashley reporting

---

[10] *Thoughts on Ed.* 165–6.
[11] Clarke to Locke (23 May 1687: iii, no. 935).
[12] Cooper to Locke (12 Dec. 1687: iii, no. 984).

back to Locke accounts of his travels and plans, we now find two friends engaged in a discussion of Locke's forthcoming *Essay concerning Human Understanding*. The problem of the nature of the soul was the particular topic of a meeting between the two in 1689; and in August of that year, Ashley 'bethought myself of the Practice you have so often advised me to', and wrote to Locke of his objections to the idea of the soul as immaterial substance. Ashley always appreciated Locke's open manner and affability, his willingness to include him in his serious philo-sophical pursuits—even when, as in the above instance, Ashley disagreed with him. 'You were used to treat mee att that Rate,' he told Locke in 1692, 'dealt with me so like a freind in every strictest Relation, Seem'd to seek my Company for my Company's sake, and conferr'd with mee upon Subjects as though you were really better for not being alone.' In *Some Thoughts concerning Education*, Locke would call for the tutor gradually to become the student's friend as the most efficacious means of winning the respect and bringing out the best efforts of the child. This dictum had proved an unqualified success in Ashley's case; the former student not only had an immense respect for his 'friend and foster-father', but had also developed a strong sympathy for Locke's educational ideas and the epistemological assumptions on which they were grounded.[13]

Ashley's Lockean views are best exemplified in his handling of an emerging family problem. Soon after his return from the continent, he felt obliged to give his father some advice on dealing with the education of his younger brother Maurice. Maurice had followed Ashley to Winchester, but was more successful in coping with the taunting of his schoolmates. His social accomplishments at the school were so great, in fact, that he had apparently frittered away the better part of his time there in revelling and ill-conduct, failing to learn even the rudiments of Latin grammar. The father was at a loss as to the reason for the failure; the eldest brother, however, had no doubts about the root cause of this debauchery. Maurice's 'natural temper', his 'perfect good nature', had been poisoned by constant bad

---

[13] Cooper to Locke (21 Nov. 1689: iii, no. 980; Aug. 1689: ibid. no. 1169; 3 Mar. 1692: iv, no. 1475); *Thoughts on Ed.* 145. For a discussion of the August 1689 letter see Voitle, op. cit. 65. Shaftesbury refers to Locke as his 'friend and foster-father' in a letter to Le Clerc (8 Feb. 1705: in Cooper, *Life*, 332).

example: 'so great a change of nature as this cannot have been worked but with the corruption of his mind, and by the untoward notions that have got into him by means of his idle company'.[14] In his letter, Ashley asked his father whether he had not noticed a radical change in Maurice's thought and behaviour, whether his 'trusty sincere plain dealing' had not become 'something of a surliness and a rugged conversation, not so open free or true hearted'. He was suggesting here that Maurice's essential character, his original make-up before the start of formal education, was in essence good. And in saying this he was assuming, it seems, the moral-sense doctrine which has traditionally been ascribed to him and which won considerable favour in the eighteenth century.[15] But whatever Ashley may have thought about the moral sense at this early date, one thing is clear: he did not consider Maurice's 'perfect good nature' powerful enough to withstand the attractions of vice and error that life at Winchester afforded. 'It is impossible but some example should lead him', he wrote; 'a very young life is formed after it, and there is but the good and the bad, so if the first be foresaken, the consequences you know.'[16] Without constant good example to guide him, in other words, the child would invariably succumb to that which was in opposition to the inclination of the moral sense. Locke, of course, had denied the existence of a separate moral sense when he abolished innate ideas in the *Essay*, hoping instead to ground morality on the basis of natural law discovered through the exercise of reason. Yet he could not have agreed more with Ashley's conclusions here in respect to the power of example for good or ill. Ashley's refusal to rest content with whatever 'good nature' we might possess at birth indicates his affinity for Lockean rigour in the educational process and his distrust of man's capacity and inclination for pursuing the good even with the moral sense operative at all times. His moral-sense doctrine, then, was really no more efficacious in furthering the interests of morality than were the innate ideas of Locke's most virulent opponents, the

[14] Cooper to second earl of Shaftesbury (July, 1689: ibid. 281).
[15] Ibid. 282. C. A. Moore, ('Shaftesbury and the Ethical Poets in England, 1700–1750', *Publications of the Modern Language Association*, 31 (1916), 264–325) traces Shaftesbury's influence in the eighteenth century.
[16] Cooper, op. cit. 281.

men who argued that Lockean epistemology undermined universal morality and obscured divine superintendence.

As for the hapless Maurice, Ashley contended that he must immediately be removed from Winchester and placed under the absolute direction of a private tutor of irreproachable reputation (he naturally suggested his own former governor Daniel Denoune as the best candidate). In other words, the only workable remedy at this late stage was a thoroughly Lockean one. The second earl assented to this recommendation of his eldest son and Denoune was given charge of Maurice's rehabilitation. His brother's education remained uppermost in Ashley's mind for some time to come, however. He consulted Locke concerning the boy's situation on more than one occasion, at one point asking Locke whether foreign travel would be best for Maurice's training and Denoune's failing health. Locke doubtlessly concurred with Ashley's designs for the education of his brother; his awareness that Ashley's views on this important subject were in accord with his own is reflected in the fact that he later solicited Ashley's advice on a suitable tutor for the son of his close friend Damaris Masham.[17] Both men were sensitive to the immense power of example in the educational process; and although Locke continued to insist upon the *tabula-rasa* mind at birth, while Ashley slowly formulated the notion of a connatural moral sense, neither individual was in the least bit naïve about mankind's penchant for ill whenever the steadying hand of the enlightened pedagogue was removed. Ashley's awareness of this unfortunate brute fact of human nature became clearer during the 1690s.

When he returned from the continent in the summer of 1689, Ashley was asked to stand for the Parliament which was to meet in March 1690, but he politely refused, preferring to focus his energies on family matters and private study. While we have no precise details, he undoubtedly concentrated on the classics, and especially on Greek philosophy—hoping, as he told Locke, to learn 'what Mankind has been heretofore, in former ages, and under former Revolutions; that I may Guess the better at what

---

[17] Cooper to Locke (21 Jan. 1692: iv, no. 1451); Locke to Cooper (7 July 1692: iv, no. 1512). Locke and Ashley had discussed the qualifications of a possible tutor for Masham earlier at Locke's home at Oates: see Cooper to Locke (25 Feb. 1692: iv, no. 1470).

they are, and may be expected to bee, in such a Turn of an Age and Time as is this present one'.[18] It was during these years that Ashley was engaged in writing the work which would later be published surreptitiously by the Deist John Toland under the title *An Inquiry Concerning Virtue and Merit*. Here the former student for the first time raised serious doubts about a view of man which had come to predominate in English thought, a view not entirely at odds with the outlook of John Locke.

Locke's *Essay concerning Human Understanding* was published in December 1689, and the ethical hedonism propounded therein, which Locke had adopted only after long reflection on the actual state of human nature, was rejected in the strongest terms by Ashley as a doctrine which made Christianity (so he believed) no better than a purely mercenary creed. Many seventeenth-century thinkers, as we have seen, had taken up a position which approximated to Locke's view. Puritans and more liberal churchmen had long emphasized the pleasures of heavenly reward, and while stressing the depravity of men and their inability to merit salvation, both had none the less continued to insist on the absolute necessity of good behaviour in accordance with the laws of God. But more than anyone else, Hobbes was the best known (and the most infamous) exponent of selfish individualism; and it was Hobbesian ethical relativism that Ashley would continue to associate with Locke's very different Christian doctrine.[19] In the *Essay*, Locke was willing to concede that whenever men perform their duties and live a peaceable life in hope of future reward, they were acting in a manner which approximated to true virtue. He had few scruples about drafting what were essentially man's less meritorious character traits into the service of morality. Ashley, however, was uneasy about this dubious compromise. To him it appeared

---

[18] Cooper to Locke (8 Sept. 1694: v, no. 1783). Shaftesbury's connection with Greek philosophy is discussed by E. Tiffany, 'Shaftesbury as Stoic', *Publications of the Modern Language Association*, 38 (1923), 642–84.

[19] As late as 1709 he told Michael Ainsworth that Locke had followed 'in the self-same tract' as Hobbes, banishing the idea of God and of all true virtue out of the universe: Cooper to Michael Ainsworth (3 June 1709: in Cooper, *Several Letters*, 38). See also R. Voitle, 'Shaftesbury's Moral Sense', *Studies in Philology*, 52 (1955), 34–5; D. Krook, *Three Traditions of Moral Thought* (Cambridge: University Press, 1959), 94–113; W. Alderman, 'The Significance of Shaftesbury in English Speculation', *Publications of the Modern Language Association*, 38 (1923), 137; Brett, *Third Earl*, 30.

more than a little shameful, dishonest even, to engage what everyone acknowledged were unattractive and often downright harmful elements of the human personality as the basis for moral action. The whole thing smacked of Hobbesianism to Ashley, and, to all appearances, he rejected it out of hand. Clearly, he thought, one could not be a truly good man when the only incentive to right behaviour was the promise of supernatural sanction, whether retribution or reward. To settle for this was tantamount to calling an otherwise wicked individual good 'when his hands are ty'd which hinders him from doing the harm that he has a mind to do'.[20] The good man, Ashley believed, could only be one who is convinced that right behaviour is worthy of a rational being—regardless of the inducements of heaven or the threats of hell—and who has as the immediate object of his affections both the good of his species and the wider system of creation of which he is a part.

His seriousness about this matter was emphasized to Locke soon after a visit which the young man made in 1691 to Locke's residence at Oates, Lady Masham's home in Essex. He informed his host that he had reached a point in his intellectual life at which it was impossible for him to respect anyone who acted 'without Love to Mankind, and Zeal for the Publick, and Impartiallity to Truth'. In his view, only absolute freedom from pride, 'the Plain Appearance of disinterestedness' could qualify a man as truly virtuous. And during the following summer, when Locke questioned him about the character of a possible tutor for Lady Masham's son, Ashley insisted that he could recommend no one who failed to demonstrate a sincere concern 'for somewhat more in Nature then what is meerly calld Ones self'. Because the sense of right and wrong was natural to man, 'being a first principle in our Constitution and Make', there was really no excuse for the person who pursued selfish interests without the least regard for the public good.[21]

This was obviously a very demanding standard by which to measure men, and Ashley recognized it as one that would be virtually impossible for the vast majority of his contemporaries

---

[20] Cooper, *An Inquiry Concerning Virtue* (London: A. Bell, 1699), 17. This is the Toland edition.

[21] Cooper to Locke, (31 Dec. 1691: iv, no. 1443; 7 July 1692: ibid. no. 1512); Cooper, *Inquiry Concerning Virtue*, 44.

to satisfy. For in the same letter where he established this lofty criterion, he admitted that men of his conviction would find life to be no easy passage: 'Now, doe but Consider the World as It is, and then say if I am not in a fine Case, and if I am not likely to have a pretty Time of Itt, if this goes on.' His despair about the unwillingness of men to act in a disinterested manner, to pursue the good out of the simple recognition that virtuous behaviour was most consonant with their rational nature, was again demonstrated almost three years later in a letter where Ashley had to turn down another invitation to visit Oates. In one sense his words can be viewed as the end product of his years of private study, of learning what 'man has been heretofore . . . and may be expected to bee'. He gloomily informed Locke that

the greatest part of what I doe in the world is not because I hope any thing; but because I think I must be doing. I can assure You I doe not act out of any Friendship to the Age, or to Mankind such as they are att present. were there no Principle to Engage mee to serve them, besides their own Meritt, besides their Characters, besides the opinion I had of them and the Esteem I bore them; upon my word it would fare ill with them, for any thing I were ever likely to doe in their behalf, tho in ever so pressing an occasion. I fancy that I am not apt to make to my self too flattering a Picture of the World. And I believe that whatever this public that you talk of, is like to have of my service; Itt will never have over much of my Respect.[22]

The obligation to serve was an immutable one for Ashley, always to be answered, even though it often appeared none too palatable, even though the bulk of humanity seemed ill-disposed to follow that same natural moral obligation. Only two months earlier he had confessed to Locke just how difficult it was to live up to this exacting standard, just how much 'Thought Exercize, and a Continuall Application' was necessary before one could begin to realize and sustain mankind's true potential for selfless devotion to the species.[23] Yet struggle one must, for to reject the goal was to repudiate man's essential nature, to fall headlong into the clutches of Puritan pessimism. Here was that tenacious faith in the moral sense which so animated the *Inquiry Concerning Virtue and Merit*, and which has so often been emphasized by students of Shaftesbury's philosophy—that

[22] Cooper to Locke (31 Dec. 1691: iv, no. 1443; 22 Nov. 1694: v, no. 1816).
[23] Cooper to Locke (8 Sept. 1694: v, no. 1783).

dogged insistence that men can, by an act of will, put service to their fellows into the forefront of their desires. And here too, although less widely recognized, was a distressed acknowledgement of practical reality, of the deep depravity of most men in a world made sometimes cruelly unbearable by pure dint of selfish effort. By this point in his life Ashley may have abandoned the Pauline theory of original sin; but many of the practical facts about man that it had been formulated to explain remained unavoidable and disturbing truths in his view of the world.

While the moral-sense doctrine was necessary, according to Ashley, if men were to become better Christians, this special sense was an extremely fragile thing—one which, in the absence of special training about its use for the humanity it existed to create, could, it seemed, all too easily lose its power over that small fraction of mankind for whom it was still compelling. Maurice had provided Ashley with his most poignant example of this harsh fact. And while Ashley continued to view man's basic nature at birth as good, his sense of right and wrong 'being an Affection of first rise and production in the affectionate part, the Soul or Temper', he conceded that there existed in everyone other contrary affections which could, if carelessly ignored, overwhelm the infant moral sense. Ashley identified three specific types, all jealously competing for possession of man, and all very familiar to Locke: the natural affections were those which led to the good of the public; the self-affections undertook to advance the interests of the private person; and the unnatural affections tended to nothing but evil, working constantly to service the irrational and the destructive in man. The task required of each person, and by implication of each educator, was to root out entirely the third type of affection while striking a delicate balance between the other two. Only then would one possess a 'natural temper' in Ashley's meaning of the term. 'What I count True Learning', he told an undoubtedly sympathetic Locke, 'is to know ourselves, what it is that makes us Low, and Base, Stubborn against Reason, to be Corrupted and Drawn away from Vertue.'[24] For while 'the highest

---

[24] Cooper to Locke (29 Sept. 1694: v, no. 1794); Cooper, *Inquiry Concerning Virtue*, 44. Basil Willey (*The Eighteenth Century Background* (Boston: Beacon Press, 1966), 69) is right to argue that for Shaftesbury 'the natural condition of a thing, and so of man, is not its original state, but rather that state in which it realizes most fully its inner intention, or individuating principle'.

improvements of temper are made in human kind, so the greatest corruptions and degeneracies are discoverable in this race'. It was an indisputable fact, Ashley maintained, that all 'worth and virtue depend on a knowledge of right and wrong, and on a use of reason, sufficient to secure a right application of the affections'. Locke, it should be mentioned, had been saying much the same thing for the previous thirty years.[25]

This was no easy matter, however. For Ashley, as for Locke, the arbiter of what constituted a proper balance had to be the faculty of mature reason. Like his former tutor, Ashley firmly believed that man was born a rational being, but that the simple provision of reason did not guarantee its continuous exercise and enlargement. Again like Locke, he insisted that man's inherent rationality would be of little use unless the power of reasoning was fully developed. All men were 'capable' of framing in their minds 'rational Objects of moral Good', but this potential had to be realized through proper education. A 'natural temper', said Ashley, was something to be learned over the course of many years; one might possess a rudimentary natural sense of right and wrong at birth, but this was unlikely, without training, to be of much help in a world of many difficult choices, where the individual was constantly buffeted by conflicting interests, and where the apparent good might only be just that. And if this education in the use of reason were neglected, then the unnatural and the self-affections would inevitably gain mastery over all, for 'It is most certain that by what proportion the natural and good Affections are lost or wanting in any Creature, by that proportion the ill and unnatural must prevail. It is the nature of every Passion by use and exercise to grow stronger and more confirm'd.' Ashley referred to this eclipse of the natural affections as a form of slavery whereby men eventually lose all character and steadiness of purpose in their lives, a view with which Locke would have heartily concurred.[26] In fact, aside

---

[25] Cooper, *Inquiry Concerning Virtue and Merit*, in *Characteristics of Men, Manners, Times*, ed. Robertson, i. 255, 291. Voitle (*Third Earl*, 125) writes that 'the moral sense is basically an activity of rational reflection and emotion'. See also L. Whitney, *Primitivism and the Idea of Progress* (New York: Octagon Books, 1934), 30; A. O. Aldridge, *Shaftesbury and the Deist Manifesto* (Philadelphia, Pa.: American Philosophical Society, 1951), 312. In *Thoughts on Ed.* 244 Locke insisted that 'few of Adam's children are so happy, as not to be born with some Byass in their natural Temper, which it is the Business of Education either to take off, or counter-balance'.

[26] Cooper, *Inquiry Concerning Virtue*, 35, 123, 177, 183.

from their disagreement over the existence of the moral sense, there was a great deal of similarity between their respective ideas at this date. Both believed that men were rational beings who had the capacity to develop the power of reason; both identified the good individual as one whose every thought and action was under the unerring guidance of reason; both emphasized the necessity of formal individualized education as a prerequisite to developing this God-given power; and, perhaps most revealingly, both despaired of ever seeing more than a tiny minority of men actually live according to reason's dictates.

Ashley even retreated from his steadfast refusal to recognize the possible service which the selfish instincts might contribute in the quest after virtue. In religion, he grudgingly accepted the need for other-worldly sanctions, for 'however servile soever it may be accounted', fear of God's wrath 'must prove a seasonable remedy against vice, and be in a particular manner advantageous to virtue'. And when discussing the best means for educating youth into the practice of disinterested benevolence, Ashley suggested—in words filled with Lockean overtones—that rewards and punishments might be of some use after all: the master of each household, 'using proper rewards and gentle punishments towards his children, teaches them goodness, and by this help instructs them in a virtue, which afterwards they practice upon other grounds, and without thinking of a penalty or a bribe'.[27] The thorny issue of just how the child would graduate from expectation of reward to disinterested service was left unclear, of course, but Ashley's concession to self-interest, at least in the case of the child who lacked the full use of mature reason, says a good deal about the author's understanding of the inherent impotence of the moral sense. That sense, he seems to have realized, was for all practical purposes inconsequential, of little use by itself in the pursuit of morality. The hypothesis of its existence embodied all of the weaknesses alleged against the theory of innate ideas by Locke in the *Essay*, and Ashley seems to admit as much. For while, by Ashley's account, all other creatures live effortlessly according to nature, 'Man in the mean

---

[27] Cooper, *Inquiry Concerning Virtue and Merit* (*Characteristics*, i. 270, 273). See the passages on reward in *Thoughts on Ed.* 153, 155–6, where Locke argued that while 'Reputation' based on praise and commendation was not the 'true principle and measure of Virtue . . . it is the proper Guide and Encouragement of Children, till they grow able to judge for themselves, and to find what is right by their own Reason'.

time, vicious and unconsonant man, lives out of all rule and proportion, contradicts his Principles, breaks the Order and Economy of all his Passions, and lives at odds with his whole Species, and with Nature: so that it is next to a Prodigy to see a Man in the world who lives Naturally, and as a Man.'[28]

The third earl's true position on this matter became clearer with the publication of the *Characteristics of Men, Manners, Times* in 1711. Locke had died in 1704, but the impression which he had made upon Shaftesbury's mind remained evident. For while it is on the basis of this collection of short pieces that Shaftesbury's philosophy is most often contrasted to that of Locke, if we look beyond the divergence of opinion over innate ideas and seek out the whole of what Shaftesbury was saying about human nature in these essays, we discover that nothing much had changed since the early 1690s. The same insistence upon the difficulty of moral conduct, and of the process by which it might be achieved, continued unabated.

Writing in 1709 on the problem posed by some recently arrived French religious extremists, Shaftesbury repeated a conviction originally stated by Locke and borne out by the entire sweep of seventeenth-century history, especially in England: that the self-deception men continuously engaged in had its root in excessive passion, in the failure of judicious self-restraint. 'One would think', he observed, 'it were in reality no hard thing to know our own weaknesses at first sight, and distinguish the features of human frailty, with which we are so well acquainted.' At this stage of his life Shaftesbury expressed little sense of surprise at the ingrained depravity of mankind. The will of most men, despite its much-lauded freedom, was for all practical purposes irretrievably under the governance of 'Humour and Fancy'. Without the constant supervision of a 'certain inspector or auditor established within us', religious fanaticism could never be eliminated.[29] The *Essay concerning*

---

[28] Cooper, *Inquiry Concerning Virtue*, 99.

[29] Cooper, *A Letter Concerning Enthusiasm to my Lord Somers*, in *Characteristics*, i. 28; id., *Soliloquy: or Advice to An Author* (ibid. 122). In the *Essay*, 2. 21. 38, Locke admitted that while reason should guide the will, 'that it is not so is visible in Experience. The infinitely greatest confessed good being often neglected, to satisfy the successive uneasiness of our desire pursuing trifles.' On the plight of the French Protestants known as Camisards and Shaftesbury's reaction, see D. Schlegel, *Shaftesbury and the French Deists* (Chapel Hill, NC: University of North Carolina Press, 1956), 3; R. Knox, *Enthusiasm* (New York: Oxford University Press, 1950), 365–71.

Human Understanding comes to mind immediately when we hear this partisan of the moral sense declare that 'As cruel a court as the Inquisition appears; there must, it seems, be full as formidable a one, erected in our selves' if mankind is to hold firm to one will, one mind, one purpose. But Shaftesbury had no illusions about the prospects for the establishment of reason's judicature; he regarded the peccant appetites as reason's elder and stronger brothers. Time and again they would overwhelm the will and nullify the adjudicative claims of reason and the moral sense. Only men of 'liberal education', of 'thorough good breeding', could hope to resist this usurpation. And even amongst this select group, only that small minority 'who Early in their youth have learnt their exercises, and form'd their notions under the best masters' could emerge the victors in this endless contest for possession of one's own soul. To succeed, Shaftesbury believed, they must thoroughly examine all their ideas before acting—a procedure that Locke would heartily have endorsed. Either expel the suggestions of fancy in all circumstances, Shaftesbury concluded, or 'she must be judg of all'.[30]

For most of humanity, the condition that Shaftesbury had earlier associated with slavery had now become by his reckoning sheer 'madness', a state of affairs where men had lost the only freedom with which they had been endowed by a benevolent Creator: their lives, it appeared, attested the accuracy of Pauline theology. According to Shaftesbury's moral-sense hypothesis, men were not predisposed to do evil in the world, but the facts of daily living told a different story—one which for us should raise serious questions about the primacy of that hypothesis in Shaftesbury's thought. 'The misfortune of Youth,' he wrote in 1707, 'and not of Youth only, but of Human Nature, is such, that it is a thousand Times easier to frame the highest Idea of Virtue and Goodness, then to practice the least Part.' Because he was forced to concede that the fancies and passions in men were irremovable and apparently uncontrollable parts of their physical and intellectual make-up, and that, consequently,

---

[30] Cooper, *Soliloquy*, 122, 123; id., *Essay on the Freedom of Wit and Humour*, in *Characteristics*, i. 84, 86. See also his *Miscellaneous Reflections* (ibid. ii. 280), and 'Philosophical Regimen' (*Life*, 177, 254).

the 'mere vulgar of mankind' would always stand in need of 'such a rectifying object as the gallows before their eyes', the outlook of this philosopher of good sense strikes us, as it probably struck him towards the end of his life, not as the confident and reassuring one that it initially promises to be, but as a troubled and unsettling one—again, surprisingly similar to Locke's.[31] To the degree that this important fact is overlooked, Shaftesbury's philosophy is misunderstood. All this is not to deny that his chief aim in the *Characteristics* was to restore credibility to man's more generous instincts and to demonstrate the natural advantages which accrue from following those instincts. Nor is it to ignore the fact that a legitimate difference of opinion existed between Shaftesbury and Locke over the moral-sense issue: there is no question that the spectre of Hobbes and his own erroneous reading of Locke in this area was the central concern of everything that Shaftesbury published after his friend's death: it is only to argue that saying this is not enough, that the resulting picture is incomplete and unnecessarily distorted. His disagreement with Locke was significant, but only in the context of his failure, shared by so many others in the late seventeenth century, to understand Locke's position on the origins of universal morality. His concurrence with Locke on the even more basic problems of man's nature and of the springs of action was of equal, if not greater, significance.

In order to rehabilitate human nature in the eyes of his contemporaries, Shaftesbury had broken with the orthodox Christian notion of Christ as redeemer, along with the understanding that man's need for prevenient grace made it impossible for him in any way to measure up to the high standard of conduct necessary for salvation under the law. Perfection in the Christian sense, after all, had traditionally meant being redeemed by Christ's unique sacrifice, being freed from the infinite demands of the law, and perfected by his grace, not simply imitating his good example in our lives. But in abolishing man's absolute dependence upon God, in making the Creator a supernumerary by discovering the moral law within each individual at birth, in holding out the possibility that man

---

[31] Cooper to Michael Ainsworth (19 Nov. 1707: in Cooper, *Several Letters*, no. 3); Cooper, *Soliloquy*, 208; id., *Essay on the Freedom of Wit and Humour*, 84. See also his 'Philosophical Regimen', 118.

might work towards perfection without assistance, Shaftesbury was removing whatever help the Christian might have called upon in the orthodox scheme of things. And given his doubts about the willingness of most men to do what was necessary in this world, and his effective removal of any hope for prevenient grace to aid men in pursuing the good, the burdens of this life became all the more onerous and the chances for substantive improvement terribly remote, except possibly for a few virtuosi like himself.[32] The orthodox Christian's corrupt tendencies could at least be counteracted through the unmerited infusion of Christ's saving grace: it was this bedrock faith which had made Reformed Christianity so dynamic and appealing during the course of the sixteenth and seventeenth centuries, appealing even to those like Locke who questioned so much of long-standing Christian tradition. With Shaftesbury, the situation was otherwise: each Christian was entirely on his own, come what may, in the difficult search for perfection.

Still, the consciousness of the moral struggle, always an integral part of the orthodox faith, and of original sin as understood by the orthodox, was there in Shaftesbury as well, in the never-ending pull and tug between the clamorous appetites and the dictates of right reason. So, too, was the recognition that more often than not reason would fail to master the situation. But the orthodox (and Locke is included here) at least had reason for some hope in the face of this hard fact: Shaftesbury could have little. In his pains to elevate man's essential nature and to discredit the Hobbesian and the Puritan positions, he had, perhaps unwittingly, raised the stakes of the game enormously. Like Pelagianism, Shaftesbury's system left no excuse for failure—for sin—no way around its terrible consequences. Each individual possessed complete free will and the natural power to triumph over the evil within his heart. Each was very much alone in this best of all possible worlds; and while the faculty of God-given reason, together with the operation of the moral sense, appeared to justify a measure of guarded optimism, the most cursory glance at the facts of experience as outlined by Shaftesbury exposed that appearance for the mirage it was.

[32] J. B. Broadbent, 'Shaftesbury's Horses of Instruction', in *The English Mind: Studies in the English Moralists Presented to Basil Willey*, ed. H. S. Davies and G. Watson (Cambridge: University Press, 1964), 79–80.

Conclusion: School-time for Locke

THE problem of depravity and its relationship to the thought of Locke was never really an issue for the eighteenth century, nor has it seriously engaged the attention of our own. Perhaps this state of affairs was inevitable, given that the *Essay*, when read, as it normally was, in isolation from the rest of Locke's private and public thoughts (excepting possibly the popular *Thoughts concerning Education*), did readily lend itself to the most sanguine of interpretations. By those who succeeded him, Lockean epistemology was viewed as revolutionary not only in its assumptions about the nature of man, but also in its attitude towards the institution of the family and, more importantly, towards the role and responsibility of the parent as educator. We are informed by scholars that prior to Locke's work the theory and practice of child-rearing had generally emphasized control over the youngster's inherently evil nature, stressing the importance of obedience, restraint, authority, and even fear; by the end of the eighteenth century, however, the emphasis had, under Locke's influence, shifted: child-rearing was now viewed as a pursuit of rational behaviour on the part of the child, with the family as educative agency, and the parent as gentle preceptor, affectionate counsellor, and sympathetic guide. And whereas in the world of Locke's youth individual failings— moral obliquity, deliberate sinfulness, acts of wilful inhumanity—would all normally have been ascribed to the inborn depravity of the perpetrator, a century later these same actions would usually be considered a result of circumstances external to the child, of parental dereliction of duty rather than of childhood degeneracy. In other words, by the beginning of the nineteenth century, if not sooner, the ultimate responsibility for the sinful behaviour of a child was no longer regarded as lying with the sinner, but rather with those charged with bringing the child into the exercise of benevolent reason.[1] This change in attitude was without much question an intellectual metamorphosis of fundamental import, at bottom nothing less than an absolute repudiation of original sin; and while it had enormous implications for the possible reform of society and the improvement, nay, the perfection of man, with this revolution in ideas Locke, we have argued, had very little to do.

The evidence, or at least that side of the evidence with which we are most familiar, seems to demand the opposite conclusion. Locke, after all, had clearly stated in *Some Thoughts concerning Education* that all children were exceedingly malleable beings possessed of empty-cabinet minds 'as easily turned this or that way, as Water itself'. And in the posthumous *Conduct of the Understanding*, a rather lengthy piece that he intended to include as a final chapter to the *Essay*, Locke even advanced the claim that the radical empiricism of the *Essay* had important implications for the amelioration of the human condition through careful education. For there he argued that 'most men come very short of what they might attain unto in their several degrees by a neglect of their understandings', suggesting that all might be set right by proper attention to the formation of character.[2] Indeed, Locke's whole career as an educator—first at Christ Church, then in Shaftesbury's household, later in France as a tutor to the son of the English financier Sir John Banks, and finally in his advice to friends like Edward Clarke and Lady Masham—helped to give him a clear insight into the dynamics of the learning process. His unfailing confidence in the determinative power of custom and habit pointed, or so it appeared, clearly in the direction of a changed outlook on human nature, one which stressed the relationship between environment and personality instead of mankind's fixed nature

[1] J. Fliegelman, *Prodigals and Pilgrims: The American Revolution against Patriarchal Authority, 1750–1800* (New York: Cambridge University Press, 1982), 9–35; J. H. Plumb, 'The New World of Children in the Eighteenth Century', *Past and Present*, 67 (1975), 64–71; L. Stone, *The Family, Sex and Marriage in England, 1500–1800* (New York: Harper and Row, 1977), 174–8, 232–9, 405–15; P. Aries, *Centuries of Childhood*, trans. R. Baldick (New York: Knopf, 1962). A similar argument is made for nineteenth-century America by Bernard Wishy, *The Child and the Republic* (Philadelphia, Pa.: University of Pennsylvania Press, 1968).

[2] Locke, *Thoughts on Ed.* 115; id., *Conduct of the Understanding*, 5. Locke's plan to incorporate the *Conduct* into the larger *Essay* was revealed in a letter to Molyneux (10 Apr. 1697: vi, no. 2243).

or, more properly speaking, the historic Christian view of man.

Others have already surveyed the influence of Lockean ideas on the thought of the eighteenth century. From *Cato's Letters* to the pages of the *Spectator* and *Tatler*, in Richardson's *Pamela* and in Sterne's *Tristram Shandy*, as over the educational theories of John Clarke, Isaac Watts, Philip Doddridge, and James Burgh, the epistemology of the *Essay* and the perceived optimism of *Some Thoughts concerning Education* exercised a special influence. William Warburton's boast in 1759 that 'Locke is universal' was surely an exaggeration, but one suspects that the basis of the claim was firm enough. It is, in fact, not difficult to imagine how the way of ideas could lead men in a progressively more radical direction—how, for example, the tentative Lockeanism of the converted Voltaire in the 1720s could ultimately become the thoroughgoing sensationalism of a Condillac in the 1740s or a Helvetius in the 1760s. Ernst Cassirer has described the spirited efforts of the later *philosophes* to get rid of the dualism of sensation and reflection peculiar to Locke's theory, to simplify the learning process even further, to help make a repackaged Locke appear convincing in the guise of the great liberator.[3] These matters, however, take us well beyond our present concern. What we have attempted to consider is the possibility that Locke would have found all these efforts on behalf of his philosophy ultimately unsatisfying and too far removed from his original intentions to meet with endorsement. We have tried to picture a man working throughout his adult life, with unflagging dedication, to articulate and defend what was still very much a Christian view of human nature and human potential: a view

---

[3] G. E. Smock, 'John Locke and the Augustan Age of Literature', *Philosophical Review*, 55 (1946), 246–81; E. Tuveson, 'Locke and the Dissolution of the Ego', *Modern Philology*, 52 (1955), 159–74; Maclean, *Locke and English Literature*; Pickering, *Locke and Children's Books*; Ezell, 'Locke's Images of Childhood', 139–55; G. Buchdahl, *The Image of Newton and Locke in the Age of Reason* (New York: Sheed and Ward, 1961); L. Cremin, *American Education: The Colonial Experience* (New York: Harper and Row, 1978), 273–86; M. Curti, 'The Great Mr Locke: America's Philosopher, 1783–1861', *Huntington Library Bulletin*, 11 (1937), 107–51; J. J. Chambliss, 'Reason, Conduct and Revelation in the Educational Theory of Locke, Watts and Burgh', *Educational Theory*, 26 (1976), 372–87; J. Lawson, 'An Early Disciple of Locke: John Clarke, Educator and Moralist', *Durham Research Review*, 4 (1962), 30–7; Voltaire, *Lettres philosophiques* (Paris: Librairie Garnier Frères, 1944), 61–70; Condillac, *Essay on Origin of Human Knowledge*; Helvetius, *Treatise on Man*; E. Cassirer, *The Philosophy of the Enlightenment* (Princeton, Pa.: University Press, 1979), 99–101. Bishop Warburton is quoted in Cragg, *Reason and Authority*, 6.

that was shared, as we have seen, by many of his contemporaries, even those who opposed him on other issues of great concern to the Christian faith. If, as we have argued, Locke's view of man was closer to that, say, of William Perkins than to that of William Godwin, then one would naturally expect elements of the former perspective to have been clearly evident in the one work Locke devoted exclusively to education—an undertaking begun almost inadvertently in 1684 but refined and rewritten again and again in the 1690s. That evidence, I believe, is there, and it is to be gleaned not so much from specific passages within the work (although there are many) that counterbalance the more extreme environmentalist statements, but rather from the assumptions which inform the spirit of the book as a whole: assumptions never plainly articulated because they were a part of the common intellectual inheritance of the late seventeenth century, the very warp and woof of a long-standing world view.[4] *Some Thoughts concerning Education* reflected Locke's deep concern for the state of moral conduct in his country, especially amongst the middle and upper classes, and the very fact that he consented to publish anonymously what were, after all, personal and private thoughts intended to aid in the upbringing of a gentleman's son, testifies to the depth of his concern both for his own generation and for those yet unborn.

We must be reminded, however, that *Some Thoughts concerning Education* was written specifically for a gentleman's son. This important fact is unhappily often overlooked: indeed, many eighteenth-century thinkers at times simply ignored it. Locke, like most men of his particular social station, cared little for the vast majority, the ninety per cent of the population that he often referred to in language which seems, to our ears, cruelly insensitive.[5] But cruel towards his social inferiors he was not, nor

---

[4] 'It is the beliefs which are so much a matter of course that they are rather tacitly presupposed than formally expressed and argued for, the ways of thinking which seem so natural and inevitable that they are not scrutinized with the eye of logical self-consciousness, that are often most decisive of the character of a philosopher's doctrine, and still oftener of the dominant intellectual tendencies of an age' (Lovejoy, *Great Chain of Being*, 7).

[5] See above, p. 125; J. L. Gorn, 'The Strange Case of Edward Clarke, Jr.: Attending Physician—John Locke, Gent.', *Educational Theory*, 17 (1967), 298–316. Neal Wood, (*The Politics of Locke's Philosophy* (Berkeley, Calif.: University of California Press, 1983), 35) argues that 'Locke believed that the laboring majority were definitely a breed apart, an order of men inferior to the propertied minority.' See also Hundert, 'Making of *Homo Faber*', 5.

even contemptuous in any meaningful sense of the word. He simply believed, as did most of his peers, that those who held leadership positions in society were there because they deserved to be there, that the privileged few who set the tone in politics and in economic life should also do the same in the sphere of morality. Assumptions about leadership in seventeenth-century England, about power and its proper exercise, were inextricably linked to a set of religious values which subtly, and perhaps perniciously, comforted those amongst the fortunate few with assurances that their present station was no fluke of nature, no unmerited caprice, but rather a clear sign of God's good favour and design. One did not need to identify oneself with all things Puritan to share such assumptions, although this might well have been Locke's firmest bond with his Puritan past. They were part of an attitude easily compatible with any religious perspective, a powerful point of view where poverty, as Professor Tawney has written, was no longer considered the best policy for the serious Christian. The change of values in such matters as the role of wealth in Christian eschatology, begun in the sixteenth century, had by Locke's day been completed. The poor were by then regarded as having no one but themselves to blame, both for their exiguous existence here on earth and for the bleak prospects which awaited them beyond things known. And so when Locke wrote in his journal that 'The three great things that governe mankind are Reason, Passion and Superstition', his further observation that 'The first govern[s] a few, the last two share the bulk of man kinde and possess them in their turns', was entirely consistent with an outlook which extended little hope for voluntary improvement in the lives of most, and which led easily to schemes for the forceable employment of the poor like the one that Locke drew up in 1697 as a member of the Board of Trade.[6]

If, as indicated in that rather infamous proposal, Locke could regard the increase in the number of poor as due to nothing else 'but the relaxation of discipline and corruption of manners', if beggars under the age of fourteen found outside their parish

---

[6] Tawney, *Religion and Rise of Capitalism*, 253–73. See also C. Hill, *Change and Continuity in Seventeenth Century England* (Cambridge, Mass.: Harvard University Press, 1975), 81–102; Schlatter, *Social Ideas of Religious Leaders*, 187–205; MS Locke f. 5, fol. 59 (journal entry for 16 May 1681).

were to be sent to workhouses, 'there to be soundly whipped and kept at work till evening', and if in these workhouses (Locke titled them 'working schools') poor children between the ages of three and fourteen were to learn spinning and knitting only, then the author must have regarded the *tabula-rasa* psychology as of little or no practical significance for children who, like those paupers, were part of the great majority of the population. These children might through the school be 'brought into some sense of religion', might 'from infancy be inured to work', and might at least find employment once released; but beyond this Locke expected little.[7] Pierre Coste, who translated *Some Thoughts* into French during 1695, remarked in his preface that while the book 'was particularly designed for the education of Gentlemen . . . this does not prevent its serving also for the education of all sorts of Children, of whatever class they are'. Excepting those passages applicable specifically to a gentleman, asserted Coste, 'nearly all the rules that he gives, are universal'.[8] This may be so, but the fact remains that Locke himself expected few, if any, below the rank of gentleman to have the opportunity to put his principles to the test. Like the poet Milton, he considered most men

> but a herd confus'd,
> A miscellaneous rabble, who extol
> Things vulgar, and well weigh'd scarce worth the praise.[9]

The aristocrat Shaftesbury was more hopeful here, although even his expectations were, as we have seen, quite limited; and, like Locke, he never conceived the possibility of a world without rigid class distinctions. *Some Thoughts concerning Education* was plainly conceived and written in the tradition of English courtesy literature; and like Thomas Elyot, the author of the first important work in that genre, *The Book of the Governor*, Locke was far more interested in guaranteeing the status of the gentleman, in making education relevant to the needs of that tiny minority of men who 'owned most of the wealth, wielded

---

[7] Locke's Poor Law reform proposal is printed in Fox Bourne, *Locke*, ii. 377–90: quotations are from pp. 378, 381, 384, 385. For a useful discussion, see W. A. Bruneau, 'Towards a History of Moral Education: Some Fundamental Considerations and a Case Study', *Paedagogica Historica*, 15 (1975), 375–7.

[8] Coste is quoted in *Thoughts on Ed.* 52.

[9] *Paradise Regain'd*, iii. 49–51 (ed. cit. ii. 44).

the power and made all the decisions, political, economic and social for the national whole', than he ever was in freeing the likes of the Pensford peasantry from their endless round of backbreaking toil on properties owned by men of quality like himself.[10]

His bifurcated conception of human roles did not, however, mean that Locke was inconsistent on the subject of human nature. Privileged gentlemen might be moulded into great exemplars of Christian morality, but with respect to their standing in the search for salvation they possessed no special advantage. Even the extended leisure which wealth made possible was more a burden for the gentleman than an advantage, because the enhanced opportunities that resulted for them to demonstrate rational behaviour made apostasy all the more serious. One is reminded here of Locke's discussion of the apostles in the *Reasonableness of Christianity*, where he notes that 'a company of poor, ignorant, illiterate men' was chosen by Christ above the 'wise and prudent' to deliver the message of forgiveness and salvation. Those better situated to know and to question, Locke wrote in an obvious reference to the sin of pride, 'would hardly have been kept from prying into his [Christ's] design and conduct; or from questioning him about the ways and measures he would take, for ascending the throne; and what means were to be used towards it, and when they should in earnest set about it'. He seemed to imply in those references that ignorance and low station were clear advantages in religion, a position at odds with the otherwise inquisitive temper of the book. The point that Locke was making here, one that he had made as early as 1678 when a rather bothersome clergyman by the name of Richard Grenville wrote seeking advice on the limits of duty for men of leisure, had to do with the special responsibilities that were, despite the fact that they shared a common nature with those of a lesser rank, incumbent upon persons of Locke's (and Grenville's) own social status. Those responsibilities could be discharged—and a gentleman achieve salvation—not by mastering the rules of scholastic logic, not by immersing onself in pedantic erudition, but only by practising

---

[10] P. Laslett, *The World We Have Lost* (New York: Scribner's Sons, 1967), 27. Elyot's goals are discussed by S. E. Lehmberg, *Sir Thomas Elyot: Tudor Humanist* (Austin, Tex.: University of Texas Press, 1960), 36–51.

learned virtue, by 'denying our selves the Satisfaction of our own Desires, when Reason does not authorize them'.[11]

We have already seen how Locke's proposals for pedagogical and curricular reform, together with his emphasis on the role of habit and custom, were anticipated by men who had very little sympathy for Pelagian principles, and how Locke could speak on behalf of *tabula rasa* and still remain within the boundaries of Latitudinarian doctrine on the Fall. That Locke's opinion that 'all the men we meet with, nine parts of ten, or perhaps ninety nine of one hundred, are what they are, good or evil, useful or not, by their education'—surely one of the most over-used and abused excerpts from his *Thoughts concerning Education*—could be somehow consistent with the general import of Articles 9–13 of the Church of England may seem difficult to imagine, if what is emphasized concerns pre-existent guilt, as opposed to inevitable but none the less deliberate transgression against God's law. Locke's deep conviction—his faith—that the sin of Adam, while not charged directly to his posterity, had none the less nullified their chances of ever obeying to the fullest extent the law of their own nature, meant that the goodness to be acquired through education was a thing of very limited proportion, and, by itself, ultimately of no value in overcoming the consequences of Adam's act of disobedience. Still, it was obviously necessary if the saving grace of Christ were to raise men up from the depths of their sinful condition. Locke's successors were consumed by the positive implications of *tabula rasa*; Locke himself, however, was acutely conscious both of what the gentleman could become under the guidance of an enlightened tutor and of what (because of his association with the first man) he would become without it. For Locke, then, education was a holding action, an exhausting and never-ending struggle to check our natural proclivity for that which was forbidden us. *Some Thoughts concerning Education* would have been an unnecessary work for Locke, a waste of time better employed otherwise in the service of his Creator, had it not been for the fact that he believed all men to be, by their own choice, obnoxious to God—had he not, that is, been a believing Christian.

---

[11] *Locke, Reasonableness (Works*, vii. 83); *Thoughts on Ed.* 143, 241; Locke to Grenville (13 Mar. 1678: i, no. 374).

Thus, when his book on education became popular in the years after Locke's death, it became so substantially because men treated it the way they treated his other published works: they took from it those elements most compatible with a new vision of humanity that would have been considered empirically invalid by Locke in his own day. Where the author wanted 'to make the best of what nature has given', others set out to recreate nature itself. Where he cautioned that a child's natural love of 'dominion', and his unbridled quest for 'Propriety and Possession' constituted 'two Roots of almost all the Injustice and Contention, that so disturb Humane Life', others blamed these failings on context or environment. And when at last he sought to qualify the applicability of his more general observations, insisting that 'There are a thousand other things, that may need consideration; especially if one should take in the various Tempers, different Inclinations, and particular Defaults, that are to be found in Children', succeeding generations confidently ignored him. 'For few of Adam's Children are so happy,' Locke wrote to an increasingly unreceptive audience, 'as not to be born with some Byass in their natural Temper, which it is the Business of Education either to take off, or counterbalance.'[12] Here was the unmistakable voice of seventeenth-century Christianity, an axiomatic statement for men convinced that the Adam story provided the only viable framework for understanding their lamentable and contingent condition. But what had Adam to do with the eighteenth century? Not, as it turned out, a very great deal. What had enlightened education to do with counter-balancing evil bias if in fact the child were *tabula rasa*? What business had Locke meddling with such false Augustinian notions? Evidently it was decided by many of the theorists who followed him that it was best not to trouble themselves over such potentially embarrassing matters.

But Locke troubled himself over them—worried, questioned, wrote—and was honest enough to admit that the situation often

---

[12] *Thoughts on Ed.* 159, 207, 244, 325. In *Two Treatises* 2. 3. 17 Locke described wilful possessiveness as 'a State of War': 'And hence it is, that he who attempts to get another Man into his Absolute Power, does thereby put himself into a State of War with him; It being to be understood as a Declaration of a Design upon his Life.' On the child's natural desire for dominion over others, see N. Tarkov, *Locke's Education for Liberty* (Chicago: University Press, 1984), 130–2.

defied plain reason and eluded education. Over the winter of
1700–1, Benjamin Furly's youngest son Arent, whom the father
described as 'extraordinarily dilligent, and covetous, not of
mony, but learning', and for whom Locke had developed an
especial fondness during his stay under Furly's roof in the last
two years of his exile, visited Locke at Oates. The father was
unsure at this time about the fifteen-year-old's future; Arent
preferred the life of a scholar, but Furly was worried that this
course could guarantee his son only unremitting penury. Furly
asked Locke his advice on the matter, hoping that the former
tutor and educational theorist might provide some special
insights. Locke's response was unfortunately of little help to
Furly, but it is of some importance to us. For instead of directing
his observations to the immediate problem at hand, the old man
quickly undertook a long digression on the corruption and
dissolution of English society at the turn of the eighteenth
century. The reformation of this state of affairs, he ruefully
noted, had 'seldom if ever been brought about in the world
without great and public calamities'. And the difficulty, as he
saw it, was that 'Old as well as younger boys are seldom
amended without scourging. and noe thing but overturnings
bring depraved [hearts] from fashionable and growing
immoralitys.'[13] Adam had much to do with the eighteenth
century, only the eighteenth century preferred not to concern
itself. Locke's ideas on education facilitated that disengagement,
but only after the ideas, or rather certain of them, had been
dexterously fitted into a new matrix. Granted, this was no
difficult work to accomplish; that has never been in dispute.
What is in dispute is whether or not Locke would have agreed
with the new fitting; and we have I hope come to see how he may
have entertained more than a few doubts, how he might have
regarded the popularizers of his educational thought in much
the same way as he regarded those Deists like Toland who
thought of themselves as faithful exponents of the master's
religious principles. Locke cannot be separated from the wider
context of early Latitudinarian theology if we wish to remain
true to the purport of his thought. Arguments about infinite

---

[13] Furly to Locke (16 Mar. 1700: vii, no. 2690; 9 Aug. 1700: ibid. no. 2754; 14 May
1701: ibid. no. 2919). Locke to Furly (30 May 1701: ibid. no. 2932). Arent eventually
became a bookseller.

malleability, about children at birth with no nature, good or ill, about the absence of original sin—arguments such as these have their roots not in the seventeenth century, not in the mind of Locke, but elsewhere in the history of ideas.[14] Damaris Masham, who understood the texture of that mind better than most, knew like her friend and house guest that 'Vertue is not (tho often so misrepresented) included in Innocency.' For her, as for Locke, the Christian faith was 'the only sufficient ground or solid support of Vertue' and both the inculcation and efforts to obtain obedience to the special values of this faith had to be accompanied by the threat of punishment and the lure of reward lest men ignore those values altogether. Her own strictures against the extremes of Calvinism and Deism clearly reflected those of the man she had known for some twenty years. Both positions, she argued, vitiated the urgency and rigour of true Christianity, the former negating work towards reform and the latter dismissing the necessity of free grace. Only the Latitudinarian solution, the theology of Whichcote, Hales, Chillingworth, Patrick, Tillotson, Barrow, Fowler—and Locke—only this could restore the just meaning of the primitive faith and make men responsible once again for their sins.[15] There is no denying the exacting nature of this theological perspective in the minds of those who espoused it, and any attempt on our part to understand its inner essence solely by comparing, not contrasting, it to the lifeless moralizing of eighteenth-century Deism obfuscates for us the character of Locke's century—which was, still very much an age of faith.

And so Locke remained, throughout his adult life, loyal to the Christian view of man's essential nature as it was understood by so many of his Latitudinarian friends, and by not a few of his Puritan enemies. 'Everything good, and everything evil . . .'— the lure of untrammelled Pelagianism was indeed an attractive one in Locke's era, and towards the end of his days younger men who identified themselves with his way of ideas eagerly took the plunge beyond the pale of orthodoxy. Not Locke: for him, the

---

[14] Greene ('Augustinianism and Empiricism') discusses the continuing influence of the doctrine of original sin in 18th-cent. literature.

[15] Damaris Masham, *Occasional Thoughts in Reference to a Vertuous or Christian Life* (London: A. and J. Churchill, 1705), 11, 27, 105–9. She referred the reader to Locke's *Reasonableness of Christianity* for confirmation of this fact.

very attractiveness of the Pelagian heresy reconfirmed in the starkest terms the insuperable nature of the sin of pride which Christians since the time of Paul had struggled, mostly in vain, to overcome. He understood, much like the Augustan poet Alexander Pope, the impiety and contumacy that lay at the root of any and every theory of human perfection. And Locke shared with Pope a picture of humankind not to be confused with that painted by many in the Century of Enlightenment—for in Locke's portrait of humanity, as in Pope's, man remained

> in doubt to act or rest;
> In doubt to deem himself a God, or Beast;
> In doubt his Mind or Body to prefer;
> Born but to die, and reas'ning but to err;
> Alike in ignorance, his reason such,
> Whether he thinks too little, or too much:
> Chaos of Thought and Passion, all confus'd;
> Still by himself abus'd, or disabus'd;
> Created half to rise, and half to fall;
> Great lord of all things, yet a prey to all;
> Sole judge of Truth, in endless Error hurl'd:
> The glory, jest, and riddle of the world![16]

John Locke did not need St Augustine to inform him about mankind's natural disinclination for the good which was God's love. The whole of his experience since the days at Christ Church provided more than sufficient evidence for him to establish that difficult fact of life. If others were willing to stare experience in the face and declare for the Pelagian perspective, well, that was their affair. Locke had little in common with such men. That we have lost cognizance of this fact is perhaps understandable, but for those interested in an accurate comprehension of the past, the resulting distortion of Locke's thought must, in the end, be as unacceptable as the extremes of Pelagianism and Augustinianism were for Locke himself.

---

[16] *Essay on Man*, Epistle II, 8–18.

Bibliography

Primary Sources

Manuscript Collection

Bodleian Library, Oxford University: Lovelace Collection of the papers of John Locke.

Books

ALLESTREE, RICHARD, *The Practice of Christian Graces, or the Whole Duty of Man* (London: T. Garthwait, 1659).

—— *The Gentleman's Calling* (London: T. Garthwait, 1660).

—— WALKER, OBADIAH, and WOODHEAD, ABRAHAM, *A Paraphrase and Annotations Upon the Epistles of St Paul* (Oxford: At the Theatre, 1675).

ANDREWES, LANCELOT, *Works*, 11 vols. (Oxford: Henry Parks, 1854).

AQUINAS, THOMAS, *The Basic Writings of St Thomas Aquinas*, ed. A. C. Pegis, 2 vols. (New York: Random House, 1945).

ARISTOTLE, *The Nicomachean Ethics*, trans. D. P. Chase (London: Dent, 1920).

AUBREY, JOHN, *Brief Lives*, ed. A. Clark, 2 vols. (Oxford: Clarendon Press, 1898).

AUGUSTINE, *City of God*, trans. John Healey, 2 vols. (London: Dent, 1945).

—— *The Basic Writings of Saint Augustine*, ed. W. J. Oates, 2 vols. (New York: Random House, 1949).

BACON, Sir FRANCIS, *The Advancement of Learning*, ed. J. Devey (New York: P. F. Collier and Son, 1905).

BARROW, ISAAC, *The Theological Works of Isaac Barrow*, ed. A. Napier, 9 vols. (Cambridge: University Press, 1859).

BENTLEY, RICHARD, *Works*, 3 vols. (London: Francis Macpherson, 1838).

BOLD, SAMUEL, *A Brief Account of the First Rise of the Name Protestant* (London: n.p., 1688).

—— *A Short Discourse of the True Knowledge of Christ Jesus* (London: A. and J. Churchill, 1697).

—— *Some Considerations on the Principal Objections and Arguments against Mr Locke's Essay* (London: A. Churchill, 1699).

—— *A Discourse Concerning the Resurrection of the Same Body* (London: S. Holt, 1705).

BOYLE, ROBERT, *Works*, 6 vols. (London: W. Johnston *et al.*, 1772).

BRATHWAIT, RICHARD, *The English Gentleman* (London: I. Dawson, 1641).

BROKESBY, FRANCIS, *Of Education* (London: John Hartley, 1701).

BURNET, GILBERT, *A Sermon Preached at the Funeral of the Honourable Robert Boyle* (London: R. Chiswell, 1692).

—— *History of His Own Time*, 4 vols. (London: R. H. Evans, 1809).

—— 'Thoughts on Education', in *Bishop Burnet as Educationist*, ed. J. Clarke (Aberdeen: University Press, 1914).

BURNET, THOMAS, *Remarks Upon an Essay Concerning Human Understanding in a Letter Addressed to the Author* (London: M. Wotton, 1697).

—— *Third Remarks Upon an Essay Concerning Human Understanding* (London: M. Wotton, 1699).

BURTHOGGE, RICHARD, *Divine Goodness Explicated and Asserted from the Exceptions of the Atheist* (London: S. and B. Griffen, 1672).

—— *Causa Dei: or An Apology for God* (London: Lewis Punchard, 1675).

—— *Organum Vetus et Novum* (London: Sam Crouch, 1678).

—— *Christianity a Revealed Mystery* (London: Lockyer Davis, 1755).

—— *The Philosophical Writings of Richard Burthogge,* ed. M. W. Landes (Chicago: Open Court, 1921).

CALVIN, JOHN, *Commentary upon the Epistles of Saint Paul to the Romans*, ed. H. Beveridge, trans. C. Rosdell (Edinburgh: Calvin Translation Society, 1844).

—— *Institutes of the Christian Religion*, trans. H. Beveridge, 3 vols. (Edinburgh: Calvin Translation Society, 1865).

CHILLINGWORTH, WILLIAM, *Works*, 3 vols. (Oxford: University Press, 1838).

CLARKE, SAMUEL, *A Demonstration of the Being and Attributes of God, the Obligation of Natural Religion, and the Truth and Certainty of the Christian Revelation* (London: W. Botham, 1728).

CONDILLAC, ÉTIENNE BONNOT DE, *An Essay on the Origin of Human Knowledge*, trans. T. Nugent (Gainesville: Scholars' Facsimiles, 1971).

COOPER, ANTHONY ASHLEY, Earl of Shaftesbury, *An Inquiry Concerning Virtue* (London: A. Bell, 1699).

—— *Several Letters Written by a Noble Lord to a Young Man at the University* (London: J. Roberts, 1716).

—— *The Life, Unpublished Letters, and Philosophical Regimen of Anthony, Earl of Shaftesbury*, ed. B. Rand (New York: Macmillan, 1900).

—— *Characteristics of Men, Manners, Times*, ed. J. M. Robertson, 2 vols. (New York: Bobbs-Merrill, 1964).

CUDWORTH, RALPH, *A Treatise Concerning Eternal and Immutable Morality* (London: James and John Knapton, 1731).

—— *Works of Ralph Cudworth*, 4 vols. (Oxford: D. A. Talboys, 1829).

—— *The True Intellectual System of the Universe*, ed. Thomas Birch, 2 vols. (New York: Gould and Newman, 1838).

DARRELL, WILLIAM, *A Gentleman Instructed* (London: E. Evets, 1704).

EDWARDS, JOHN, *The Plague of the Heart* (Cambridge: n.p., 1665).

—— *Cometamantia: A Discourse of Comets* (London: n.p., 1684).

—— *Brief Remarks on Mr Whiston's New Theory of the Earth* (London: n.p., 1693).

—— *Some Thoughts Concerning the Several Causes and Occasions of Atheism* (London: J. Robinson, 1695).

—— *A Demonstration of the Existence of God from the Contemplation of the Visible Structure of the Greater and Lesser World* (London: n.p., 1696).

—— *Socinianism Unmasked* (London: J. Robinson, 1696).

—— *A Brief Vindication of the Fundamental Articles of the Christian Faith* (London: n.p., 1697).

—— *The Socinian Creed* (London: J. Robinson, 1697).

—— *Sermons on Special Occasions and Subjects* (London: n.p., 1698).

——*The Eternal and Intrinsick Reasons of Good and Evil* (Cambridge: University Press, 1699).

—— *A Free Discourse Concerning Truth and Error* (London: n.p., 1701).

—— *The Arminian Doctrines Condemn'd by the Holy Scriptures* (London: n.p., 1711).

—— *Some New Discoveries on the Uncertainty, Deficiency and Corruptions of Human Knowledge and Learning* (London: n.p., 1714).

EDWARDS, JONATHAN, *The Doctrine of Original Sin* (Oxford: Henry Clements, 1711).

ELLIS, CLEMENT, *The Gentle Sinner* (Oxford: Henry Hall, 1660).

EVELYN, JOHN, *Diary*, ed. W. Bray, 2 vols. (London: Walter Dunne, 1901).

FOWLER, EDWARD, *The Design of Christianity* (London: Tyler and Holt, 1671).

—— *Libertas Evangelica* (London: R. Norton, 1680).

GAILHARD, JEAN, *The Complete Gentleman: or Directions for the Education of Youth* (London: Thomas Newcombe, 1678).

GLANVILL, JOSEPH, *Scepsis Scientifica: or Confest Ignorance, the Way to Science* (London: E. Cotes, 1665).

—— *Plus Ultra: or, the Progress and Advancement of Knowledge Since the Days of Aristotle* (London: James Collins, 1668).

GRENVILLE, DENIS, *Counsel and Directions Divine and Moral* (London: Robert Clavell, 1685).

HALES, JOHN, *The Works of the Ever Memorable Mr John Hales of Eton*, 3 vols. (Glasgow: R. and A. Foulis, 1765).

HARTCLIFFE, JOHN, *Sermon Preached at the Oxfordshire Feast* (London: Ralph Holt, 1684).

—— *A Discourse Against Purgatory* (London: Brabazon Almer, 1685).

—— *A Treatise of Moral and Intellectual Virtues* (London: C. Harper, 1691).

HELVETIUS, C. A., *A Treatise on Man: His Intellectual Faculties and His Education*, ed. and trans. W. Hooper, 2 vols. (London: Albion Press, 1810).

HOOKER, RICHARD, *The Works of Mr Richard Hooker*, 2 vols. (Oxford: Clarendon Press, 1865).

HOOKER, THOMAS, *Thomas Hooker: Writings in England and Holland*, ed. G. H. Williams *et al.* (Cambridge, Mass.: Harvard University Press, 1975).

HYDE, EDWARD, Earl of Clarendon, *A Collection of Tracts of the Right Honorable Edward, Earl of Clarendon* (London: T. Woodward, 1727).

—— *A History of the Rebellion and Civil Wars in England*, ed. W. D. Macray, 6 vols. (Oxford: Clarendon Press, 1888).

LAUD, WILLIAM, *Works*, 7 vols. (Oxford: J. H. Parker, 1847).

LIMBORCH, PHILIP van, *Theologia Christiana*, trans. W. Jones as *A Complete System or Body of Divinity, both Speculative and Practical, founded on Scripture and Reason*, 2 vols. (London: John Darby, 1713).

—— *History of the Inquisition*, trans. Samuel Chandler, 2 vols. (London: J. Gray, 1731).

LINGARD, RICHARD, *A Letter of Advice to a Young Gentleman*, ed. F. Erb (New York: McAuliffe and Booth, 1907).

LOCKE, JOHN, *An Early Draft of Locke's Essay, Together with Excerpts from his Journals*, ed. R. Aaron and J. Gibb (Oxford: University Press, 1936).

—— *An Essay Concerning Human Understanding*, ed. A. C. Fraser, 2 vols. (Oxford: University Press, 1894).

—— *An Essay Concerning Human Understanding*, ed. M. W. Calkins (Chicago: Open Court, 1917).

—— *An Essay concerning Human Understanding*, ed. P. H. Nidditch (Oxford: Clarendon Press, 1975).

—— *An Essay Concerning the Understanding, Knowledge, Opinion and Assent*, ed. B. Rand (Cambridge, Mass.: Harvard University Press, 1931).

—— *Conduct of the Understanding*, ed. T. Fowler (New York: Burt Franklin, 1970).

—— *Epistola de Tolerantia*, ed. and trans. J. W. Gough and R. Klibansky (Oxford: Clarendon Press, 1968).

—— *Essays on the Law of Nature*, ed. W. von Leyden (Oxford: Clarendon Press, 1954).

—— *Paraphrase and Notes on the Epistles of St Paul*, ed. A. W. Wainwright (Oxford: Clarendon Press, 1987).

—— *The Correspondence of John Locke,* ed. E. S. De Beer, 8 vols. (Oxford: Clarendon Press, 1973–7).

—— *The Educational Writings of John Locke,* ed. W. Adamson (Cambridge: University Press, 1922).

—— *The Educational Writings of John Locke,* ed. J. Axtell (Cambridge: University Press, 1968).

—— *Two Tracts on Government,* ed. P. Abrams (Cambridge: University Press, 1969).

—— *Two Treatises of Government,* ed. P. Laslett (Cambridge: University Press, 1965).

—— *Works,* 10 vols. (London: Thomas Tegg, 1823).

LOWDE, JAMES, *The Reasonableness of the Christian Religion* (London: Walter Kettilby, 1684).

—— *A Discourse Concerning the Nature of Man* (London: Walter Kettilby, 1694).

MASHAM, DAMARIS, *Occasional Thoughts in Reference to a Vertuous or Christian Life* (London: A. and J. Churchill, 1705).

MILNER, JOHN, *An Account of Mr Lock's Religion* (London: J. Nutt, 1700).

MILTON, JOHN, *Works,* ed. F. A. Paterson, 18 vols. (New York: Columbia University Press, 1931–8).

MOLYNEUX, WILLIAM, *Dioptrica Nova* (London: B. Tooke, 1692).

MORE, HENRY, *An Account of Virtue: or Dr More's Abridgement of Morals, put into English* (London: Benjamin Tooke, 1690).

—— *A Collection of Aphorisms* (London: J. Downing, 1704).

NORRIS, JOHN, *The Theory and Regulation of Love* (Oxford: Henry Clements, 1688).

—— *Reason and Religion* (London: S. Manship, 1689).

—— *Christian Blessedness: or Discourses Upon the Beatitudes* (London: S. Manship, 1690).

—— *Reflections Upon the Conduct of Human Life* (London: S. Manship, 1690).

—— *Practical Discourses Upon Several Divine Subjects* (London: S. Manship, 1691).

—— *Practical Discourses Upon Several Subjects,* 3 vols. (London: S. Manship, 1693).

—— *An Account of Reason and Faith* (London: S. Manship, 1697).

—— *Treatises Upon Several Subjects* (London: S. Manship, 1697).

—— *An Essay Towards the Theory of the Ideal or Intelligible World,* 2 vols. (London: S. Manship, 1701, 1704).

—— *Letters Concerning the Love of God* (London: S. Manship, 1705).

—— *A Practical Treatise Concerning Humility* (London: S. Manship, 1707).

—— *A Treatise Concerning Christian Prudence* (London: S. Manship, 1710).

—— *A Collection of Miscellanies* (London: S. Manship, 1717).

—— 'Letter from Mr Norris to Corinna for the Direction of Her Studies', in *Pylades and Corinna*, ed. R. Gwinnett (London: n.p., 1732).

—— *Cursory Reflections upon a Book call'd, An Essay Concerning Human Understanding*, ed. G. P. McEwen (Los Angeles: Augustan Reprint Society, 1961).

NYE, STEPHEN, *Discourse Concerning Natural and Revealed Religion* (London: Jonathan Robinson, 1696).

OWEN, JOHN, *Works*, 6 vols. (Philadelphia, Pa.: Protestant Episcopal Book Society, 1860).

PATRICK, SIMON, *The Works of Simon Patrick*, ed. A. Taylor, 9 vols. (Oxford: University Press, 1858).

PENTON, STEPHEN, *The Guardian's Instruction* (London: n.p., 1688).

PEPYS, SAMUEL, *The Diary of Samuel Pepys*, ed. R. Latham and W. Matthews, 11 vols. (Berkeley, Calif.: University of California Press, and London: Bell and Hyman, 1970–83).

PERKINS, WILLIAM, *Works*, 3 vols. (Cambridge: John Legate, 1608).

POPE, ALEXANDER, *An Essay on Man*, ed. Mack (London: Methuen, 1970).

POPPLE, WILLIAM, *A Rational Catechism* (London: Andrew Sowle, 1687).

—— *A Discourse of Human Reason* (London: A. Churchill, 1690).

RAMESEY, WILLIAM, *The Gentleman's Companion* (London: n.p., 1676).

REYNOLDS, EDWARD, *A Treatise of the Passions and Faculties of the Soule of Man* (London: Robert Buistock, 1640).

—— *Works* (London: Thomas Newcomb, 1679).

RICHARDSON, SAMUEL, *Pamela*, 2 vols. (London: Dent, 1931).

SHERLOCK, WILLIAM, *Discourse Concerning the Happiness of Good Men* (London: W. Rogers, 1704).

SMITH, JOHN, *Select Discourses of John Smith* (London: F. Flesher, 1660).

SPRAT, THOMAS, *A History of the Royal Society of London, for the Improving of Natural Knowledge*, ed. J. I. Cope and H. W. Jones (St Louis: Washington University Press, 1959).

STANHOPE, PHILIP DORMER, Earl of Chesterfield, *Letters Written by Lord Chesterfield to His Son*, 2 vols. (London: W. Tegg, 1879).

STILLINGFLEET, EDWARD, *Works*, 6 vols. (London: n.p., 1707–10).

TAYLOR, JEREMY, *The Whole Works of the Right Reverend Jeremy Taylor*, ed. R. Heber, 15 vols. (London: Ogle, Duncan, and Co., 1822).

TILLOTSON, JOHN, *The Rule of Faith* (London, n.p., 1666).

—— *Works*, ed. T. Birch, 10 vols. (London: J. F. Dove, 1820).

TOLAND, JOHN, *Christianity Not Mysterious* (London: n.p., 1696).

TOWERSON, GABRIEL, *An Explication of the Decalogue or Ten Command-ments, with Reference to the Catechism of the Church of England* (London: J. Macock, 1676).

TYRRELL, JAMES, *A Brief Disquisition of the Law of Nature* (London: Richard Baldwin, 1692).

VOLTAIRE, F. M. A., *Lettres philosophiques* (Paris: Librairie Garnier Frères, 1944).

WALKER, OBADIAH, *Of Education, Especially of a Young Gentleman* (Oxford: n.p., 1673).

WHICHCOTE, BENJAMIN, *Select Sermons of Dr. Whichcote* (London: A. and J. Churchill, 1699).

—— *Works*, 4 vols. (Aberdeen: J. Chalmers, 1751).

—— *Moral and Religious Aphorisms*, ed. Samuel Slater (London: J. Payne, 1753).

WHITBY, DANIEL, *A Paraphrase and Commentary Upon All the Epistles of the New Testament* (London: W. Bowyer, 1700).

—— *A Discourse Concerning the True Import of the Words Election and Reprobation* (London: John Wyat, 1710).

—— *A Full Answer to the Arguments of the Reverend Dr Jonathan Edwards* (London: John Wyat, 1712).

WOOD, ANTHONY, *Athenae Oxonienses*, ed. P. Bliss, 4 vols. (London: n.p., 1820).

—— *Life and Times*, ed. A. Clark, 5 vols. (Oxford: Clarendon Press for Oxford Historical Society, 1891–1900).

Secondary Sources

AARON, R. I, 'The Limits of Locke's Rationalism' in *Seventeenth Century Studies Presented to Sir Herbert Grierson* (Oxford: Clarendon Press, 1938).

—— *John Locke* (Oxford: University Press, 1955).

AARSLEFF, H., 'The State of Nature and the Nature of Man in Locke', in *John Locke: Problems and Perspectives*, ed. John Yolton (Cambridge: University Press, 1969).

ACWORTH, R., 'Locke's First Reply to John Norris, *Locke Newsletter*, 2 (1971), 7–11.

—— *The Philosophy of John Norris of Bemerton, 1657–1712* (New York: Hildesheim, 1979).

AIRY, R., *Westminster* (London: Bell, 1902).

ALDERMAN, W., 'The Significance of Shaftesbury in English Specula-tion', *Publications of the Modern Language Association*, 38 (1923), 175–95.

ALDRIDGE, A. O., *Shaftesbury and the Deist Manifesto* (Philadelphia, Pa.: American Philosophical Society, 1951).

ALEXANDER, F., *Our Age of Unreason: A Study of the Irrational Forces in Social Life* (New York: J. B. Lippincourt, 1942).

ALLISON, C. F., *The Rise of Moralism: The Proclamation of the Gospel from Hooker to Baxter* (New York: Seabury Press, 1966).

ANDREWS, C. M., *The Colonial Period in American History*, 4 vols. (New Haven, Conn.: Yale University Press, 1934–8).

ANGLIM, J., 'On Locke's State of Nature', *Political Studies*, 26 (1978), 78–90.

ARIES, P., *Centuries of Childhood*, trans. R. Baldick (New York: Knopf, 1962).

ARONSON, J., 'Shaftesbury on Locke', *American Political Science Review*, 53 (1959), 1101–4.

ASHCRAFT, R., 'Faith and Knowledge in Locke's Philosophy', in *John Locke: Problems and Perspectives*, ed. J. Yolton (Cambridge: University Press, 1969).

BAKER, H., *The Dignity of Man: Studies in the Persistence of an Idea* (Cambridge, Mass.: Harvard University Press, 1947).

—— *The Wars of Truth* (Cambridge, Mass.: Harvard University Press, 1964).

BANGS, C., *Arminius: A Study in the Dutch Reformation* (Nashville, Tenn.: Abington Press, 1973).

BARCLAY, W., *The Mind of St Paul* (New York: Harper and Row, 1975).

BARKER, G. F. R., *Memoir of Richard Busby, D.D.: With Some Account of Westminster School in the Seventeenth Century* (London: Lawrence and Buller, 1895).

BARNES, T. G., *Somerset, 1625–1640* (Cambridge, Mass.: Harvard University Press, 1961).

BARRETT, C. K., *A Commentary on the Epistle to the Romans* (London: A. and C. Black, 1957).

—— *From First Adam to Last: A Study in Pauline Anthropology* (New York: Scribner's Sons, 1962).

—— *A Commentary on the First Epistle to the Corinthians* (New York: Harper and Row, 1968).

BECKER, C., *The Heavenly City of the Eighteenth Century Philosophers* (New Haven, Conn.: Yale University Press, 1932).

BENNETT, J., *Locke, Berkeley, Hume: Central Themes* (Oxford: Clarendon Press, 1977).

BERNSTEIN, J. A., 'Shaftesbury's Reformation of the Reformation: Reflections on the Relation between Deism and Pauline Christianity', *Journal of Religion and Ethics*, 6 (1978), 257–78.

BICKNELL, E. J., *A Theological Introduction to the Thirty-Nine Articles* (London: Longman, 1919).

BIDDLE, J. C., 'Locke's Critique of Innate Principles and Toland's Deism', *Journal of the History of Ideas*, 37 (1976), 411–22.

BLOK, P. J., *History of the People of the Netherlands*, trans. R. Putnam, 5 vols. (New York: Putnam's Sons, 1898–1912).

BOLGER, R. R., *The Classical Heritage and Its Beneficiaries* (Cambridge: University Press, 1954).

BOURKE, V. J., *St Thomas and the Greek Moralists* (Milwaukee: Marquette University Press, 1947).

BOURNE, E. C. E., *The Anglicanism of William Laud* (London: SPCK, 1947).

BRAUR, G. L., *The Education of a Gentleman: Theories of Gentlemanly Education in England, 1660–1675* (New York: Bookman Associates, 1959).

BRETT, R. L., *The Third Earl of Shaftesbury: A Study in Eighteenth Century Literary Theory* (London: Hutchison's University Library, 1951).

BRINDENBAUGH, C., *Vexed and Troubled Englishmen, 1590–1642* (New York: Oxford University Press, 1968).

BROADBENT, J. B., 'Shaftesbury's Horses of Instruction', in *The English Mind: Studies in the English Moralists Presented to Basil Willey*, ed. H. S. Davies and G. Watson (Cambridge: University Press, 1964).

BROWNING, A., ed., *English Historical Documents, 1660–1714* (London: Eyre and Spottiswoode, 1953).

BRUNEAU, W. A., 'Towards a History of Moral Education: Some Fundamental Considerations and a Case Study', *Paedagogica Historica*, 15. 2 (1975), 375–7.

BUCHDAHL, G., *The Image of Newton and Locke in the Age of Reason* (New York: Sheed and Ward, 1961).

BULTMANN, R., *Primitive Christianity in its Contemporary Setting*, trans. R. H. Fuller (New York: Meridian Books, 1956).

—— *The Old and the New Man*, trans. K. R. Crim (Richmond, Va.: John Knox Press, 1967).

BURKILL, T. A., *The Evolution of Christian Thought* (Ithaca, NY: Cornell University Press, 1978).

BURTT, E. A., *Man Seeks the Divine: A Study in the History and Comparison of Religions* (New York: Harper and Brothers, 1957).

—— *The Metaphysical Foundations of Modern Physical Science* (Garden City, NJ: Doubleday, 1960).

BUSH, D., *Paradise Lost in Our Time* (Gloucester, Mass.: P. Smith, 1957).

BUTTERFIELD, H., *Christianity and History* (London: Bell, 1949).

CARRE, M. H., *Phases of Thought in England* (Oxford: Clarendon Press, 1949).

CARROLL, R. T., *The Common-Sense Philosophy of Bishop Edward Stillingfleet* (The Hague: Nijhoff, 1975).

CASPARI, F., *Humanism and the Social Order in Tudor England* (Chicago: University Press, 1954).

CASSIRER, E., *The Platonic Renaissance in England*, trans. J. P. Pettegrove (New York: Nelson, 1953).

—— *The Philosophy of the Enlightenment* (Princeton, NJ: University Press, 1979).

CAVE, S., *The Christian Estimate of Man* (London: Duckworth, 1946).

CHADWICK, H., *The Early Church* (Reading: Penguin, 1984).

—— *Augustine* (Oxford: University Press, 1986).

CHAMBLISS, J. J., 'Reason, Conduct and Revelation in the Educational Theory of Locke, Watts and Burgh', *Educational Theory*, 26 (1976), 372–87.

CLARK, G. N., *The Later Stuarts* (Oxford: Clarendon Press, 1934).

—— *Science and Social Welfare in the Age of Newton* (Oxford: Clarendon Press, 1937).

CLARKE, M. L., *Classical Education in Britain, 1500–1900* (Cambridge: University Press, 1959).

COBBAN, A., *In Search of Humanity: The Role of the Enlightenment in Modern History* (New York: G. Braziller, 1960).

COLIE, R. L., *Light and Enlightenment: A Study of the Cambridge Platonists and Dutch Arminians* (Cambridge: University Press, 1957).

—— 'John Locke in the Republic of Letters', in *Britain and the Netherlands*, ed. J. S. Bromley and E. H. Kossman (London: Chatto and Windus, 1960).

COLLINSON, P., *The Elizabethan Puritan Movement* (London: Cape, 1967).

COLMAN, J., *John Locke's Moral Philosophy* (Edinburgh: University Press, 1983).

CONANT, J. B., 'The Advancement of Learning During the Puritan Commonwealth', *Proceedings of the Massachusetts Historical Society*, 65 (1942), 3–31.

COOLIDGE, J. S., *The Pauline Renaissance in England: Puritanism and the Bible* (Oxford: Clarendon Press, 1970).

COPLESTON, F. C., *Aquinas* (Harmondsworth: Penguin Books, 1982).

CORY, D. M., *Faustus Socinus* (Boston: Beacon Press, 1932).

COSTELLO, W., *The Scholastic Curriculum at Early Seventeenth Century Cambridge* (Cambridge, Mass.: Harvard University Press, 1958).

COX, R., *Locke on War and Peace* (Oxford: Clarendon Press, 1960).

CRAGG, G. R., *From Puritanism to the Age of Reason* (Cambridge: University Press, 1950).

—— *Puritanism in the Period of the Great Persecution, 1660–1688* (Cambridge: University Press, 1957).

—— *Reason and Authority in the Eighteenth Century* (Cambridge: University Press, 1964).

CRANE, R. S., *The Idea of the Humanities and Other Essays*, 2 vols. (Chicago: University Press, 1967).

CRANFIELD, C. E. B., *Romans: A Shorter Commentary* (Grand Rapids, Mich.: Eerdmans Publishing Co., 1985).

CRANSTON, M., *John Locke: A Biography* (London: Longman, 1957).

CREMIN, L., *American Education: The Colonial Experience* (New York: Harper and Row, 1978).

CURTI, M., 'The Great Mr Locke: America's Philosopher, 1783–1861', *Huntington Library Bulletin*, (1937), 107–51.

CURTIS, M., *Oxford and Cambridge in Transition, 1558–1642* (Oxford: Clarendon Press, 1959).

DAVENPORT, P. M., *Moral Divinity with a Tincture of Christ?: An Interpretation of the Theology of Benjamin Whichcote* (Nijmegen: n.p., 1972).

DAVIES, G., *The Restoration of Charles II* (San Marino, Calif.: Huntington Library, 1955).

DAVIES, H., *Worship and Theology in England: From Cranmer to Hooker, 1534–1603* (Princeton, NJ: University Press, 1970).

—— *Worship and Theology in England: From Andrewes to Baxter and Fox, 1603–1690* (Princeton, NJ: University Press, 1975).

DEPAULEY, W. C., *The Candle of the Lord* (London: SPCK, 1937).

DEWHURST, K., *John Locke, Physician and Philosopher: A Medical Biography* (London: Wellcome Historical Medical Library, 1963).

DRISCOLL, E. A., 'The Influence of Gassendi on Locke's Hedonism', *International Philosophical Quarterly*, 12 (1972), 87–110.

DRURY, J. B., 'John Locke, Natural Law and Innate Ideas', *Dialogue*, 19 (1950), 531–45.

DUNN, J., *The Political Thought of John Locke* (Cambridge: University Press, 1969).

—— *John Locke* (Oxford: University Press, 1984).

ELSON, J. H., *John Hales of Eton* (New York: King's Crown Press, 1948).

ELTON, G. R., *Reformation Europe, 1517–1559* (New York: Harper and Row, 1963).

EVENNETT, H. O., *The Spirit of the Counter-Reformation* (Notre Dame, Ind.: University Press, 1970).

EVERY, G., *The High Church Party, 1688–1718* (London: SPCK, 1956).

EZELL, M. J. M., 'Locke's Images of Childhood: Early Eighteenth Century Responses to Some Thoughts Concerning Education', *Eighteenth Century Studies*, 17 (1983–4), 139–55.

FERGUSON, A. B., *The Articulate Citizen and the English Renaissance* (Durham, NC: Duke University Press, 1965).

FERGUSON, J., *Pelagius* (Cambridge: Heffer, 1956).

FISHER, G. P., *A History of Christian Doctrine* (New York: Scribner's Sons, 1901).

FISHER, K., *History of Modern Philosophy: Descartes and His School*, trans. G. P. Gordy (New York: Scribner's Sons, 1887).

FLEW, R. N., *The Idea of Perfection in Christian Theology* (Oxford: University Press, 1934).

FLIEGELMAN, J., *Prodigals and Pilgrims: The American Revolution against Patriarchal Authority, 1750–1800* (New York: Cambridge University Press, 1982).

FOGELKLOU, E., *James Nayler: The Rebel Saint*, trans. L. K. Yapp (London: Benn, 1931).

FOWLER, T., *Shaftesbury and Hutcheson* (London: Sampson Low, 1882).

FOX BOURNE, H. L., *The Life of John Locke*, 2 vols. (London: H. King, 1876).

FOXCROFT, H. C., ed., *A Supplement to Burnet's History* (Oxford: Clarendon Press, 1902).

FRERE, W. H., *A History of the English Church in the Reigns of Elizabeth and James I, 1558–1615* (London: Macmillan, 1904).

FROUDE, J. H., *Lectures on the Council of Trent* (London: Longman, 1896).

GARDINER, S. R., *History of England*, 10 vols. (London: Longman, 1883).

—— *History of the Commwealth and Protectorate*, 3 vols. (London: Longman, 1897).

GAUTHIER, D., 'Why Ought one Obey God? Reflections on Hobbes and Locke', *Canadian Journal of Philosophy*, 7 (1977), 425–46.

GAY, P., *The Enlightenment: An Interpretation*, 2 vols. (New York: Norton, 1969).

GEORGE, C. AND K., *The Protestant Mind of the English Reformation, 1570–1640* (Princeton, NJ: University Press, 1961).

GEORGE, E. A., *Seventeenth Century Men of Latitude* (New York: Scribner's Sons, 1908).

GEYS, P., *The Netherlands in the Seventeenth Century, 1609–1648* (London: Benn, 1961).

GILSON, E., *The Spirit of Medieval Philosophy*, trans. A. H. C. Downes (London: Sheed and Ward, 1936).

—— *A History of Christian Philosophy in the Middle Ages* (New York: Random House, 1955).

—— *The Christian Philosophy of St Augustine* (New York: Random House, 1960).

GORN, J. L., 'The Strange Case of Edward Clarke, Jr.: Attending Physician—John Locke, Gent', *Educational Theory*, 17 (1967), 298–316.

GOUGH, J. H., *John Locke's Political Philosophy* (Oxford: Clarendon Press, 1950).

—— 'James Tyrrell: Whig Historian and Friend of Locke', *Historical Journal*, 19 (1976), 581–610.

GRAVE, S. A., *Locke and Burnet* (East Freemantle: Westover Press, 1981).

GREAN, S., *Shaftesbury's Philosophy of Religion and Ethics* (New York: Ohio University Press, 1967).

GREAVES, R. L., *The Puritan Revolution and Educational Thought* (New Brunswick, NJ: Rutgers University Press, 1969).

GREENE, D., 'Augustinianism and Empiricism: A Note on Eighteenth Century English Intellectual History', *Eighteenth Century Studies*, 1 (1967), 33–68.

GREENLEE, D., 'Locke and the Controversy over Innate Ideas', *Journal of the History of Ideas*, 38 (1977), 251–64.

HALEY, K. H. D., *The First Earl of Shaftesbury* (Oxford: Clarendon Press, 1968).

HALL, A. R., *The Scientific Revolution, 1500–1800* (London: Longman, 1954).

HALLER, W., *The Rise of Puritanism* (New York: Columbia University Press, 1938).

HAMLET, D. M., *One Greater Man: Justice and Damnation in Paradise Lost* (Lewisburg: Bucknell University Press, 1973).

HAMLIN, H. P., 'A Critical Evaluation of John Locke's Philosophy of Religion' (University of Georgia Ph. D. thesis, 1972).

HARGREAVES-MAWDSLEY, W. N., *Oxford in the Age of John Locke* (Norman, Okla.: University of Oklahoma Press, 1973).

HARNACK, A., *History of Dogma*, 7 vols. (New York: Dover, 1961).

HARRIS, M., *The Rise of Anthropological Theory* (New York: Cornell University Press, 1968).

HAZARD, P., *The European Mind, 1680–1715* (New York: Meridian, 1960).

HEFELBOWER, S. G., *The Relation of John Locke to English Deism* (Chicago: University Press, 1918).

HEFELE, C. J., *A History of the Councils of the Church, from the Original Documents*, 5 vols. (Edinburgh: T. and T. Clark, 1876).

HEINEMANN, F. H., 'John Toland and the Age of Enlightenment', *Review of English Studies*, 20 (1944), 125–46.

HICK, J., *Evil and the Love of God* (New York: Harper and Row, 1966).

HILL, C., *The Intellectual Origins of the English Revolution* (Oxford: Clarendon Press, 1965).

—— *Society and Puritanism in Pre-Revolutionary England* (London: Panther Books, 1969).

—— *God's Englishman: Oliver Cromwell and the English Revolution* (New York: Harper Torchbooks, 1970).

—— *Puritanism and Revolution* (New York: Schocken Books, 1970).

——*The World Turned Upside Down: Radical Ideas During the English Revolution* (New York: Viking, 1972).

—— *Change and Continuity in Seventeenth Century England* (Cambridge, Mass.: Harvard University Press, 1975).

—— *Milton and the English Revolution* (London: Faber, 1977).

—— *The Experience of Defeat: Milton and Some Contemporaries* (New York: Viking, 1984).

HOOPES, R., *Right Reason in the English Renaissance* (Cambridge: University Press, 1962).

HOPPEN, T., 'The Dublin Philosophical Society and the New Learning in Ireland', *Irish Historical Studies*, 14 (1964), 99–118.

—— *The Common Scientist in the Seventeenth Century: A Study of the Dublin Philosophical Society, 1683–1708* (Charlottesville, Va.: University of Virginia Press, 1970).

HUEHNS, G., *Antinomianism in English History* (London: Cresset Press, 1951).

HULL, W. I., *Benjamin Furly and Quakerism in Rotterdam* (Lancaster, Pa.: Lancaster Press, 1941).

HUNDERT, E. J., 'The Making of *Homo Faber:* John Locke between Ideology and History', *Journal of the History of Ideas*, 33 (1972), 3–22.

HUNT, R. M., *The Place of Religion in the Science of Robert Boyle* (Pittsburgh, Pa.: University Press, 1955).

HUNTER, M., *Science and Society in Restoration England* (New York: Cambridge University Press, 1981).

HURSTFIELD, J., 'Church and State 1558–1612: the Task of the Cecils', in *Freedom, Corruption and Government in Elizabethan England* (Cambridge, Mass.: Harvard University Press, 1973).

HUTCHINSON, F. E., *Milton and the English Mind* (New York: Macmillan, 1948).

HUTTON, R., *The Restoration: A Political and Religious History of England and Wales, 1658–1667* (Oxford: Clarendon Press, 1985).

JACOB, J. R., *Henry Stubbe: Radical Protestantism and the Early Enlightenment* (Cambridge: University Press, 1983).

JACOB, M., *The Newtonians and the English Revolution* (Ithaca, NY: Cornell University Press, 1976).

JAEGER, W., *Humanism and Theology* (Milwaukee, Wis.: Marquette University Press, 1943).

—— *Early Christianity and Greek Paideia* (Cambridge, Mass.: Belknap Press, 1961).

JAMES, D. G., *The Life of Reason: Hobbes, Locke, Bolingbroke* (London: Longman, 1949).

JEFFREYS, M. V. C., *John Locke: Prophet of Common Sense* (London: Methuen, 1967).

JOHNSON, C., 'Locke's Examination of Malebranche and John Norris', *Journal of the History of Ideas*, 19 (1958), 551–8.

JOHNSON, M., *Locke on Freedom* (Austin, Te.: Best Printing Co., 1977).

JONES, J. R., *The First Whigs: The Politics of the Exclusion Crisis, 1678–1683* (Oxford: University Press, 1961).

—— *Country and Court* (Cambridge: University Press, 1979).

JORDON, W. K., *The Development of Religious Toleration in England*, 4 vols. (London: Allen and Unwin, 1938).

KATO, T., 'The *Reasonableness* in the Historical Light of the *Essay, Locke Newsletter*, 12 (1981), 45–57.

KELLY, P., 'Locke and Molyneux: the Anatomy of a Friendship, *Hermathena*, 126 (1979), 99–118.

KENYON, J. P., ed., *The Stuart Constitution* (Cambridge: University Press, 1966).

KING, P., *The Life of John Locke* (Oxford: University Press, 1829).

KIPPIS, A., *Biographia Britannica*, 7 vols. (London: n.p., 1747).

KIRK, K. E., *The Vision of God: The Christian Doctrine of the Summum Bonum* (London: Longman, 1931).

KNAPPEN, M. M., 'The Early Puritanism of Lancelot Andrewes', *Church History*, 2 (1933), 95–107.

—— *Tudor Puritanism: A Chapter in the History of Idealism* (Chicago: University Press, 1939).

KNOX, R., *Enthusiasm* (New York: Oxford University Press, 1950).

KOYRE, A., *From the Closed World to the Infinite Universe* (Baltimore, Md.: Johns Hopkins University Press, 1957).

KRAUSE, P., 'Locke's Negative Hedonism', *Locke Newsletter*, 15 (1984), 43–63.

KRAYNAK, R., 'John Locke: From Absolutism to Toleration', *American Political Science Review*, 74 (1980), 55–60.

KROOK, D., *Three Traditions of Moral Thought* (Cambridge: University Press, 1959).

LAMPRECHT, S., *The Moral and Political Philosophy of John Locke* (New York: Russell and Russell, 1962).

LASLETT, P., 'Masham of Otes: The Rise and Fall of an English Family', *History Today*, 3 (1953), 535–43.

—— *The World We Have Lost* (New York: Scribner's Sons, 1967).

—— and HARRISON, J., eds., *The Library of John Locke* (Oxford: Clarendon Press, 1971).

LATOURETTE, K. S., *A History of Christianity*, 2 vols. (New York: Harper and Row, 1975).

LAWSON, J., 'An Early Disciple of Locke: John Clarke, Educator and Moralist', *Durham Research Review*, 4 (1962), 30–7.

LEARY, D. E., 'The Intentions and Heritage of Descartes and Locke: Toward a Recognition of the Moral Basis of Modern Psychology', *Journal of General Psychology*, 102 (1980), 281–91.

LEHMBERG, S. E., *Sir Thomas Elyot: Tudor Humanist* (Austin, Tex.: University of Texas Press, 1960).

LEITH, J. H., ed., *Creeds of the Churches* (Atlanta, Ga.: John Knox Press, 1977).

LEVINE, J. M., 'Ancients, Moderns and History: The Continuity of English Historical Writing in the Later Eighteenth Century', in *Studies in Change and Revolution: Aspects of English Intellectual History, 1640–1800*, ed. P. Korshin (Menston: Scolar Press, 1972).

LICHTENSTEIN, A., *Henry More: The Rational Theology of a Cambridge Platonist* (Cambridge: Harvard University Press, 1962).

LINDER, R. D., 'Calvinism and Humanism: The First Generation', *Church History*, 44. 2 (1975), 167–81.

LOCKE, L. G., *Tillotson: A Study in Seventeenth Century Literature* (Copenhagen: Rosenkilde and Bagger, 1954).

LOUGH, J., ed., *Locke's Travels in France* (Cambridge: University Press, 1954).

LOVEJOY, A. O., *The Great Chain of Being* (Cambridge, Mass.: Harvard University Press, 1936).

—— *Essays in the History of Ideas* (Baltimore, Md.: Johns Hopkins Press, 1948).

—— *Reflections on Human Nature* (Baltimore, Md.: Johns Hopkins Press, 1961).

MABBOTT, J. D., *John Locke* (Oxford: University Press, 1970).

McADOO, H. R., *The Structure of Caroline Moral Theology* (London: Longman, 1949).

—— *The Spirit of Anglicanism* (London: Longman, 1965).

MACAULAY, T. B., *History of England*, 2 vols. (London: Longman, 1873).

MacCAFFREY, W., *The Shaping of the Elizabethan Regime* (Princeton, NJ: University Press, 1968).

McGEE, J. S., *The Godly Man in Stuart England* (New Haven, Conn.: Yale University Press, 1976).

McGIFFERT, A. C., *Protestant Thought Before Kant* (London: Duckworth, 1911).

MACKINNON, F. I., *The Philosophy of John Norris of Bemerton* (Baltimore, Md.: Review Publishing Co., 1910).

McLACHLAN, H., *The Religious Opinions of Milton, Locke and Newton* (Manchester: University Press, 1941).

—— *Socinianism in Seventeenth-Century England* (Oxford: University Press, 1951).

MACLEAN, K., *John Locke and English Literature of the Eighteenth Century* (New Haven, Conn.: Yale University Press, 1936).

MACPHERSON, C. B., *The Political Theory of Possessive Individualism* (Oxford: University Press, 1979).

MALLET, C., *A History of the University of Oxford*, 3 vols. (New York: Longman, 1924).

MANUEL, F., *A Portrait of Isaac Newton* (Cambridge, Mass.: Belknap Press, 1968).

—— *The Religion of Isaac Newton* (Oxford: Clarendon Press, 1974).

MARSHALL, J. S., *Hooker and the Anglican Tradition: An Historical and Theological Study of Hooker's Ecclesiastical Polity* (London: A. and C. Black, 1963).

MARTINEAU, J., *Types of Ethical Theory*, 2 vols. (Oxford: Clarendon Press, 1885).

MASON, J. G., 'A Critical Interpretation of the Educational Thought of John Locke' (University of Nottingham Ph. D. thesis, 1960).

—— 'John Locke's Experience of Education and its Bearing on his Educational Thought', *Journal of Educational Administration and History*, 3 (1971), 1–24.

MATTHEWS, A. G., ed., *Calamy Revised* (Oxford: Clarendon Press, 1934).

MERTON, R. K., *Science, Technology and Society in Seventeenth Century England* (New York: Harper Torchbooks, 1970).

MEYER, C. S., *Elizabeth I and the Religious Settlement of 1559* (St Louis, Mo.: Concordia Press, 1960).

MILLER, J., *Popery and Politics in England* (Cambridge: University Press, 1973).

—— *James II* (Hove: Wayland Publishers, 1977).

MILLER, P., *The New England Mind: The Seventeenth Century* (Boston: Beacon Press, 1964).

—— and JOHNSON, T., eds., *The Puritans* (Boston: American Book Co., 1938).

MINTZ, S., *The Hunting of Leviathan: Seventeenth Century Reactions to the Materialism and Moral Philosophy of Thomas Hobbes* (Cambridge: University Press, 1962).

MOORE, C. A., 'Shaftesbury and the Ethical Poets in England, 1700–1750', *Publications of the Modern Language Association*, 31 (1916), 264–325.

MOORE, J. T., 'Locke's Concept of Faith' (University of Kansas Ph. D. thesis, 1970).

—— 'Locke's Analysis of Language and the Assent to Scripture', *Journal of the History of Ideas*, 37. 4 (1976), 707–14.

—— 'Locke on the Moral Need for Christianity', *Southwestern Journal of Philosophy*, 1 (1980), 25–30.

MORE, L. T., *The Life and Works of Robert Boyle* (New York: Oxford University Press, 1944).

MORGAN, E., *The Puritan Dilemma* (New Haven, Conn.: Yale University Press, 1958).

—— *Visible Saints: The History of a Puritan Idea* (New York: New York University Press, 1963).

MUIRHEAD, J. H., *The Platonic Tradition in Anglo-Saxon Philosophy* (London: Allen and Unwin, 1931).

MULLETT, C. F., 'Toleration and Persecution in England, 1660–1689', *Church History*, 18 (1949), 18–43.

MUSGROVE, F., 'Two Educational Controversies in the Eighteenth Century: Nature and Nurture: Private and Public Education', *Paedagogica Historica*, 2 (1962), 81–94.

NANKIVELL, J., *Edward Stillingfleet, Bishop of Worcester* (Worcester: Ebenezer Bayliss and Son, 1946).

NEALE, J. E., *Elizabeth I and her Parliaments*, 2 vols. (London: J. Cape, 1953).

NEW, J. F. H., *Anglican and Puritan: The Basis of their Opposition, 1558–1640* (Stanford, Calif.: University Press, 1964).

NICHOLSON, M., 'Christ's College and the Latitude Men', *Modern Philology*, 27 (1929), 35–53.

NIEBUHR, R., *Beyond Tragedy* (New York: Scribner's Sons, 1941).

—— *The Nature and Destiny of Man*, 2 vols. (London: Nisbet and Co., 1945).

NOTESTEIN, W., *The English People on the Eve of Colonization* (New York: Harper Torchbooks, 1962).

NUTTAL, G. F., 'James Nayler: A Fresh Approach', *Journal of the Friends Historical Society*, Supplement 26 (1954).

O'BRIEN, J., 'Commonwealth Schemes for the Advancement of Learning', *British Journal of Educational Studies*, 16 (1968), 30–42.

O'CONNELL, M. R., *The Counter-Reformation* (New York: Harper and Row, 1974).

OGG, D., *England in the Reigns of James II and William III* (Oxford: University Press, 1969).

—— *England in the Reign of Charles II* (Oxford: University Press, 1972).

OGILVIE, R. M., *Latin and Greek: A History of the Influence of the Classics on English Life from 1600 to 1900* (London: Routledge and Kegan Paul, 1964).

ORR, R. R., *Reason and Authority: The Thought of William Chillingworth* (Oxford: Clarendon Press, 1967).

OSMOND, P. H., *Isaac Barrow: His Life and Time* (London: SPCK, 1944).

OVERTON, J. H., *Life in the English Church* (London: Longman, 1885).

PARRY, G., *John Locke* (London: Allen and Unwin, 1978).

PASSMORE, J., *Ralph Cudworth: An Interpretation* (Cambridge: University Press, 1951).

—— 'The Malleability of Man in Eighteenth Century Thought' in *Aspects of the Eighteenth Century*, ed. E. R. Wasserman (Baltimore, Md.: Johns Hopkins Press, 1965).

—— *The Perfectibility of Man* (London: Duckworth, 1970).

—— 'Locke and the Ethics of Belief', *Proceedings of the British Academy*, 64 (1978), 185–208.

PATRIDES, C., ed., *The Cambridge Platonists* (Cambridge: University Press, 1971).

PATTISON, M., *Essays*, 2 vols. (Oxford: Clarendon Press, 1898).

PEARSON, S. C., Jr., 'The Religion of John Locke and the Character of His Thought', *Journal of Religion*, 58 (1978), 253–6.

PELIKAN, J., *The Growth of Medieval Theology, 600–1300* (Chicago: University Press, 1978).

PETRYSZAK, N. G., 'Tabula Rasa: Its Origins and Implications', *Journal of the History of the Behavioral Sciences*, 17 (1981), 15–27.

PETTIT, N., *The Heart Prepared: Grace and the Conversion Process in Puritan Spiritual Life* (New Haven, Conn.: Yale University Press, 1966).

PICKERING, S. F., *John Locke and Children's Books in Eighteenth Century England* (Knoxville, Tenn.: University of Tennessee Press, 1981).

PLACHER, W. C., *A History of Christian Theology* (Philadelphia, Pa.: Westminster Press, 1983).

PLUMB, J. H., *The Growth of Political Stability in England, 1675–1715* (London: Peregrine Books, 1969).

—— 'The New World of Children in the Eighteenth Century', *Past and Present*, 67 (1975), 64–93.

POLIN, R., 'Locke's Conception of Freedom', in *John Locke: Problems and Perspectives*, ed. J. Yolton (Cambridge: University Press, 1969).

POPE, H., *St Augustine of Hippo* (New York: Image Books, 1961).

POPKIN, R., 'The Philosophy of Edward Stillingfleet', *Journal of the History of Philosophy*, 9 (1971), 303–19.

—— *The History of Scepticism from Erasmus to Spinoza* (London: University of California Press, 1979).

PORTER, H. C., *Reformation and Reaction at Tudor Cambridge* (Cambridge: University Press, 1958).

PORTER, N. 'Marginalia Lockeana', *New Englander and Yale Review*, 11 (1877), 33–49.

POWICKE, F. J., *A Dissertation on John Norris of Bemerton* (London: George Philip and Son, 1894).

—— *The Cambridge Platonists* (London: Dent, 1926).

POWICKE, M., *The Reformation in England* (Oxford: University Press, 1961).

PUGH, R. B., ed., *Victoria County History: Staffordshire*, viii. (London: Oxford University Press, 1963).

QUINTANA, R., *Two Augustans: John Locke and Jonathan Swift* (Madison, Wis.: University of Wisconsin Press, 1978).

REDWOOD, J., *Reason, Ridicule and Religion: The Age of Enlightenment in England, 1660–1750* (Cambridge, Mass.: Harvard University Press, 1976).

ROBBINS, C., 'Absolute Liberty: The Life and Thought of William Popple', *William and Mary Quarterly*, 3rd ser. 24 (1967), 190–223.

—— *The Eighteenth Century Commonwealthman* (New York: Atheneum, 1968).

ROBERTS, J. D., *From Puritanism to Platonism in Seventeenth Century England* (The Hague: Nijhoff, 1968).

ROBINSON, H. W., *The Christian Doctrine of Man* (Edinburgh: T. and T. Clark, 1947).

ROGERS, G. A. J., 'Boyle, Locke and Reason', *Journal of the History of Ideas*, 27 (1966), 205–16.

—— 'Locke, Newton and the Cambridge Platonists', *Journal of the History of Ideas*, 15 (1979), 195–205.

ROMANELL, P., *John Locke and Medicine: A New Key to Locke* (Buffalo, NY: Prometheus Books, 1984).

ROSSI, P., *Francis Bacon: From Magic to Science* (Chicago: University Press, 1968).

RUSK, R. R., *Doctrines of the Great Educators* (New York: St Martin's Press, 1967).

RUSSELL, C., *The Crisis of Parliaments* (New York: Oxford University Press, 1971).

—— *Parliaments and English Politics* (Oxford: Clarendon Press, 1979).

SAHAKIAN, W. S. and M. L., *John Locke* (Boston: Twayne Publishers, 1975).

SALMON, V., 'Problems of Language Teaching: A Discussion among Hartlib's Friends', *Modern Language Review*, 59 (1954), 13–24.

SARGEAUNT, J., *Annals of Westminster School* (London: Methuen, 1898).

SCHLATTER, R., *The Social Ideas of Religious Leaders, 1660–1688* (Oxford: University Press, 1940).

SCHLEGEL, D., *Shaftesbury and the French Deists* (Chapel Hill, NC: University of North Carolina Press, 1956).

SCOTT, D. R., *Christ, Sin and Redemption* (London: James Clarke and Co., 1927).

SCROGGS, R., *The Last Adam: A Study in Pauline Anthropology* (Philadelphia, Pa.: Fortress Press, 1966).

SEATON, A. A., *The Theory of Toleration under the Later Stuarts* (Cambridge: University Press, 1911).

SHAPIRO, B., *Probability and Certainty in Seventeenth Century England* (Princeton, NJ: University Press, 1983).

SHIRLEY, F. J., *Richard Hooker and Contemporary Political Ideas* (London: SPCK, 1949).

SIMON, I., ed., *Three Restoration Divines: Barrow, South, Tillotson* (Paris: n.p., 1952).

SIMON, J., *Education and Society in Tudor England* (Cambridge: University Press, 1979).

SKINNER, Q., 'The Ideological Context of Hobbes's Political Thought', *Historical Journal*, 7 (1966), 286–317.

SMITH, E., *Some Versions of the Fall* (Chatham: W. and T. Macay Ltd., 1973).

SMOCK, G. E., 'John Locke and the Augustan Age of Literature', *Philosophical Review*, 55 (1946), 246–81.

SNOOK, I. A., 'John Locke's Moral Theory of Education', *Educational Theory*, 20 (1976), 364–7.

SNYDER, D., 'Faith and Reason in Locke's *Essay*' *Journal of the History of Ideas*, 47 (1986), 197–213.

SPENSER, T., *Shakespeare and the Nature of Man* (New York: Macmillan, 1942).

STEPHEN, L., *Essays in Freethinking and Plainspeaking* (New York: Putnam's Sons, 1905).

—— *History of English Thought in the Eighteenth Century*, 2 vols. (New York: Harbinger, 1962).

STEWART, M. A., 'Locke's Professional Contacts with Robert Boyle', *Locke Newsletter*, 12 (1981), 19–44.

STOEVER, W. K. B., *A Faire and Easie Way to Heaven: Covenant Theology and Antinominanism in Early Massachusetts* (Middletown, Conn.: Wesleyan University Press, 1978).

STONE, L., *The Crisis of the Aristocracy* (Oxford: Clarendon Press, 1965).

—— *The Family, Sex and Marriage in England, 1500–1800* (New York: Harper and Row, 1977).

STRANKS, C. J., *The Life and Writings of Jeremy Taylor* (London: SPCK, 1952).

—— *Anglican Devotion* (London: SCM Press, 1961).

STRAUSS, L., *Natural Right and History* (Chicago: University Press, 1953).

STROMBERG, R., *Religious Liberalism in Eighteenth-Century England* (Oxford: University Press, 1954).

SWABEY, W. C., *Ethical Theory From Hobbes to Kant* (New York: Greenwood Press, 1969).

TARKOV, N., *Locke's Education for Liberty* (Chicago: University Press, 1984).

TAWNEY, R. H., *Religion and the Rise of Capitalism* (Gloucester, Mass.: P. Smith, 1962).

TAYLOR, J. J., *A Retrospect of the Religious Life of England* (London: Trubner, 1876).

TENNANT, F. R., *The Sources of the Doctrines of the Fall and Original Sin* (Cambridge: University Press, 1903).

THOMAS, K., *Religion and the Decline of Magic* (Harmondsworth: Penguin Books, 1984).

THOMPSON, H. L., *Christ Church* (London: F. E. Robinson and Co., 1900).

THOMPSON, O. T., 'The Freewillers in the English Reformation', *Church History*, 37 (1968), 271–80.

TIFFANY, E., 'Shaftesbury as Stoic', *Publications of the Modern Language Association*, 38 (1923), 642–84.

TILLICH, P., *A History of Christian Thought* (New York: Harper and Row, 1968).

TILLYARD, E. M. W., *The Elizabethan World Picture* (London: Chatto and Windus, 1943).

TOOLE, R., 'The Concepts of Freedom and Necessity in Shaftesbury's Philosophy', *Studia Leibnitiana*, 9 (1977), 190–211.

TOON, P., *God's Statesman: The Life and Work of John Owen* (Grand Rapids, Mich.: Zondervan Publishing, 1973).

TOYNBEE, A., *An Historian's Approach to Religion* (New York: Oxford University Press, 1956).

TREVOR-ROPER, H., *Archbishop Laud, 1573–1645* (London: Macmillan, 1940).

—— *The Crisis of the Seventeenth Century* (New York: Harper and Row, 1968).

TROELTSCH, E., *The Social Teachings of the Christian Churches*, trans. O. Wyon, 2 vols. (London: Allen and Unwin, 1931).

TULLOCH, J., *Rational Theology and Christian Philosophy in England*, 2 vols. (Edinburgh: Blackwood, 1872).

—— *The Christian Doctrine of Man* (New York: Scribner, Armstrong, and Co., 1875).

TULLY, J., *A Discourse on Property: John Locke and his Adversaries* (Cambridge: University Press, 1980).

TURNBULL, G. H., *Samuel Hartlib: A Sketch of his Life* (Oxford: University Press, 1920).

—— 'The Visit of Comenius to England in 1641', *Notes and Queries*, 196 (1951), 137–40.

TURNER, W., *Lives of Eminent Unitarians*, 2 vols. (London: Unitarian Association, 1840).

TUVESON, E., 'Locke and the Dissolution of the Ego', *Modern Philology*, 52. 3 (1955), 159–74.

—— 'Shaftesbury on the Not So Simple Plan of Human Nature', *Studies in English Literature*, 5 (1965), 403–34.

TYACK, N., 'Puritanism, Arminianism and Counter-Revolution', in *The Origins of the English Civil War*, ed. C. Russell (New York: Barnes and Noble, 1973).

VAN LEEUWEN, H. G., *The Problem of Certainty in English Thought, 1630–1690* (The Hague: Nijhoff, 1970).

VINCENT, W. A. L., *The State and School Education in England and Wales, 1640–1660* (London: n.p., 1958).

VINER, J., *The Role of Providence in the Social Order* (Philadelphia, Pa.: American Philosophical Society, 1970).

VOITLE, R., 'Shaftesbury's Moral Sense', *Studies in Philology*, 52 (1955), 17–38.

—— *The Third Earl of Shaftesbury* (Baton Rouge, La.: Louisiana State University Press, 1984).

VON LEYDEN, W., 'John Locke and Natural Law', *Philosophy*, 31 (1956), 23–35.

—— *Hobbes and Locke: The Politics of Freedom and Obligation* (New York: St Martin's Press, 1982).

WALKER, D. P., *The Decline of Hell: Seventeenth Century Discussions of Eternal Torment* (Chicago: University Press, 1964).

—— *The Ancient Theology: Studies in Christian Platonism from the Fifteenth to the Eighteenth Century* (Ithaca, NY: Cornell University Press, 1972).

WALLACE, D. D., Jr., 'The Doctrine of Predestination in the Early English Reformation', *Church History*, 43. 2 (1974), 201–15.

—— *Puritans and Predestination: Grace in English Protestant Theology* (Chapel Hill, NC: University of North Carolina Press, 1982).

WALLACE, R., *Antitrinitarian Biography*, 3 vols. (London: E. T. Whitfield, 1850).

WARFIELD, B. B., *Two Studies in the History of Doctrine* (New York: Christian Literature Co., 1897).

WATSON, F., 'The State and Education during the Commonwealth', *English Historical Review*, 15 (1900), 58–72.

—— *The English Grammar Schools to 1660* (New York: Frank Cass and Co., 1908).

—— *The Beginnings of the Teaching of Modern Subjects in England* (London: Pitman, 1909).

WEBB, S. S., *The Governors-General: The English Army and the Definition of the Empire* (Chapel Hill, NC: University of North Carolina Press, 1979).

WEDGWOOD, C. V., *The King's War, 1641–1647* (London: Collins, 1958).

WESTFALL, R., *Science and Religion in Seventeenth Century England* (Ann Arbor, Mich.: University of Michigan Press, 1973).

WHITE, M., 'Original Sin, Natural Law, and Politics', *Partisan Review*, 2 (1956), 218–36.
—— *Science and Sentiment in America* (New York: Oxford University Press, 1972).
WHITE, R. J., *Dr Bentley* (London: Eyre and Spottiswoode, 1965).
WHITNEY, L., *Primitivism and the Idea of Progress* (New York: Octagon Books, 1934).
WILLEY, B., *The Seventeenth Century Background* (London: Chatto and Windus, 1934).
—— *The English Moralists* (London: Chatto and Windus, 1964).
—— *The Eighteenth Century Background* (Boston: Beacon Press, 1966).
WILLIAMS, N. P., *The Ideas of the Fall and Original Sin* (London: Longman, 1929).
WILLIAMSON, H. R., *Jeremy Taylor* (London: D. Dobson Ltd., 1951).
WISHY, B., *The Child and the Republic* (Philadelphia, Pa.: University of Pennsylvania Press, 1968).
WOOD, N., *The Politics of Locke's Philosophy* (Berkeley, Calif.: University of California Press, 1983).
WOOD, T., *English Casuistical Divinity During the Seventeenth Century* (London: SPCK, 1952).
WOOLHOUSE, R. S., *John Locke* (Brighton: Harvester Press, 1983).
WORMALD, B. H. G., *Clarendon* (Cambridge: University Press, 1951).
YOLTON, J., *John Locke and the Way of Ideas* (Oxford: Clarendon Press, 1956).
—— 'Locke on the Law of Nature', *Philosophical Review*, 67 (1958), 477–98.
—— 'Locke's Concept of Experience', in *Locke and Berkeley: A Collection of Critical Essays*, ed. C. B. Martin and D. M. Armstrong (Notre Dame, Ind.: University Press, 1968).
—— *John Locke and the Compass of the Human Understanding* (Cambridge: University Press, 1970).
—— 'The Science of Nature', in *John Locke: Problems and Perspectives*, ed. J. Yolton (Cambridge: University Press, 1969).
——*John Locke: An Introduction* (Oxford: Blackwell, 1985).
ZAGORIN, P., *The Court and the Country: The Beginning of the English Revolution* (New York: Atheneum, 1971).

Index